LAWLESS V IRELAND (1957–1961): THE FIRST CASE BEFORE THE EUROPEAN COURT OF HUMAN RIGHTS

Dedication

This work is dedicated to
Sean MacBride,
Thomas J. Connolly
Seamus Sorahan
Patrick C. Moore
Ciaran MacAnally
who
without reward and at professional and personal expense
represented Gerard Lawless before
the European Commission and European Court of Human Rights
in defence of the rights chartered in
the European Convention of Human Rights
and thereby rendered
a signal service to the cause of international human rights

Lawless v Ireland (1957–1961): The First Case Before the European Court of Human Rights

An international miscarriage of justice?

BRIAN DOOLAN, Ph.D., Barrister
Senior Lecturer in Legal Studies, Faculty of Business,
Dublin Institute of Technology

Routledge
Taylor & Francis Group
LONDON AND NEW YORK

First published 2001 by Ashgate Publishing

Published 2019 by Routledge
2 Park Square, Milton Park, Abingdon, Oxon, OX14 4RN
605 Third Avenue, New York, NY 10017

Routledge is an imprint of the Taylor & Francis Group, an informa business

A Library of Congress record exists under LC control number:

ISBN 13: 978-1-138-63536-4 (hbk)
ISBN 13: 978-1-315-20460-4 (ebk)

Contents

Sources

Unpublished Sources

The bulk of the unpublished material in this book is to be found in files on the Lawless case in the National Archives, Dublin. A series of Department of Foreign Affairs files are available; though unfortunately two critical files are missing. A series of Department of Justice files contain the full pleadings and the verbatim records of the hearings and the full decisions of the European Commission and European Court. It was necessary to make application to view the Department of Justice policy files. A number of material files from the Department of the Taoiseach are available though other relevant files remained closed. It was necessary to make application to view the files that were held in the Office of the Attorney General. Understandably there is a considerable amount of overlap between all these various files. Files in the Public Records Office, London, are also of interest. Appropriate references to the particular files are made in the endnotes. Unfortunately, the files on the case that were retained by the firm of P.C.Moore & Co., solicitors, who acted for Lawless, were destroyed in a fire in the mid-1980s. The documents in the Lawless case deposited with the Council of Europe are closed to public access except those that have been authorised to be published.

Published Sources

The Council of Europe issued two publications on the Lawless case. The first, the Series A documents, contains the full judgments of the European Court of Human Rights. The Series B publication contains a wide range of documents such as the complete written pleadings and oral submissions before the European Court and an edited version of the proceedings before the European Commission.

Preface

The European Convention of Human Rights was signed in November 1950. With the passage of fifty years since that event, it is a timely moment to publish a study of the first case in which the European Court of Human Rights exercised its jurisdiction. This study was only possible when the Irish archives, which had been closed for thirty years, were released. Thus the entire pleadings and the verbatim records were revealed for the very first time. The picture that emerges is crucially different in vital aspects to the picture in the heavily edited material published by the Council of Europe shortly after the case concluded. A critical analysis of the entire material leads to the conclusion that the proceedings before the Strasbourg institution were so flawed as to amount to an international miscarriage of justice. This may be an uncomfortable finding for the Strasbourg institutions but such a statement must be understood in a historical context. The Strasbourg institutions can hardly expect to escape the rigorous scrutiny that the decisions of national courts are subjected to. Incidentally, the Council of Europe files remain closed. The Council of Europe should consider the introduction of some system whereby materials in the cases become automatically available after some specific time period. This would permit a comprehensive study of the various cases, either individually or collectively, to evaluate the effectiveness of the Strasbourg institutions. Such a system of disclosure must be in the interest of the peoples of Europe.

This book is also timely for a more pressing contemporary reason. International criminal tribunals with specific geographical effect are operating and there are proposals for the establishment of a permanent international criminal court. Careful thought will be given to the jurisdiction and composition of such a court and to the investigation and prosecution processes. Care will be taken to afford those before such a tribunal the adequate protections needed to insure a fair trial. But what mechanisms will be put in place to remedy a miscarriage of justice discovered possibly long after the guilty verdict has been delivered and the condemned person has suffered undeserved punishment? International justice will not be without its flaws and faults. As national jurists are only too well aware, it is a gigantic task to remedy a miscarriage of justice though all national legal systems are dotted with such victories. But the efforts needed to right a legal wrong are usually long and arduous and those who suffer from such miscarriages of justice are generally irrevocably damaged. Irrespective of the herculean effort the righting of an international wrong may demand, the international jurist must emulate his or her national counterpart in this regard. This work is a minute step in that direction.

This work was originally presented as a doctoral thesis to the University of Dublin. I must express my appreciation to Dr. Gerard Hogan for his initial willingness to supervise the project and later for his expert guidance and immeasurable assistance. Professor William Binchy, Head of the Law School, encouraged and supported the project. Dr. Gerry Whyte offered some useful advice. Professor Conor Gearty of King's College London gave important support when this book approached publication. The late Mr. Justice Brian Walsh and Mr. Ciaran MacAnally, participants in the Lawless case so many years ago, gave whatever information they could. The staff of the National Archives in Dublin, particularly Ms. Catriona Crowe, a mine of information, were extremely helpful and always courteous. The Departments of the Taoiseach, of Foreign Affairs, of Justice and the office of the Attorney General made files available to me that were not on general release at the time.

I could neither have undertaken nor sustained this work without the generous support of the Dublin Institute of Technology. In particular, I place on record my appreciation to the President, Dr. Brendan Goldsmith. Within the Business Faculty, I must mention the gratitude due to the Director, Mr. Paul O'Sullivan, who granted me the necessary time to prepare the thesis for publication. Dr. Nicola Timony gave me her support in my many moments of doubt.

Maud Halferty provided help with translations from French. Deirdre Ni Bhroin traced source material. A very special word of thanks must go to Eamon Byrne for his assistance with the complex and tedious (for me) technical side of producing the original thesis.

Finally, I must record my thanks to the Institut Catholique d'Etudes Superieures in La Roche sur Yon for providing me with a quiet corner of their library while I made the final adjustments to the text.

Brian Doolan
Mareuil sur Lay
22nd July 2000

Abbreviations

AC	Appeal Cases
AG	Attorney General
BL	Barrister at Law
BPRO	British Public Records Office
BYIL	British Yearbook of International Law
CA	Court of Appeal
Camb.LJ	Cambridge Law Journal
CE	Council of Europe
CJ	Chief Justice
CRO	Commonwealth Relations Office (British)
DD	Dail Debates
DEA	Department of External Affairs
DF	Department of Finance
DFA	Department of Foreign Affairs
DJ	Department of Justice
DO	Dominions Office (British)
DT	Department of the Taoiseach
FO	Foreign Office (British)
HRJ	Human Rights Journal
ICJR	International Court of Justice Reports
ICLQ	International Comparative Law Quarterly
IJ	Irish Jurist
ILRM	Irish Law Reports Monthly
ILT	Irish Law Times
ILTR	Irish Law Times Reports
IR	Irish Reports
J	Justice/Judge of the Supreme Court/High Court
KB	King's Bench
KC	King's Counsel
P	President of the High Court
SC	Senior Counsel
SD	Seanad Debates
TD	Teachta Dala: member of Dail Eireann
YBECHR	Yearbook of the European Convention of Human Rights

1 European Convention of Human Rights and Ireland

Introduction

Following the conclusion of the terrible conflict in Europe, the establishment of the Council of Europe was the first genuine result of co-operation between European states, which was to become a regular and increasing feature of European political life. The most tangible outcome of this greater European *entente* was the endorsement of a Convention of Human Rights. Though it took a decade for the enforcement institutions envisaged in this code to come to fruition, nevertheless it was to become the most enduring and influential creation of the Council of Europe. Henceforth, the enunciation and protection of human rights in European states was to exist on two levels, the first on a domestic level and the second on a European level which was superimposed on the first. As will be seen in the unfolding chapters, Lawless was to fully exploit both sets of rights. The foundation of the Council of Europe, the background to the adoption of the European Convention of Human Rights and the establishment of the enforcement institutions are discussed in this chapter. Ireland's role in these events, taken from archival material, is discussed here for the first time.

Ireland: Founding Member of the Council of Europe

The desire never again to witness the suffering and destruction of Europe, which had occurred in two terrible wars fought within thirty years of each other, was the impetus which led to the foundation, in 1949, of the Council of Europe, as an organisation to foster greater unity and co-operation between the people and nations of Europe. In May 1948 over 700 delegates from sixteen countries and observers from ten additional countries attended a 'Congress of Europe' in The Hague which called for a united Europe, and in particular for a European Assembly and a Charter and Court of Human Rights. The European Movement, an unofficial organisation that promoted the union of Europe, developed these proposals.[1] On 7 March 1949 a formal invitation was received from London inviting the Government of Ireland to attend a conference of Foreign Ministers of European countries to be held later that month. A draft statute for the new organisation was prepared and approved which provided machinery for contact between European states at government and at parliamentary levels and with headquarters in the French Rhineland city of Strasbourg to symbolise post-war reconciliation. The Consultative Assembly[2] was to hold its first meeting on 11 August 1949 subsequent to a meeting of the Committee of Ministers on 8 August. Representatives on behalf of France, Britain, Italy, Sweden, the Netherlands, Belgium, Ireland, Norway, Denmark and Luxembourg signed the Statute of the Council of Europe at a formal ceremony in St. James's Palace, London, on 5 May 1949.[3] Ernest Bevin, the British Foreign Minister, who presided, described the occasion as an historic one and said that the agreement laid the foundation of something new and hopeful in European life.

For Ireland, Sean MacBride, Minister for External Affairs, signed the Statute. The signature of this Statute, within two weeks or so of the coming into force of the Republic of Ireland Act 1948,[4] which had broken the single remaining constitutional and political link with Britain,[5] was the first international agreement entered into by the Irish State without reference to Britain. By becoming a member of the Council of Europe, Ireland's close links with Europe, which had existed up until the end of the 17th century, were re-established. These links had drastically declined following the Act of Union in 1800 - which had abolished the Irish parliament and created a single parliament for Great Britain and Ireland. Membership of this European body emphasised Ireland's co-equal status with other states, particularly Britain, in a wider European context. It gave Ireland a platform in a multinational organisation at a time when membership of mondial organisations, such as the United Nations, had been denied. While the Irish print media recorded the event, greater prominence was given to the more immediate issues of the day. The civil war in China in which the communists were to triumph was the dominant international event of the day. The story that dominated the domestic news was the continuing opposition of all political parties[6] to the Ireland Bill[7] then progressing through the British parliament. This measure was Britain's response to the enactment in Ireland of the Republic of Ireland Act 1948.

The Government decided[8] that prior to ratification, the Statute should be given parliamentary approval by both Houses of the Oireachtas.[9] The Minister for External Affairs, on 12 July 1949, moved a motion in Dail Eireann, the popularly elected House of the Oireachtas, "that the Dail approve of the Statute of the Council of Europe, signed at London on 5

May 1949...". The debate was short, with only three serious contributions.[10] MacBride reviewed the historical efforts to unify Europe and explained the institutions established under the Statute. Eamon de Valera, the leader of the Opposition, concentrated on economic aspects, though he wondered why the State was referred to as the "Irish Republic". The remaining contributor was the only speaker to mention human rights. In reply, MacBride explained that the Statute had been drafted before the enactment of the Republic of Ireland Act 1948 and that the description Irish Republic was used in the same way as the French Republic had been used to describe France. Dail Eireann approved the motion without a vote on 13 July 1949. Ireland deposited the instrument of ratification on 30 July 1949 and the Statute of the Council of Europe came into force on 4 August 1949 upon being ratified by seven of its signatories.

Drafting a Human Rights Convention

One of the stated objectives of the Statute of the Council of Europe was that every member of the Council of Europe must accept the principle of the rule of law and of the enjoyment by all persons within their jurisdictions of human rights and fundamental freedoms. Thus, from the initial discussions on European unity, the protection of human rights was a central and dominating feature. The Juridical Committee of the European Movement submitted its preliminary draft Convention to the Committee of Ministers of the Council of Europe. This desire further manifested itself at 1st Ordinary Session of the Consultative Assembly, held in Strasbourg in August and September 1949. An item on the agenda was "measures for the fulfilment of the declared aims of the Council of Europe...in regard to the maintenance and further realisation of human rights". At the conclusion of this debate, the Consultative Assembly recommended to the Committee of Ministers that a draft Convention be drawn up as quickly as possible providing for a collective guarantee designed to ensure the effective engagement of human rights to all persons residing within the Council of Europe states. An outline was submitted of the form such a Convention should take and contained a simple enumeration of the rights essential to guarantee personal independence and human dignity.

To ensure the observance of these engagements, it was recommended that a Commission of Human Rights and a Court of Human Rights be established with a suggested outline of their composition and powers. To assist in the process, the Committee of Ministers convened meetings of legal experts and of senior government officials. Following its session in August 1950, the Committee of Ministers transmitted to the Consultative

Assembly a draft Convention for its views. The Assembly, animated by a desire to have the Convention signed as early as possible, strongly urged that the text be modified in the manner of a number of proposed amendments, which were concerned with a Preamble, the peaceful enjoyment of possessions rights, to education and political rights. The Consultative Assembly adopted the draft Convention, despite these reservations, at its 2nd Session in August 1950 by all 111 representatives voting in favour. The general attitude of the four Irish representatives was that, even with the additions proposed by the Assembly, the draft fell far short of the ideals which the peoples of Western Europe should prize. Nevertheless, it should be accepted as a first step on the road towards the complete protection of human rights.[11]

Ireland's Minister for External Affairs shared the view that the draft Convention had many imperfections, on property, education and political rights, which were only partially cured by the amendments proposed by the Consultative Assembly. In view of the shortcomings of the text, the Minister reserved his position when the matter was discussed at the August session of the Committee of Ministers. Nevertheless, he formed the opinion from discussions with colleagues that there was opposition to the amendments proposed by the Assembly and that it was unlikely that any substantial changes would be made in the draft Convention. The matter was to come before the Committee of Ministers at its next meeting, in Rome, in November and a number of governments suggested that the Convention should be signed during that meeting. The Consultative Assembly attached the highest importance to the early signature of the Convention and to its entry into force at the earliest possible date. The Convention would be the first concrete result of the work of the Council of Europe and would increase the confidence of Western Europe peoples in its effectiveness and in its practical approach to the problems confronting the Western nations. The Convention was also generally regarded as a means of bringing home to the peoples of Eastern Europe the fundamental differences between the Western democracies and the regimes under which they existed. Politically, Ireland's signature of the Convention was of prime importance even though the draft had not satisfied all the Irish representatives' aspirations. Any reluctance to sign might be construed as a lack of interest in a problem that was very real to those peoples of Western Europe who had suffered under totalitarian regimes.

The Government authorised the Minister for External Affairs to sign the Convention on the understanding that every endeavour would be made to have the amendments proposed by the Consultative Assembly accepted by the Committee of Ministers and incorporated into the final draft text at their forthcoming meeting on 3 November 1950. The question was pondered as to whether the Convention was inter-government or inter-state, and a query was addressed to the Secretary General of the Council of Europe, who replied that it was intended to add a Preamble to make clear the inter-government character of the Convention.[12]

The Department of Justice[13] expressed annoyance that it had not been given an opportunity of expressing its views on the Convention before its submission to Government. The important question was whether the proposed Article 5[14] restricted the power of the executive to intern persons without trial under the Offences Against the State (Amendment) Act 1940. It may be that there was nothing inconsistent between Article 15 and the 1940 Act though there was some doubt on this. The view was expressed that even if the 1940 Act was *ultra vires* the Convention, Ireland would not be guilty of any violation by merely allowing the statute to remain on the statute book so long as the Government did not take any action under the Act. It was very doubtful whether the Minister for Justice would be prepared to introduce any legislation to amend the 1940 Act. It was also noted that if that Act ran counter to the Convention, propaganda could be used against Ireland for leaving it on the statute book even if it never operated. The Department of Justice also feared that there might be a breach of Article 6 because there was no system of legal assistance in criminal cases, except in capital cases. Any procedure which entitled a private individual or an organisation to make complaint to an international commission, would provide publicity for malicious and groundless charges against governments and might injure the reputation of states. Apparently, the Council of Europe countries were anxious to have a Human Rights Convention published without delay to focus attention on the freedoms enjoyed in Western Europe as compared with "Iron Curtain" countries. The Minister for External Affairs in the Committee of Ministers and the Irish representatives in the Consultative Assembly had strongly supported the draft Convention. Therefore it seemed, that even if the Convention restricted the executive's powers under the 1940 Act, the Department of Justice recorded the view that the Government would consider it prudent to sign the Convention. Thus, the available archival records show that very little debate took place, and even less disagreement was noted, apart from the Department of Justice's prophetic concern about whether the detention of persons without trial contravened the draft Convention.[15] This precise question was to arise in the Lawless case some ten years later.

Signature of the European Convention of Human Rights

The European Convention for the Protection of Human Rights and Fundamental Freedoms was signed in Rome on 4 November 1950, by representatives from Belgium, Denmark, France, Federal Republic of Germany, Iceland, Ireland, Italy, Luxembourg, Netherlands, Norway, Saar,[16] Turkey and the United Kingdom. The Minister for External Affairs, Sean MacBride, on the occasion said, "the present struggle is one which is largely being fought in the minds and consciences of mankind. In this struggle...we lack a clearly defined charter which sets out unambiguously the rights which we democrats guarantee to our people. This Convention is a step in that direction." MacBride had made strenuous, though largely unsuccessful, efforts to have the amendments proposed by the Consultative Assembly accepted for incorporation into the final text. The Council of Ministers agreed to the addition of a Preamble, and the reduction to eight of the number of states required to accept the jurisdiction of the European Court of Human Right as a prerequisite to the establishment of the court. The other amendments proposed by the Consultative Assembly were referred to the Committee of Legal Experts for further study.

Ratification of Convention and Lodgement of Declarations by Ireland

In accordance with Article 29 of the Irish Constitution,[17] a copy of the Convention was laid before Dail Eireann on 14 February 1951. In view of the important nature of the Convention, and the active part played by the Irish representatives to the Consultative Assembly during the drafting stages, the Minister for External Affairs proposed to Government that an opportunity be afforded to Dail Eireann for a debate. Leave to move the motion "that Dail Eireann approves the terms of the Convention for Protection of Human Rights and Fundamental Freedoms..." was sought. Strictly speaking, the approval of Dail Eireann was not essential, presumably because implementation of the Convention did not involve a charge on public funds.[18] Such a debate never took place, nor has the Convention ever been approved by Dail Eireann, nor has its terms been incorporated into domestic law.[19] The reason this motion was not taken at that time can be explained by the fact that the body politic in Ireland was by then engulfed by the famous "Mother and Child" crisis when state authorities clashed with church authorities with regard to a proposed governmental health measure.[20] MacBride played a central role in these events and the signature of the Convention was the most that could have been achieved in these circumstances.

It was envisaged that following approval by Dail Eireann, which as already noted never occurred, Ireland should ratify the Convention forthwith. Towards this end, the Attorney General, the legal adviser to the Government, indicated that no new legislation was required and the Department of Justice indicated that no reservation was necessary, at the time of depositing the instrument of ratification, in respect of any existing legislation. The Minister for External Affairs was of opinion that Ireland should make the necessary declaration as to individual petition. This was in light of the attitude of the Irish representatives both in the Committee of Ministers and in the Consultative Assembly in urging that the Convention did not go far enough in the protection of human rights. If such a declaration was not made, Ireland would appear to be unwilling to fully implement the existing Convention whilst at the same time urging extensive amendments. The practical safeguard of the necessity to exhaust domestic remedies was noted. The Department of Justice differed from this view and expressed the opinion that the State should not make the declaration with regard to the right of individual petition. It was not clear whether States would be expected to make such declaration in the absence of complaints against them by private individuals or organisations. The Attorney General was of opinion that if a citizen on recourse to the Commission or the Court obtained some relief that was denied by Irish courts, the prerogative of mercy or executive action would be available to give effect to any compromise arrived at. It was interesting to note the view taken by the Department of External Affairs on the future role the Convention might play in the development of human rights in Ireland. A memorandum wryly noted that "in practice, however, the likelihood of this country being brought before the Commission or the Court is very remote, as all the 'rights' set out in the Convention are already conceded here".[21]

The Minister for External Affairs sought to take, on behalf of the Government, such steps as might be necessary for the ratification of the Convention. Consideration was given to the question of making the declarations as specified in Articles 25 and 46 respectively of the Convention. The Department of External Affairs, in consultation with the Attorney General, was to settle their terms and if necessary the Secretary General of the Council of Europe should be consulted on the form of the declarations. The Government agreed that the declarations should be made. At this time, the Department of Justice raised a reservation that it was not prepared to sponsor any proposal for the provision of free legal assistance for all poor persons who were charged with offences. On 18 February 1953, the declaration required under Article 25 of the Convention was deposited. This declared that "the Government of Ireland recognised the competence of the European Commission of Human Rights to receive petitions addressed to the Secretary General of the Council of Europe from any person, non government organisation or group of individuals claiming to be victims of a violation by one of the High Contracting parties of the rights set forth in the said Convention". The further declaration required under Article 46 was also deposited. This recited that "the Government of Ireland recognises the jurisdiction of the European Court of Human Rights as compulsory ipso facto and without special agreement in all matters concerning the interpretation and application of the said Convention, for a period of five years and thereafter until such time as notice of withdrawal of the recognition may be given". Ireland was the first signatory state to make this declaration. The instrument of ratification was deposited on 25 February 1953. This stated that "the Government of Ireland do hereby confirm and ratify the aforesaid Convention and undertake faithfully to perform and carry out all the stipulations therein contained subject to the reservations that they do not interpret Article 6 (3) (c) of the Convention as requiring the provision of free legal assistance to any wider extent that is now provided in Ireland".[22]

Coming into Force of the European Convention of Human Rights

The Convention came into force when the tenth ratification was supplied on 3 September 1953.[23] To ensure the observance of the engagements undertaken by the states a Commission of Human Rights and a Court of Human Rights were to be established.

Establishment of the European Commission of Human Rights

The European Human Rights Commission[24] was to be elected by the Committee of Ministers from names submitted by national delegations in the Consultative Assembly. It was to be composed of persons of high moral character possessed of qualifications required for appointment to high judicial office or have a recognised competence in national or international law. The members must sit in an individual capacity and hold office for six years and were eligible for re-election. The Commission could only exercise the jurisdiction to hear individual petitions when at least six states were bound by such declarations, a condition not satisfied until 5 July

1955,[25] though the Commission could hear inter-state applications from 3 September 1953, the date of the Convention's inception.

The first Commission election took place on 18 May 1954. William Black[26] was elected in respect of Ireland and was one of the members, chosen by lot, whose term of office was to expire at the end of the initial period of three years. At the unanimous request of his colleagues, Paul Faber of Luxembourg acted as President during the 1st Session of the Commission when the Rules of Procedure were adopted.[27] On 15 December, Prof. C.H.M. Waldock[28] of the United Kingdom[29] and Prof. C. Th.Eustathiades of Greece[30] were elected president and vice-president respectively. On 16 April 1956, during a session of the Consultative Assembly[31] in which he was one of Ireland's parliamentary delegates, James Crosbie[32] was unanimously elected by the Committee of Ministers to fill the vacancy caused by William Black's resignation. On 6 April 1957, the Committee of Ministers re-elected the six outgoing members including Crosbie.

The Commission held regular sessions between July 1955 and 31 December 1957. During that period 343 individual applications were lodged though none had advanced beyond the stage of determining its admissibility. Of these applications, 277 were declared inadmissible and 15 struck off the list, in most cases owing to withdrawal. The other 51 remained pending, either because the exchange of observations between the parties was still in progress, or because the Commission had ordered further investigation before reaching a decision or had yet to consider the case. A sub-Commission had been established to examine the first inter-state application, brought by Greece against the United Kingdom.[33]

Establishment of the European Court of Human Rights

The Court,[34] when established, was to consist of a number of judges equal to that of the members of the Council of Europe. No two judges must be nationals of the same state. The judges, of high moral character, must either possess the qualifications required for appointment to high judicial office or be jurisconsuls of recognised competence and were to be elected for nine years by the Consultative Assembly. Membership of the Court was to be renewed one-third at a time and judges could be re-elected. Each state was entitled to nominate three candidates; two at least must be its nationals. The establishment of the Court, and the first election of members, could not take place until the jurisdiction of the Court had been accepted by eight states and no case could be brought to the Court before that election. At the time Lawless submitted his claim, in November 1957, the jurisdiction of the Court had been recognised by only five States. Subsequently, this condition was fulfilled on 3 September 1958,[35] which enabled the first election to take place on 21 January 1959.[36] Ireland nominated three candidates, Richard McGonigal SC,[37] John Kenny SC,[38] and Prof. Herman Mosler.[39] Both McGonigal and Mosler were elected, with McGonigal's term of office being set at three years instead of the usual nine years because he was one of the members chosen by lot whose terms were to expire at the end of three years. The formal inauguration of the Court[40] took place on 20 April 1959. This event coincided with the 10th Anniversary of the founding of the Council of Europe. The Court,[41] at its 3rd plenary session,[42] adopted rules, and elected, as doyen d'age, Lord McNair of the United Kingdom[43] as President and Rene Cassin of France[44] as Vice-President.

The Court had to wait almost a year for a case, that of Lawless v Ireland, to be referred to it on 1 April 1960 and a further six months before the Court sat to hear argument in the case on 3 October 1960. History was made with the referral of that case to the Court. Not alone was Lawless's case the first one to come before the European Court of Human Rights for hearing but this was the first occasion when an international tribunal of this stature was called upon to adjudicate in a human rights dispute between an individual and his State.

Notes

[1] YBECHR 1955-56-57, pp. 92-95, outlines these events.

[2] 87 delegates attended: France (18), Britain (18), Italy (18) Sweden (6), Belgium (6), Netherlands (6), Ireland (4), Norway (4), Denmark (4) and Luxembourg (3).

[3] YBECHR.1955-56-57, pp. 275-351 for a brief historical account.

[4] Repealed External Relations Act 1936, s.3. which had provided "that...the king... continues to act..for the purposes of the appointment of diplomatic...representatives and the conclusion of international agreements...and...on behalf of Saorstat Eireann [the Irish Free State] for the like purposes as and when advised by the Executive Council so to do".

[5] Republic of Ireland Act 1948 came into force on 18 April 1949.

[6] Dail Eireann (10 May 1949: 115 DD 785-825), and Seanad Eireann (11 May 1949: 36 SD 1022-1043) passed unanimous motions that, *inter alia*, "places on record its indignant protest against the introduction in the British Parliament of legislation purporting to ensure and continue the existing partition of Ireland".

[7] This became law on 2 June 1949. It declared (1), that the part of Ireland heretofore known as Eire ceased to be a part of His Majesty's dominions; and (2), that Northern Ireland

remained part of His Majesty's dominions and of the UK and that in no event will Northern Ireland cease to be part...of the UK without the consent of the parliament of Northern Ireland; and (3), that part of Ireland already referred to as Eire is to be referred to by the name attributed thereto by law, that is to say, as the Republic of Ireland.

[8] Cabinet Minute. 7 June 1949. Cab.2/11.

[9] Article 29.5.2° of the Constitution provides: "The State shall not be bound by any international agreement involving a charge upon public funds unless the terms of the agreement shall have been approved by Dail Eireann."

[10] 117 DD 694-714 and 741-748.

[11] The information in this section is contained in DT File S.14921A.

[12] "The governments signatory...as governments of European countries.." Preamble to the Convention.

[13] The Department of State responsible for internal security.

[14] See Appendix 1 for articles of the Convention.

[15] Unlike in Britain where politicians and administrators divided sharply. See *Fundamental Rights: The UK Isolated.* A.Lester. Public Law. (1984). pp.46-72.

[16] The Saar was integrated into the Federal Republic of Germany on 1 January 1957.

[17] "Every international agreement to which the State becomes a party shall be laid before Dail Eireann."

[18] See footnote 9, supra.

[19] A central issue in the Lawless case in the Irish courts: see pp.52-54.

[20] See *Church & State in Modern Ireland 1923-1979*, J.H.Whyte (2nd edn) p.228.

[21] For similar views by other states, see p.254, footnotes 15 and 16.

[22] Free legal assistance was only given in capital cases. The Criminal Justice (Legal Aid) Act 1962 now provides a scheme of criminal legal assistance: see The State (Healy) v Donoghue [1976] IR 325.

[23] United Kingdom (8 March 1951); Norway (15 January 1952); Sweden (4 February 1952); Germany (5 December 1952); Saar (14 January 1953); Ireland (25 February 1953); Greece (28 March 1953); Denmark (13 April 1953); Iceland (29 June 1953) and Luxembourg (3 September 1953).

[24] Articles 20-37 of the Convention.

[25] Sweden (4 February 1952); Ireland (25 February 1953); Denmark (13 May 1953); Iceland (29 March 1955); Federal Republic of Germany and Belgium (5 July 1955).

[26] A retired judge of the Supreme Court of Justice.

[27] On 2 April 1955. YBECHR 1955-56-57, pp.58-86. These rules, applicable in the Lawless case, were amended in September 1955, July 1957 and June 1959.

[28] See Appendix 2 for biographical note on members of the Commission.

[29] The UK did not recognise the right of individual petition until 14 January 1966.

[30] Greece did not recognise the right of individual petition until 20 November 1985.

[31] On 20 April 1956, the Consultative Assembly, decided (Resolution 96) that "a representative to the Consultative Assembly shall be at liberty to become a member of the Commission of Human Rights". On this issue of incompatibility, H.Golsong, later Deputy-Registrar of the Court, accepted this change as proper, though argued that a Commission member could not at the same time hold office in any other control body under the Convention, such as the Court, the Committee of Ministers, the Secretary-Generalship or be

a member of any government of a contracting state and as such likely to be responsible for that State's attitude in proceedings before the Commission: *International Protection of Human Rights.* 110 Recueil des Cours. (1963) pp.1-151 at p.73.

32 James Crosbie remained a member of Seanad Eireann until May 1957. According to SD (46:16 May 1956-19 December 1956) he made debating contributions though Volume 47 (16 January 1957-28 March 1957) records no contributions. The Consultative Assembly probably took the decision it did (see previous footnote) to cover Crosbie's election to the Commission. Golsong missed the point that what may have been incompatible was the election to Commission membership of a serving parliamentarian because such a person may have voted for a measure which may later be called into question, or may be called upon to exercise some supervisory role over governmental action which is later challenged as a breach of the Convention before the Commission.

33 YBECHR 1955-56-57. pp.132-134.

34 Articles 38-56 of the Convention.

35 Ireland (25 February 1953); Denmark (13 April 1953); Netherlands (31 August 1954); Germany and Belgium (5 July 1955); Luxembourg (28 April 1958); Austria and Iceland (3 September 1958).

36 YBECHR 1958-59, pp.118-156.

37 See Appendix 2 for biographical notes on members of the Court. Since the court was not a whole time tribunal McGonigal's appointment did not affect his practice at the Irish Bar. Indeed, McGonigal appeared for the State, during this period, in many constitutional cases.

38 Later a judge of the High Court and Supreme Court.

39 Professor of law at Heidelberg University. Nominated also by Germany.

40 The full Court was composed of: Mosler (Germany); Ross (Denmark); Arik (Turkey); Verdross (Austria); Cassin (France); Wold (Norway); McGonigal (Ireland); Holmback (Sweden); McNair (UK); Maradikis (Greece); Balladore Pallieri (Italy); van Asbeck (Netherlands); Rodenburg (Luxembourg); Arnals (Iceland) and Rolin (Belgium).

41 Lord McNair kept London informed of the early private working sessions of the Court. In his report (3 March 1959) on the first week's work, he noted "the general expectation is that the Court is unlikely to have many cases..." BPRO. FO. 371/146289/1734/7.

42 14-18 September 1959.

43 United Kingdom only recognised the compulsory jurisdiction of the Court on 14 January 1966. Incredibly, the UK held the presidency of both the Court and the Commission despite refusals to recognise the right of individual petition and the jurisdiction of the Court.

44 France recognised the compulsory jurisdiction of the Court only on 3 April 1974.

2 Ireland's Constitutional and Legal Framework

Introduction

This chapter explains the general political, constitutional and legal framework of the birth and development of the Irish State. These events formed historical and juridical backdrops to the Lawless case over a quarter of a century later. In particular, the constitutional and legal aspects of the statutory powers of detention without trial are considered as a prelude to an examination of the international human rights dimensions of these issues which were to be explored as the Lawless case unfolded.

Political Violence, Anglo Irish Treaty 1921 and Civil War 1922-1923

Political violence, and the expected British governmental responses, was a constant feature of Irish society in the 18th and 19th centuries. In the 20th century, the local but intensive Easter Rising in 1916 and the more prolonged and widespread War of Independence from 1919 to 1921, insured that some political settlement of the Irish question was guaranteed. In May 1921, a general election was held under the Government of Ireland Act 1920, which had established two political systems on the island of Ireland. One such entity, "Southern Ireland", with Dublin as its capital, was to be composed of 26 administrative counties consisting of about three-quarters of the territory of the island. The other entity, "Northern Ireland", with Belfast as its capital, was to be composed of the 6 northeastern administrative counties consisting of about one quarter of the island's territory. A consultative Council of Ireland was to consider matters of common interest.

In that election, Sinn Fein, which campaigned for independence from Britain, captured 124 of the 128 seats for the parliament of 'Southern Ireland' though the Sinn Fein members continued to meet separately in an assembly constituted as the Second Dail Eireann. Within two months a truce was arranged between the British forces in the south and the Irish Republican Army. In October 1921, delegates from the Second Dail

Eireann travelled to London to negotiate a settlement with the British Government.

On 6 December 1921, a Treaty[1] was signed which gave the 26-Counties, henceforth to be styled the Irish Free State, dominion status within the British Empire. While the treaty formally applied to the whole island of Ireland, the parliament of Northern Ireland exercised the opt-out right in May 1922. Publication of the Treaty caused an immediate split in the Sinn Fein organisation. The month of December 1921 and early January 1922 were consumed with acrimonious debate, and eventually, on 6 January 1922, the Second Dail Eireann passed the Treaty[2] by the narrow margin of 64 votes to 57. A provisional government was formed.[3] In June 1922 a general election, known as the "Pact Election" was held under considerable disturbance. The outcome was 58 treatyites, 36 anti-treatyites and 34 others. When many of the independent members declared support for the Treaty, with the result that the anti-treatyites could muster support from only 36 of the 128 members, the anti-treatyites refused to take their seats in the Third Dail Eireann.[4]

Later that month the bloody Civil War broke out and continued until April 1923.[5] The most dramatic event of that conflict was the shelling of the Four Courts, the headquarters of the Republican forces, by the Provisional Army, which forced the surrender of the embattled garrison. To quell the rebellion, the Provisional Government resorted to military courts,[6] and executions followed which were to embitter Irish political life for generations.

Constitution of the Irish Free State 1922

In January 1922, the Provisional Government established a committee to draft a new constitution,[7] which was published on 16 June 1922 - the day of the Pact Election. During September and October 1922, the Third Dail Eireann examined the draft, and "sitting as a Constituent Assembly in this Provisional Parliament",[8] enacted the Constitution of the Irish Free State (Saorstat Eireann) Act 1922, on 25 October 1922. This Constitution came into effect on 6 December 1922, one year after the Treaty was concluded. While acknowledging the constitutional, legal and political changes which had occurred, the preamble provided that if any provision, or amendment, or law made thereunder, was repugnant to the Treaty, it should be absolutely void and inoperative. All things had then to be done, including the enactment of further legislation, to implement the Treaty.

This Constitution, innovative in form and content, was a written composite document establishing the institutions of government and declaring fundamental freedoms. The Irish Free State had Dominion status within the British Empire, and the Crown was represented by a Governor General. The legislative power was vested in an Oireachtas which consisted of the King, the Senate and Dail Eireann. The executive authority was vested in the King, aided and assisted by an Executive Council, headed by a President and responsible to Dail Eireann, which was to be directly elected by popular franchise. Justice was to be administered in public courts by an independent judiciary with a final appeal to the British Privy Council. The courts had the task of deciding whether any law was invalid having regard to the Constitution. A charter of citizens' rights was incorporated. For obvious reasons a totally new system of laws could not come into effect and the practical expedient was adopted of carrying over the existing laws that were to be of full force and effect provided they were not inconsistent with the Constitution. The Constitution could be amended by ordinary legislation within eight years from its coming into operation.[9] Thereafter, it could only be amended by a referendum of the people.

Despite the Constitution of the Irish Free State being a milestone in constitutional and political history, the revolutionary and political violence that had been an ingredient of the struggle for independence for generations, has continued with varying degrees of intensity until modern times. Consequently, statutory enactments for the suppression of subversive activities, including the power of indefinite detention without trial,[10] were deemed necessary from the foundation of the Irish Free State.[11]

Constitution of Ireland 1937

With the changing political landscape, and the gradual dismantling of the Constitution of the Irish Free State, which had culminated in the abolition of the office of Governor General and the Senate, the time had come for a new written document to serve as the basic law.[12] The Constitution of Ireland, Bunreacht na hEireann, having been passed by Dail Eireann,[13] was approved by the people in a plebiscite,[14] and came into operation on 29 December 1937.

This fundamental law marked a further constitutional milestone. In the future, political and legal sovereignty would almost exclusively rest with the people. The visible connection with any external authority, notably the British Crown, which was a feature of the Irish Free State Constitution, was severed though some minor constitutional link remained.[15] In exercise of that sovereignty the people created the State, described as Ireland, and established institutions of government founded on the tripartite separation of the powers of government into legislative power, executive power and judicial power. The Constitution assigned limited functions and powers to the three institutions of government and to their constituent parts. The Constitution placed the individual in a privileged position in relation to the State and acknowledged that the individual was possessed of a collection of natural rights which the State was bound by law and action to defend, protect and vindicate. The Constitution, after a short transition period of three years,[16] could thereafter only be amended by popular referendum.[17]

Detention without Trial Powers in 1939 Law

For two years following the enactment of the Constitution there was no statutory mechanism providing for detention without trial. With the renewal of political violence, particularly when the Irish Republican Army declared war on Britain and organised a bloody bombing campaign in that country,[18] and the possibility of a wider conflict in Europe, the Offences Against the State Act 1939 was enacted[19] which cured this lacuna. Whenever actions and conduct calculated to undermine public order and the authority of the State were committed, the Government could make and publish a proclamation declaring that powers of indefinite detention without trial were necessary to secure the preservation of public peace and order.[20] Whenever the executive was satisfied that any particular person was engaged in activities calculated to prejudice the preservation of the peace, order, or security of the State, the arrest and detention of such person may be ordered. Every person so arrested shall be detained until the Act ceased to be in force or until he was released under other provisions of the Act, whichever happened first.[21] The Act contained safeguards against abuses. Dail Eireann could pass a resolution annulling the proclamation.[22] The Government must establish a Detention Commission, with a membership appointed and removable by the Government, consisting of three persons of whom one must be a barrister or solicitor of not less than seven years standing, or be or have been a judge. Any detained person may apply in writing to the Government to have his detention considered and the Government shall forthwith refer the matter to the Detention Commission, which shall make an inquiry, and shall, with all convenient speed, report thereon to the Government. If the Detention Commission reported that no reasonable grounds existed for the detention, such person shall within one week either be released or be charged according to law with an offence.[23]

Constitutional and Legal Responses to European Conflict: 1939-1945

As war clouds gathered over Europe, the Government realised that the Constitution was inadequate to deal with the scenario that was likely to unfold. War shall not be declared and the State shall not participate in any war save with the assent of Dail Eireann.[24] But the Constitution was silent as to the ramifications of a war taking place in which the State was not a belligerent but which affected the vital interests of the State. Consequently, on Saturday, 2 September 1939, the day before Britain and France declared war on Germany, the Houses of the Oireachtas engaged in a flurry of intense activity. In the space of a mere 15 hours, over a weekend, the Constitution was amended by ordinary legislation, a state of national emergency was declared, and emergency legislation was enacted.

The First Amendment of the Constitution Act[25] was passed[26] with the single purpose of extending the definition of "time of war"[27] to include "a time when there is taking place an armed conflict in which the State is not a participant but in respect of which each of the Houses of the Oireachtas shall have resolved that arising out of such armed conflict, a national emergency exists affecting the vital interests of the State...".

Immediately following the enactment of this amendment, the Houses of the Oireachtas[28] resolved "that arising out of the armed conflict then taking place in Europe that a state of national emergency existed affecting the vital interests of the State".[29] The same article of the Constitution opens with the words: "Nothing in this Constitution shall be invoked to invalidate any law enacted by the Oireachtas which is expressed to be for the purpose of securing the public safety and the preservation of the State in time or war or armed rebellion, or to nullify any act done in time of war or armed rebellion in pursuance of any such law...". Consequently, once a state of national emergency is declared to exist, and a law is enacted for the purposes set out therein, that law is immune from judicial review on the ground of constitutional invalidity. However, the courts may not be completely powerless in that they may review the facts on which these resolutions were based.[30]

In the early hours of Sunday, 3 September 1939, the Emergency Powers Act 1939 was enacted[31] to provide for securing the public safety and the preservation of the State in time of war. This statute permitted the

Government, by emergency order, *inter alia*, to authorise and provide for the indefinite detention of persons, other than natural-born Irish citizens.

Constitutional Challenge to Power of Detention without Trial

The Government, on 22 August 1939, made a proclamation, under Part VI of the Offences Against the State Act 1939, bringing the powers of detention without trial into force. On 15 September 1939, the police searched James Burke's house and found seditious and incriminating documents.[32] The next day the Minister for Justice signed a warrant for Burke's detention. On the application of Burke's brother, leave was granted in the High Court of Justice by Gavan Duffy J to serve a notice of motion for an order of *habeas corpus ad subjiciendum*, pursuant to Article 40.4.2° of the Constitution.[33] Sean MacBride,[34] counsel for Burke, in making the application, indicated that if it were contended that any act was done in pursuant of the Offences Against the State Act 1939 it would be submitted that such provisions were invalid as being repugnant to the Constitution.[35]

Following the hearing of legal argument for two days, Gavan Duffy J delivered his reserved judgment on 1 December 1939. He held for Burke on three grounds, two of which are material here. In investigating the duty of the executive under the relevant section[36] of the Act and in ascertaining its essential character, the word *satisfied* clearly suggested a serious inquiry resulting in a serious finding. Before issuing the arrest warrant the executive must reach a conclusion on certain matters of fact on evidence, though it need not be legal evidence. To have the right to intern, the executive must be satisfied that the person concerned was in fact engaged in specific activities and then must consider whether those activities were calculated to prejudice the State, as being hurtful to the public peace, public order or public security. It would be difficult, if not impossible, for a person to engage in such activities without offending the ordinary criminal law and the activities described were, by their nature, part of the criminal domain. Accordingly, the authority conferred was an authority, not merely to act judicially, but to administer criminal justice and to condemn an alleged offender without charge or hearing, and without the aid of a jury. The administration of justice was a peculiarly and distinctively judicial function which, from its essential nature, did not fall within the executive power and was not properly incidental to the performance of the appropriate functions of the executive arm of government. Consequently, a law that endowed the executive with the powers to indefinitely intern without trial was an invasion of the judicial domain and as such was repugnant to the Constitution.

The second ground for rejecting the law was that the internment without charge or hearing of a citizen was outside the great protection of criminal jurisprudence in that it did not respect his right to personal liberty as far as was practicable. Also it unjustly attacked his person because it did not require that a suspect be brought before a real court. Nor was there any impracticability in telling him, before ordering his internment, what was alleged against him and hearing his answer, a course dictated by elementary justice. The right to personal liberty and the other principles customarily summarised as the rule of law were most deliberately enshrined in a national Constitution, drawn up with the utmost care for a free people. The power to intern on suspicion or without trial was fundamentally inconsistent with the rule of law as expressed therein. The material portion of the judge's order recited that the "court being of opinion that the conferring of a power of internment...in the terms set out in the Offences Against the State Act 1939 is repugnant to the provisions of the Constitution...[and] it is ordered that the said Seamus Burke be forthwith released".

When an immediate appeal was lodged with the Supreme Court of Justice, a preliminary objection was taken by Burke's counsel as to the jurisdiction of that court to entertain such an appeal. After three days of legal argument, the court by a majority,[37] ruled on 15 December 1939, that an appeal did not lie. The single material point was whether the court could hear an appeal from the order directing the release of a person from custody that had been made under Article 40.4.2° of the Constitution. The majority held that the general words in another article,[38] which appeared to confer appellate jurisdiction in such instances, could not abrogate the settled principles and established practice.[39] This provided that once the High Court was satisfied that a detention was unlawful, and made an order for immediate release, and the person had been discharged from custody, the legality of that discharge could never be questioned on appeal. The language of Article 40.4.2° of the Constitution showed that the determination by the High Court was intended to be final.[40]

Executive and Legislative Response: New Detention Powers

On the day after the High Court gave its ruling in Burke's case, 53 detainees were released, because there was no law under which Irish citizens could be detained without trial. Following a dramatic raid by the IRA which dealt a body blow to Government morale,[41] at a time when the European conflict was intensifying, the Houses of the Oireachtas were summoned from recess, on 3 January 1940, to consider two proposals for fresh laws to provide detention powers. The first measure, the Emergency Powers (Amendment) Act 1940, was passed,[42] with the single purpose of deleting the words "other than natural-born Irish citizens" from the Emergency Powers Act 1939. By resorting to the emergency provision of the Constitution, this legislative measure was placed beyond constitutional challenge. Detention for non-citizens, mainly foreign combatants captured within the State, and political and subversive persons, was effected by these measures from 1940 to 1945.[43]

The second measure, the Offences Against the State (Amendment) Bill 1940, passed by the Houses of the Oireachtas,[44] was expressed to make provision for detention. Part II of the Bill was similar, though obviously not identical, to the provisions of Part VI of the 1939 Act. It was in the powers of arrest and detention provisions that the changes necessitated by the decision in Burke's case were to be seen. The offending section[45] was re-enacted except that the word *opinion* was substituted for the word *satisfied*.[46] The composition of the Detention Commission was slightly different in that its membership must include a commissioned officer of the Defence Forces and the Government was required to furnish the Houses of the Oireachtas with particulars of detentions every six months. The main object of enacting the Bill was to obtain from the Supreme Court an opinion as to the constitutionality of ordinary legislation that provided for detention without trial.[47] This was an academic exercise because at that time persons were detained without trial under the Emergency Powers Acts 1939 and 1940.

President Refers Proposal to Supreme Court of Justice

The President, clearly influenced by these suggestions, referred the Offences Against the State (Amendemnt) Bill to the Supreme Court of Justice on 8 January 1940. This was the first occasion that this presidential discretion had been exercised.[48] The hearing lasted five days, with argument advanced on behalf of the Attorney General in favour of the Bill, and with argument advanced against the Bill by counsel assigned by the court.

The Supreme Court,[49] by a majority, advised the President, on 8 February 1940, that the Bill was not repugnant to the Constitution or to any provision thereof. The court attached considerable weight to there being no express prohibition in the Constitution against this type of measure, whereas in many articles, the Oireachtas, in plain and unambiguous language, was prohibited from passing certain laws.[50] The contention was rejected that a Minister, when performing his functions under the Bill, was engaged in trying a criminal charge and that the detention was a punishment in respect of a criminal offence. The single essential preliminary to the exercise of the powers was that the Minister should have opinions on the matters specifically mentioned and the validity of such opinions was not a matter that could be questioned in any court.[51] Detention was not in the nature of punishment but of preventative justice, being a precautionary measure taken for the purpose of preserving the public peace and order and the security of the State. The guarantee of personal liberty, and the duty of determining the extent to which the rights of any particular citizens could properly be harmonised with the rights of citizens as a whole, was a matter peculiarly within the province of the Oireachtas. Any attempt by the court to control the legislature in the exercise of this function would be a usurpation of its authority and in breach of the doctrine of the separation of powers that was enshrined in the Constitution. If the Oireachtas enacted a law within the scope of its legal and constitutional authority it was for the courts to construe and apply such a law. A person in custody was detained in accordance with law if he was detained in accordance with a statute duly passed by the Oireachtas, subject to the qualification that such statute was not repugnant to the Constitution. The right to *habeas corpus* remained.

Following the Supreme Court decision, the President signed and promulgated the Bill as a law on 9 February 1940. This Act was not activated at that time but was brought into operation on two subsequent occasions, on 24 July 1945[52] and on 5 July 1957.

Final Constitutional Amendment and Consequences

The Oireachtas exercised its powers of constitutional amendment by ordinary legislation for the final time when it enacted the Second Amendment of the Constitution Act 1941. These amendments were deemed necessary as a consequence of issues raised both in Burke's case and Article 26 and the Offences Against the State (Amendment) Bill 1940 case. The amendment of interest here was an attempt to provide for legislative certainty and to guard against repetitive challenges to laws that had been declared to be in conformity with the Constitution.[53] Consequently, it is generally accepted that the Offences Against the State (Amendment) Act 1940 was beyond further constitutional challenge. It is universally forgotten that this additional sub-section was not part of the original Constitution, nor was it part of the Constitution when the former Supreme Court pronounced its decision. This constitutional provision, with its far-reaching consequences of granting a permanent badge of constitutionality to certain legislative measures,[54] was inserted by ordinary legislation, as late as May 1941, almost four years after the enactment of the Constitution. Thus, for over fifteen months, from 8 February 1940 - the date of the Supreme Court decision - until the signing of the law containing the constitutional amendments on 31 May 1941, the 1940 Act could have been challenged again as to its constitutionality. For practical and legal reasons such a challenge was unlikely. Since the statute was not in force during that period there was no person with the *locus standi* to challenge its provisions.[55] Had a constitutional action been taken it is probable that *stare decisis*, as then applied, would have compelled the High Court, and on appeal the Supreme Court, to follow the previous decision and to find against the litigant.

The question then arises whether the added sub-section has retrospective effect, a point not adverted to in the literature. If it has, then the court's decision would be subject to the sub-section and the legislative measure would have always been, and continue to be, beyond constitutional reproach. Alternatively, if the enactment of the sub-section had mere prospective effect it would leave the Supreme Court of Justice's decision open to a fresh constitutional challenge.[56] This is possible since the present Supreme Court is not bound by the decisions of the Supreme Court of Justice where laws are challenged as to their constitutionality.[57] In addition, regard must be had to judicial dicta, which suggests that the decision of the Supreme Court in such reference instances may not form binding precedent.[58] It must be axiomatic that the Constitution on its coming into operation was solely to have prospective effect in that circumstances cannot be envisaged whereby the Constitution could have retrospective effect. Whether a constitutional amendment has merely prospective effect may depend on the method of its enactment and its wording. An amendment to the Constitution by referendum, since it is done in such a solemn way, is a matter of serious impact, as serious as the initial enactment of the Constitution. It is arguable that because the people are without limitation on their legislative powers that they could enact an amendment with retrospective effect. That would produce the anomalous position that while the Constitution, the basic law, could not itself have retrospective effect, an amendment of the basic law could have such an effect. On the other hand, the amendments of the Constitution effected by ordinary legislation could be seen as a tidying up of the original Constitution, a process foreseen by the people. In a sense the enactment of the Constitution and these various statutory amendments were a single incident. In that case the rule of prospective effect enjoyed by the Constitution from the date of its coming into effect would extend to these statutory additions from that date. The wording of the sub-section does not expressly provide for retrospective effect - the addition of the phrase 'after the coming into operation of this Constitution' would have put the wording of the sub-section beyond doubt in this regard.[59] The inclusion of the phrase 'shall have been' may have been intended to refer to all references made to the Supreme Court since the coming into operation of the Constitution. If retrospective effect were intended, a more appropriate wording to achieve such a result would have been 'any law' or 'every law'.

An additional reason exists as to why the 1940 Act may not be beyond further constitutional challenge. There is a serious doubt as to whether the former Supreme Court of Justice had the jurisdiction to advise the President in such instances - a very novel jurisdiction - which did not have a counterpart in the Constitution of the Irish Free State. The Constitution of 1937 provided for the temporary continuance of the courts[60] pending the establishment of new courts.[61] It authorised the Supreme Court of Justice to exercise its existing jurisdiction with one expressed addition. That related solely to the determination by that court of the jurisdiction of hearing appeals from the High Court in cases where the validity of a law had been challenged. While there is some authority[62] for the view that the additional sub-section captures this consultative jurisdiction, this very much depends on interpreting the word *law* to include a *bill* – a very doubtful proposition indeed. The expression more likely refers exclusively to the exercise of appellate jurisdiction from the exercise by the High Court of its power to review laws on constitutional grounds. The Supreme Court of Justice presumed it had such jurisdiction to advice the President on the constitutionality of the Offences Against the State (Amendment) Bill. In the absence of express authority conferring such jurisdiction, the Supreme Court of Justice could not, and should not have assumed for itself any additional jurisdiction. In particular, it could not assume a jurisdiction clearly intended to be exercised exclusively by the Supreme Court which was expressly required by the Constitution to be established by laws enacted after the coming into effect of the Constitution. Prior to the enactment of such a law, almost a quarter of a century after the enactment of the Constitution,[63] the judiciary[64] insisted that the courts then in existence were those established by the Courts of Justice Act 1924.

Notes

[1] *Articles of Agreement for a Treaty between Great Britain and Ireland* are printed as a schedule to the Constitution of the Irish Free State (Saorstat Eireann) Act 1922.

[2] Article 18 of the Treaty required such approval.

[3] Ibid. Article 17 required the British Government to transfer power to this body.

[4] *Irish Elections 1918-1977*. C.O'Leary (1979).

[5] *The Irish Republic*. D.Macardle (1968).

[6] The ordinary courts refused relief to those seeking their assistance. "...A state of war had arisen in Ireland and it became the duty of the Government to take all necessary steps to suppress it...", per Molony CJ., on 23 November 1922, in R(Johnstone) v O'Sullivan [1923] 2 IR 13. (CA). "The Provisional Government is now the de jure as well as de facto the ruling authority, bound to administer the law, to preserve the peace and to repress by force, if necessary, all persons who seek by violence to overthrow it", per O'Connor MR, on the same day, in R (Childers) v Adjt.Gen.of the Provisional Forces [1923] 1 IR 5. (KB).

[7] *The Drafting of the Irish Free State Constitution*. B.Farrell. 5 (1970) IJ pp.115 and 343 and IJ 6 (1971) pp.111 and 343. See, *1922 - The Birth of Irish Democracy*. T.Garvin. (1996).

[8] Preamble of the Constitution.

[9] Extended to 16 years by Constitution (Amendment No.16) Act 1929, the validity of which was upheld in The State (Ryan) v Lennon [1935] IR 170. In the 15 years of its existence this Constitution was amended by ordinary legislation 24 times.

[10] See *Fundamental Rights in Irish Law and Constitution*. J.M.Kelly. (1967) pp.77-80.

[11] Public Safety (Emergency Powers) Act 1923 (this Act did not survive a constitutional challenge taken the day after its enactment: R (O'Brien) v Military Governor, North Dublin Union [1914] 1 IR 32 - martial law effectively ended on 1 August 1923 with this decision: see *Political Violence and the Law in Ireland*. Hogan & Walker. (1989). p.175.); Public Safety (Emergency Powers) No.2 Act 1923; Public Safety (Powers of Arrest and Detention) Temporary Act 1924 (for a discussion on these statutes see *Emergency Law in Ireland. 1918-1925*. C.Campbell. (1994). pp. 171-194); Public Safety (Emergency Powers Act 1926; Public Safety Act 1927 (survived a constitutional challenge: AG v McBride [1928] IR 451.); Constitution (Amendment No.17) Act 1931.

[12] *The Constitutional Revolution: An Analysis of the Making of the Constitution*. D.Keogh. 35 (4) Administration. (1987) pp.4-84.

[13] On 14 June 1937. 62 in favour and 48 against. 67-68 DD 434.

[14] On 1 July 1937. Total electorate: 1,775,055. Total poll: 1,346,207. Votes in favour: 685,105 (56.52%). Votes against: 526,945 (43.48%).

[15] External Relations Act 1936 remained in force (see p.10, footnote 4) and was only repealed by the Republic of Ireland Act 1948.

[16] See footnote 25, infra.

[17] Article 46 of the Constitution.

[18] Coogan. op.cit. pp.150-173.

[19] Dail Eireann: 53 votes to 8 on 27 April 1939: 75 DD 1274, and Seanad Eireann: 28 votes to 9 on 31 May 1939: 22 SD 1635. Signed by the President on 14 June 1939.
[20] Offences Against the State Act 1939, section 54 (2).
[21] Ibid. Section 55, quoted at footnote 36, infra.
[22] Ibid. Section 54 (4). A similar power is not conferred on Seanad Eireann.
[23] Ibid. Section 59.
[24] Article 28.3.1° of the Constitution.
[25] Article 51 provided that the Constitution, except Article 51 itself, may be amended by the Oireachtas within three years after the date on which the first President shall have entered into office, which occurred on 25 June 1938 when Dr. Douglas Hyde entered into office. Thus, the transitional period ended on 25 June 1941.
[26] Introduced in Dail Eireann by the Taoiseach (Prime Minister) at 3.00 pm and, after 5 contributions, was agreed to, without a vote, at 4.05 pm: 77 DD 19. Went to Seanad Eireann at 4.15 pm and, after a longer debate with over a dozen contributions, was agreed to, without a vote at 5.45 pm: 23 SD 1043. The President signed the Bill that evening, as it was not legislation but an amendment to the Constitution.
[27] Article 28.3.3° of the Constitution.
[28] Moved in Dail Eireann by the Taoiseach at 6.00 pm. Agreed to in a matter of minutes without a vote and no debate: 77 DD 19-20. Moved in Seanad Eireann at 6.30 pm and after only one serious contribution, was agreed to, without a vote at 6.45 pm: 23 SD 1044-1047.
[29] On 1 September 1976, after considerable debate, resolutions were passed that this emergency ceased to exist and that arising out of the armed conflict taking place in Northern Ireland a national emergency existed: 292 DD 3-260: 85 SD 6-212. In February 1995, resolutions were passed that this emergency ceased to exist: 448 DD 1538-1587: 141 SD 2013-2061.
[30] The Supreme Court decided, in Article 26 and the Emergency Powers Bill 1976 [1977] IR 159, that the presumption that the facts stated in the resolutions were correct had not been displaced in that case, and seemed to leave open the possibility that facts might be challenged.
[31] Dail Eireann, after debate, passed it without a vote: 77 DD 20-190. Seanad Eireann, after debate, passed it without a vote at 5.40 am on Sunday morning: 23 SD 1047-1091. A motion was agreed that, pursuant to Article 25.2.2° of the Constitution, Seanad Eireann concurred to its earlier signature by the President, which was done later that day.
[32] An offence under section 12 of the Offences Against the State Act 1939.
[33] "Upon complaint being made by or on behalf of any person that he is being unlawfully detained, the High Court and any and every judge thereof shall forthwith enquire into the same and may make an order requiring the person in whose custody such person shall be detained to produce the body of the person so detained before such court or judge without delay and to certify in writing as to the cause of the detention, and such court or judge shall thereupon order the release of such person unless satisfied that he is being detained in accordance with the law."
[34] MacBride, as Minister for External Affairs, was later to lead Ireland into the Council of Europe (see p. 2) and signed, on Ireland's behalf, the European Convention of Human Rights (see pp. 5-6). He was to lead Lawless's legal team against the Government of Ireland before the institutions established under the Convention.

[35] The State (Burke) v Lennon [1940] IR 136. The first time a claim of this kind had arisen for adjudication under the Constitution: see Gavan Duffy J at p.143.

[36] Section 55: "Whenever a Minister of State is satisfied that any particular person is engaged in activities calculated to prejudice the preservation of the peace, order, or security of the State, such Minister may by warrant under his hand, order the arrest and detention of such person under this section."

[37] Sullivan CJ., Murnaghan, Meredith, Geoghegan JJ. with Johnston J. dissenting.

[38] Article 34.4.4°: "No law shall be enacted excepting from the appellate jurisdiction of the Supreme Court cases which involve questions as to the validity of any law having regard to the provisions of this Constitution."

[39] On the authority of the British House of Lords decision in *Cox v Hakes* 15 AC 506.

[40] The present Supreme Court refused to follow this decision in The State (Browne) v Feran [1967] IR 147. In that case it held that an appeal to it did lie against the granting of an order of *habeas corpus*.

[41] On the night of 23 December 1939, the Magazine Fort in the Phoenix Park was raided by the IRA and the State's entire ammunition stock was stolen. Coogan. op.cit. pp. 177-9.

[42] By Dail Eireann, 82 votes to 9 votes. 78 DD 1309-1524 and by Seanad Eireann, without a vote: 24 SD 422-559. Signed by the President on 5 January 1940 following a resolution under Article 25.2.2° of the Constitution.

[43] This Act was repealed by the Emergency Powers (Continuance and Amendment) Act 1945, enacted on 29 July 1945.

[44] Passed in Dail Eireann by 62 votes to 7 votes on 4 January 1940: 78 DD 1527-1648 and in Seanad Eireann without a vote on 5 January 1940: 24 SD 563-672.

[45] See footnote 36, supra.

[46] Section 4 of the Bill/Act.

[47] The Taoiseach said that "the President is likely, having seen a decision of the judge of the High Court to the effect that this Act as it stood originally was unconstitutional, and being possessed of the power, before signature, to refer a Bill to the Supreme Court, we would say that he is likely to refer it": 78 DD 1351-52. The Minister for Justice noted that "the main object of the Bill..is to get an opinion from the Supreme Court". 24 SD 563.

[48] Article 26.1.1°: "The President may, after consultation with the Council of State, refer any Bill to which this article applies to the Supreme Court for a decision on the question as to whether such Bill or any specified provision or provisions of such Bill is or are repugnant to this Constitution or to any provision thereof."

[49] Sullivan CJ., Maguire P., Murnaghan, Geoghegan and O'Byrne JJ.

[50] e.g. Article 15.5 provides: "The Oireachtas shall not declare acts to be infringement of the law which were not so at the date of their commission."

[51] This portion of the judgment was later applied in In re O Laighleis [1960] IR 93 (the Lawless case in the domestic courts) by the Supreme Court of Justice. But this view of the law was expressly disapproved of by the Supreme Court in The State (Lynch) v Cooney [1982] IR 337.

[52] Ceased operation on 23 May 1947.

[53] Article 34.3.3° provides: "No court whatever shall have jurisdiction to question the validity of a law, or any provision of a law, the Bill for which shall have been referred to the Supreme Court by the President under Article 26 of this Constitution."

[54] Report of the Committee on the Constitution 1967, para.99: "The best solution would be to retain the existing provision with an amendment to the effect that the Supreme Court decision could be challenged in further legal proceedings after a period of, say, seven years." The Constitutional Review Group (1996) (p.80) recommended "on balance Art.34.3.3° should be deleted in its entirety."

[55] The modern rule as to *locus standi*, contained in Cahill v Sutton [1980] IR 269, provides that the person must have been either adversely affected, or stand in real and imminent danger of being adversely affected, by the law.

[56] This point was not argued when the Lawless case was in the Irish courts: see pp.52-54.

[57] In The State (Quinn) v Ryan [1965] IR 70, the Supreme Court refused to follow a decision of the former Supreme Court in State (Duggan) v Tapley [1952] IR 62.

[58] Ryan v AG [1965] IR 294 per Kenny J in the High Court: "the advice given by the Supreme Court to the President [does not bind] the High Court in the same way as does a decision of the Supreme Court in a case between parties."

[59] The Sixth Amendment of the Constitution (Adoption) Act 1979, which amended Article 37, opens with the words "No adoption of a person taking effect or expressed to take effect at any time after the coming into operation of this Constitution." This sub-section has not been the subject of any judicial comment.

[60] Article 58: "On and after the coming into operation of this Constitution and until otherwise determined by law, the Supreme Court of Justice..shall, subject to the provisions of the Constitution relating to the determination of questions as to the validity of any law, continue to exercise the same jurisdictions...as theretofore."

[61] *Annotated Constitution of Ireland*. Foley & Lalor. (1995). The Transitory Provisions, Articles 52-63, are omitted from official texts of the Constitution published after the date the first President entered into office: Article 52.1.

[62] Sullivan v Robinson [1954] IR 161, per O'Byrne J: "the reference of Bills to the Supreme Court was contemplated as something that might be done during the transition period before courts were set up under the Constitution."

[63] Courts (Establishment and Constitution) Act 1961, signed on 16 August 1961 and brought into effect on 29 September 1961 by Courts (Establishment and Constitution Act (Commencement) Order 1961 (S.I.217 of 1961).

[64] Sullivan v Robinson, supra, and The State (Killian) v Minister for Justice [1954] IR 207; 90 ILTR 116.

3 Governmental Responses to Resurgence of Political Violence in Ireland

Introduction

As already noted in the previous chapter, the constitutional and political partition of the island of Ireland in 1921 generated recurring political violence in every decade from that unfortunate and catastrophic event to the present day. The standard and predictable governmental response to the resurgence of such violence in the 1950s was the introduction of detention without trial. The background to these events, and the activities that culminated in Lawless's detention without trial, are outlined in this chapter. Whether the political violence that occurred could be categorised as a public emergency that threatened the life of the nation, and whether the actual response was strictly required by the exigencies of that situation, and whether Lawless's detention could be justified, were crucial issues to be resolved when these events came later to be judged in the light of the European Convention of Human Rights. The chapter ends with revelations, detailed here for the first time, of episodes whereby the executive prevented the legislature from discussing matters relating to detention without trial.

Resurgence of Political Violence

The ending of the war in 1945 brought a lull in IRA violence that had been a constant feature of life during that period. Repressive measures and the disenchantment with the lack of military success coupled with the failure to gain any credible popular support combined to weaken the interest in armed struggle as a method of achieving the political reunification of the island. The British presence in Ireland continued to be a highly emotive political issue. Despite the enactment of the Republic of Ireland Act 1948, which severed the last remaining constitutional and political link with Britain, and membership of the Council of Europe, which gave Ireland a voice in European affairs, the lull in IRA activities was merely a prelude to a resurgence of political violence. The first task facing the IRA was to re-arm, and attacks on barracks in Northern Ireland and Britain[1] yielded a large quantity of arms and ammunitions. Violent activities, sporadic at first though often deadly in nature, committed in Northern Ireland were repeatedly condemned by elected representatives in Dublin.[2]

Gerard Lawless

Gerard Richard Lawless was born on 15 August 1936, the eldest of five children, and lived in Dublin's north inner city where his father found regular employment in the docks. As was the tradition of the time he left school in his early teens and took a number of labouring jobs. At 17 years of age he enlisted in the Forsa Cosanta Aitiuil (FCA), the Army Reserve, on 11 March 1954. On joining the army he solemnly swore that he would be faithful to Ireland and loyal to the Constitution, and that he would obey all orders and not join nor be a member of nor subscribe to any secret society. There was later to be a dispute as to the length of time Lawless served in the FCA. He maintained that he attended parades for only 18 months, until late 1955. The Government maintained, to the contrary, that Lawless remained a serving soldier for two years and nine months, until the end of 1956. The importance of this point was whether Lawless, while serving in the Defence Forces, had become and remained an IRA member and taken part in subversive activity.

Also, from an early age Lawless belonged to one of a number of minor groups dedicated to a policy of physical force to end the partition of Ireland. One such group, the Irish National Brotherhood, later known as the Irish Volunteers had been organised by Lawless. This group was subsequently absorbed into the Fianna Eireann, a scout organisation with republican ideals. Lawless, on his own admission, as will be seen later in this chapter, became a member of the IRA in January 1956.

By June 1956, there was considerable disunity amongst IRA members, with some expressing strong dissatisfaction with IRA leadership for not pursuing a sufficiently militant policy. While a good deal of discussion took place, no agreement with the dissidents was possible and they severed their connection from the main IRA. This organisation, which appointed its own "Army Council" was not recognised within the republican movement, and was generally known, and is thus described throughout this work, as the "IRA splinter group". Lawless, by then a tough, violent and undisciplined agitator, left the ultra-conservative IRA he distrusted and went with the IRA splinter group leadership. In subsequent months and years, this splinter group committed a number of armed outrages though never caused death or serious injury. For example, in Northern Ireland six customs posts were destroyed in November 1956, and in May 1957 the locks on the Newry canal were blown up causing immense damage. In the Republic of Ireland, the group's activities consisted of armed raids to steal explosives, the blowing up of the Gough monument - which honoured an Irishman who had served as a soldier in the British Empire and was situated in a large public park in the city of Dublin - and the drilling of its members. The Government consistently claimed that Lawless was a member of the IRA splinter group. Lawless accepted that he was such a member but persistently claimed that he severed his links with the IRA splinter group towards the end of 1956.

On 21 September 1956, Lawless was one of four men found in a deserted house near the border between the Irish Republic and Northern Ireland in which the police found a machine gun, six rifles, six shotguns, a revolver, an automatic pistol and over 400 rounds of ammunition. The men admitted they were IRA members returning to Dublin from a ten-day training camp in County Donegal.[3] Some of these firearms had been recently stolen by armed men from the residence of a retired British Army officer. The men were charged in the Dublin District Court with possession of firearms and ammunition without a firearms certificate and possession of six firearms that had been stolen or obtained unlawfully, a charge later withdrawn. The men refused to say anything and were remanded in custody as they declined the bail that was set. During the adjourned hearing, Lawless said: "We may as well tell you we are members of the IRA and the guns were the property of the IRA." Later, another one of the group said: "As a soldier of the Irish Republican Army and as leader of these men here I do not wish to have any part in the proceedings of this court." On being asked to plead to the charges, the same man said: "On behalf of my comrades and myself I wish to state that any arms and ammunition found on us were to be used against the British forces of occupation to bring about the re-unification of our country and no Irishman or woman of any political persuasion had anything to fear from us. We hold that it is legal to possess arms and also to believe it is the duty of every Irishman to bear arms in defence of his country." Lawless subsequently said in a reply that this man spoke for him. The defendants were returned for jury trial. On 23 November 1956, these men, including Lawless, refused to recognise the jurisdiction of the Circuit Criminal Court and pleas of "not guilty" were entered. At the conclusion of the prosecution case the judge directed the jury to acquit on the ground that the technical requirements of proving that each accused did not hold a firearms certificate had not been complied with. Lawless was later to admit his involvement in these events when giving evidence before the sub-Commission of Human Rights in Strasbourg. The Attorney General was later to say, before the European Court of Human Rights, that "under the Irish system of law, an acquittal of this kind is not the subject of any appeal, but it involves no declaration of innocence".[4]

In October 1956, Military Intelligence became aware, probably as a result of his arrest on the firearm charges, that Lawless was engaged in unlawful activities and that, for security reasons, he was an undesirable person to retain in the Defence Forces. Accordingly, he was discharged with effect from 11 December 1956.

Launch of IRA Campaign

On 12 December 1956, the IRA launched what was to become known in popular history as the "Border Campaign". The IRA was composed of members from Northern Ireland and the Irish Republic. Often the territory of the Irish Republic was used as a base from which to launch attacks into Northern Ireland, and as a safe haven to return to when these missions were completed or aborted. Initially, the attacks were aimed at the destruction of buildings and bridges. Later, armed attacks on police barracks were mounted which resulted in the death of police officers. On 1 January 1957, in an attack on Brookeborough barracks, a police officer and two IRA members died. The Taoiseach, John A.Costello TD, in a radio broadcast, on 6 January, said that while there were groups hostile to one another, each group had in common only their defiance of the authority of the Government and Dail Eireann and their willingness to set Irishmen in arms against one another. Because of the duty owed to the people to avert the evils which followed when men take the law into their own hands, the Government instructed the authorities to take the necessary action to put a halt to these activities. Despite this crackdown, which resulted in many arrests and imprisonments for a variety of offences, these efforts by the authorities in the Irish Republic failed to halt the attacks.

Raids on Explosives Factories

On 12 January 1957 a late night burglary took place at a chemical store in the Republic in which one ton of explosives was stolen. The IRA denied involvement and stated that it "again emphasised that the Republican Movement regards activities of this nature as definite acts of sabotage against the campaign now in progress in the 6 Counties against British occupation". On 6 May 1957 an armed raid by six men took place at a factory, again in the Republic, in which a further quantity of explosives was stolen. Again, the IRA denied that any "branch of the Irish Republican Movement had any connection" with the raid. Some time after this second raid, the police "received from one of the participants confidential information which indicated the persons who had actually taken part in the armed raid". "Lawless's participation in [these raids] was received under a promise of secrecy from another member of this IRA group who took part in the raid[s]."[5] On 14 May nine members of the IRA splinter group were arrested, including Lawless. He was taken to a police station where, when searched, an incriminating document was found in his pocket. During a subsequent search of his home, two further documents were found which he accepted as his. During questioning he gave an account of his movements from midnight on 5 May to midnight on 6 May. Lawless was placed on an identification parade in connection with the second armed raid though he was not identified by any of the witnesses.

Despite the failure to charge Lawless with these offences, the Government repeatedly claimed that he had taken part in these two raids, claims Lawless consistently and persistently denied. Indeed, when the Attorney General had the one opportunity to cross-examine Lawless as to his alleged part in these raids, before the European sub-Commission of Human Rights, he failed to do so. That omission was not to deter, in any way, a public repetition of these allegations before the European Court of Human Rights.[6]

Lawless's Conviction for Possessing Incriminating Documents and Acquittal of Membership of an Unlawful Organisation Charge

Lawless was charged with the possession of three incriminating documents. These were: (a) a sketched map which showed the County Donegal border village of Pettigo marked to indicate a British customs post and a police barracks and on which were written the words "Infiltrate, Annihilate, Destroy"; (b) a document relating to the Ayrshire Radar Station in Britain; and (c) a document on guerrilla warfare. Lawless was convicted of this offence and was sentenced to one month's imprisonment.

At the same court hearing a charge of membership of an illegal organisation (the IRA) was preferred against Lawless. A police officer gave evidence on oath that Lawless had said on arrest "I am in nothing now". This denial was accepted and the charge was dismissed. The Government later claimed that these words were a formula devised by the IRA splinter group with the intention of conveying that since the IRA had disowned Lawless he was no longer a member of any unlawful organisation. This despite the fact that he continued, with others of the splinter group, to engage in activities of a kind which made any such organisation an illegal organisation. It was also claimed that during the hearing he questioned the authority of that court to try "Republican soldiers" and when sentenced said: "the court is merely being used to safeguard the last remnants of the British Empire". Lawless, when he appeared before the sub-Commission of Human Rights, claimed that his exact words were "whether the judge realised or not that the Special Branch [the branch of the police which dealt with subversive crime] were using the process of the court to protect the last remnants of the British Empire in Ireland". The Attorney General was later to be critical of this acquittal before the European Court of Human Rights.[7] While he explained that it was not unusual for a court, when a person was convicted on a particular charge, to dismiss other minor charges arising out of the same facts, he said that despite this practice he could not explain the acquittal decision. The Attorney General rightly said that no evidence was offered on Lawless's behalf to show that he was not an IRA member and the court did not state the reasons for his acquittal. He then disingenuously failed to mention the denial Lawless had made to the arresting police officer, which was given in court and which was not challenged by the prosecuting authority. These critical comments were part of a wider undercurrent of dissatisfaction, and even suspicion, which the executive held with regard to the judiciary of the inferior courts and which is discussed later in this chapter.

While imprisoned Lawless associated with other persons who, the Government claimed,[8] were members of the IRA splinter group on remand awaiting trial for the armed raid on one of the explosive factories. One of these associates, said to be the leader of the splinter group, later received two concurrent sentences of two months' imprisonment on charges of membership of an illegal organisation and possession of incriminating documents, though he was never detained without trial.[9] Another associate, acquitted with Lawless of possessing firearms, was later convicted of a different charge of the possession of firearms, and sentenced to three months' imprisonment, though acquitted of membership of an illegal organisation. Both these men were acquitted of the armed raid on the explosive factory by direction of the trial judge because there was insufficient evidence to sustain the charges. The Government was later to claim that the witnesses had been intimidated. Whether this prison association was by accident or by design was to become controversial later.

Lawless was to claim that he had no control over what prison, and in what part of that prison, he was to be confined in. The Government stressed that it was by design, which tended to suggest that Lawless had continued association with IRA members while in prison, long after he claimed he had dissociated himself from all unlawful organisations. Lawless was released from prison on 15 June 1957.

Government Introduces Detention without Trial

IRA action continued in Northern Ireland.[10] On 4 July 1957 a police officer was killed and another wounded. This was the final act that provoked the Irish Government into action. At its meeting on Friday 5 July the Government decided to bring into operation Part II of the Offences Against the State (Amendment) Act 1940.[11] Over the following weekend, 63 men were arrested in countrywide raids for which no official explanation was given. The first public announcement of the introduction of detention without trial was made on Monday 8 July when the following proclamation appeared in a special issue of Iris Oifigiuil, the Government Gazette, and was published widely in the media:

PROCLAMATION

The Government, in exercise of the powers conferred on it by sub-section 2 of section 3 of the Offences Against the State (Amendment) Act 1940 (No.2 of 1940), hereby declares that the powers conferred by Part II of the said Act are necessary to secure the preservation of public peace and order and that it is expedient that the said Part of said Act should come into force immediately.

Given under the official seal of the
Government this 5th day of July 1957.
Eamon de Valera, Taoiseach.

A rather terse Government statement, issued on the same day, stated that no one was arrested because of political activity. Those arrested were believed to be engaged in the activities of an organisation attempting to maintain a military or armed force in contravention of the Constitution. More detailed reasons for the introduction of detention without trial were not given publicly until 25 July 1957, some three weeks after the event. A statement, couched in very general terms, from the Government said that "no democratic State could endure - that there could be neither ordered Government, security nor progress in any community in which groups could organise, arm and equip themselves, assume powers of life and death, and arrogate to themselves the right to make war at will, in defiance of the legitimate Government and the basic law. Those against whom the Government had recently to take action were leading members of such groups, the activities of which had already led to loss of life and were likely, if continued, to embroil the Irish people not only in war with another country but in a hateful civil war as well. The Government took this action only when other means had failed. These groups were appealed to and warned over the last two or three years but all appeals and warnings were ignored, and armed activities, with loss of life, continued. To prevent error, every detained person had the right to appeal to the Detention Commission. Moreover, no one would be kept in detention who undertook to respect the Constitution and the laws and to refrain from being a member of, or assisting, any unlawful organisation".

Simultaneously with the introduction of detention without trial a practice was introduced that if a detained person gave an undertaking as to his future conduct he would be released.[12] It is useful to examine the background to this practice, which had no statutory basis, because it was to continuously percolate through the Strasbourg proceedings. Initially, this requirement of an undertaking as to future conduct arose in the context of restoring public officials and others to service and employment following conviction for subversive crimes. The Government had decided, on 28 March 1957, some months before the introduction of detention without trial, that civil servants convicted under the Offences Against the State Act 1939 should be suspended from duty and pay. In addition, such steps as were necessary to suspend from duty and pay all officers and employees of local authorities and other local bodies, including vocational education committees, committees of agriculture and harbour authorities, similarly convicted should be taken. Where the convicted person was employed by a state-sponsored body that body should be informed of the action decided upon in the cases of civil servants and officers and employees of local authorities and other local bodies. Restoration to duty of such persons should be conditional on the prior signature of an undertaking in terms to be settled after consideration by the Minister for Justice in consultation with the Attorney General.

The Government, on 9 April 1957, decided on the following: "I undertake to uphold the Constitution of Ireland and its laws, and I declare that I am not and will not become a member of, or assist, any unlawful organisation". From the available archival material it is impossible to state with certainty when it was decided that those detained without trial would be released on giving a similar undertaking. In late July 1957, it was agreed, following discussions, that the word "respect" should be substituted for "uphold" and that the expression "the laws" should be substituted for "its laws".[13] This clarification of the terms of the undertaking was a prelude to the issuing of a Government statement, on 25 July 1957, already quoted. But the Department of Justice noted that the police informed all but a few senior members of the IRA immediately on arrest that release would follow on the signing of the undertaking. A small number signed and were released but the majority refused, making contemptuous remarks. Those arrested in the early days of the introduction of the powers of detention, and this included Lawless, were asked to give the original undertaking to uphold the Constitution and its laws. Incidentally, the authority for the police to act in this manner cannot be traced and it is highly unlikely that individual police officers would have assumed this responsibility. It is very probable that such authority came from the Department of Justice. It also seems that not every detained person had been informed that release would follow the giving of an undertaking and it seems that the military authorities in charge of the place of detention had authority to release a detained person forthwith on the giving of the required undertaking.

In the interest of clarity and uniformity, the Government, on 6 August 1957, decided that each detained person should be informed individually, in writing, of the terms of the undertaking. The Minister for Justice was given discretion either (a) to order the release of a detained person without requiring an undertaking where, in his opinion, the circumstances warranted that course, or, (b) to direct that an oral undertaking should be accepted, provided that it was formally given in the presence of a witness and that a record, signed by the witness, of the giving of the undertaking was retained. The Attorney General was later to state before the European Court of Human Rights[14] that it was indicated to detained persons that their giving of an undertaking would not be disclosed to other persons and that in releasing persons from detention it would not be disclosed whether the person had in fact given an undertaking. Accordingly, on 16 August 1957, each detained person was informed in writing that he would be released forthwith on giving an undertaking "to respect the Constitution of Ireland and the laws, and not be a member of, or assist, any organisation which is an unlawful organisation under the Offences Against the State Act, 1939".[15] From the available archival material it is impossible to say how many persons were either not detained, or released from detention, on giving this undertaking. As will be noted in the next chapter, Lawless was released when he gave a modified form of this undertaking and it will be noted later that large numbers of detained persons were released without giving any form of undertaking.

The Taoiseach was later asked to state whether any threat of war against this country had been made and if so would he name the country, state the terms of the threat and the action taken.[16] He replied that no threat of war had been made against this country. This statement was to have important repercussions much later. Whether there existed at that time in Ireland a public emergency which entitled the Government to derogate from its obligations under the Convention of Human Rights, and whether the measures taken were strictly required by the exigencies of the situation, and, of equal importance, how these matters were to be proved, were to be central to the Lawless case before the Strasbourg organs.

On 20 November 1957, four months after the introduction of the powers of detention,[17] the Minister for Justice, for the first time, gave more specific reasons when replying to a motion in Dail Eireann calling for the release of those detained. The course of this motion is considered later. Within the Department of Justice there was a suspicion that some members of the District Court judiciary harboured latent support for IRA activists.[18] It was noted that some of those judges "allowed scenes and propaganda" and that others gave "perverse decisions". One judge did claim that he had been intimidated after hearing a subversion case.[19] Despite these claims, the 1956 official criminal statistics recorded that "no persons were punished" under the Offences Against the State Act 1939.[20] In 1957 "a total of 126 persons were prosecuted for [such] breaches, of whom 113 were convicted, [and] 11 were sentenced to prison without the option of a fine".[21] The charges generally preferred, such as membership of an illegal organisation,[22] failure to account for movements,[23] and possession of incriminating documents[24] were minor offences attracting relatively light sentences. It was the practice, if not the policy, to arrest suspects, question them and search for incriminating documents.[25] Convictions were thus secured in a great many cases, though the sentences were short. In other instances, failure to secure a conviction inevitably followed from the failure of the prosecution to produce the correct evidence. The more compelling reason for the lack of an increase in subversive crime was that the majority of serious offences were committed outside the jurisdiction of the Irish Republic and no mechanism existed in law for trying persons found in the Irish Republic for offences committed elsewhere.[26] There is slight evidence that at that time the establishment of special courts was considered.[27] The Department of Justice noted that if proceedings were taken in special courts, the proof required would have been as strict as in the ordinary courts. However, it was also noted that conviction of membership of an unlawful organisation in special courts carried a penalty of two years' imprisonment as against a mere three months that could be imposed in the District Court.

Looking at general life in the Irish Republic from the end of December 1956 to July 1957, one is driven to the conclusion that events were normal and tranquil. The institutions of government functioned, the Houses of the Oireachtas met regularly, indeed, a general election had been held in March 1957. The courts performed their business, and central and local government conducted their affairs as usual. Every other aspect of life continued as normal. Public events, such as the St. Patrick's Day parades and Easter parades, were held, the individual could enjoy many sporting activities, and social, cultural and religious events were held regularly and without incident. Activities associated with public emergencies, such as widespread civil disobedience, general strikes, violent actions aimed at government, etc. were never a possibility, let alone likely. The usual governmental responses to a public emergency, such as the suspension of the Constitution, the elected assembly and the courts, or the enactment of special emergency laws, the greater use of the military, curfews, travel restrictions, the banning of public meetings, censorship, etc. were all absent. The Lord Mayor of Dublin, at that time, averred that "there has been for many years now a complete absence of public disorder, riots, civil commotion or other grave disturbances of the public peace arising out of political issues of any nature".[28] Historians make merely passing reference to the period and there is no claim that events amounted to an emergency, using that expression in its ordinary sense. One historian, when referring to the period, merely notes that the Government of the Republic re-introduced internment in July 1957 and co-operated with the Belfast Government to snuff out IRA border raids.[29] Another notes, again in a passing reference, that the Dublin Government effectively dealt with the IRA in an almost routine manner and the campaign was broken before the year was out.[30] A legal commentator, writing in 1962,[31] noted that "in 1957 it must be confessed that along with the majority of his fellow inhabitants of the Irish Republic the writer was unaware of a threat which could not have been met by the ordinary law of the land". In reality, the introduction of detention without trial was an easy and crude method of dealing with the recurring consequences of the partition of Ireland, essentially a political problem, by an authoritarian figure coming to the end of a long political career, in an era that was also coming to a conclusion both at home and abroad. Within a handful of years the political, legal and social landscape was to change so drastically in Ireland and elsewhere, that detention without trial would never be used in the Irish Republic again to suppress political violence.

The Detention Commission was established by the Government on 16 July 1957.[32] This was required under section 8 of the Offences Against the State (Amendment) Act 1940. The membership was composed of Barra O Briain, a judge of the Circuit Court, Eamonn O Riain, a District Justice and Colonel John V. Joyce,[33] an officer of the Defence Forces.

The Government authorised the Minister for External Affairs to despatch a letter to inform the Secretary General of the Council of Europe that Part II of the Offences Against the State Act 1940, which conferred special powers of arrest and detention, had been brought into force. In so far as the coming into operation of the Act involved derogation from the obligations imposed by Article 5 of the Convention for the Protection of Human Rights and Fundamental Freedoms then this letter was to be regarded as notice in accordance with Article 15 (3) of the Convention.[34] It was further stated that the detention of persons was considered necessary to prevent the commission of offences against public order and to prevent the maintaining of military or armed forces other than those authorised by the Constitution. The Detention Commission had been established to inquire into the ground of detention of any person who applied to have his detention investigated. This letter was despatched on 20 July 1957.

Role of the Houses of the Oireachtas

The 1940 Act provides that it shall be lawful for Dail Eireann, at any time while the Act was in force, to pass a resolution annulling such proclamation.[35] When the Government made the proclamation on 5 July 1957, Dail Eireann was not in session, having been adjourned the previous day until 23 October 1957.[36] Dail Eireann was thus prevented from exercising its supervisory jurisdiction over this executive action. It is reasonable to assume, from the early adjournment of Dail Eireann, that the Government did not wish to risk the possibility that such a resolution might have been tabled. While such a motion would undoubtedly have been defeated, because the Government commanded the support of the majority of the members of Dail Eireann, the embarrassment it might have caused would certainly not have been welcomed. While the other House of the Oireachtas, Seanad Eireann, did not adjourn until 11 July 1957 the matter was not raised there. Thus, detention without trial, which made major inroads into the constitutional right to personal liberty and involved derogation from the European Convention of Human Rights, was in operation for two-and-a-half months before the matter could be raised in Dail Eireann, the statutory supervisory forum.

On the day Dail Eireann resumed, the 23 October 1957, a question was asked as to whether the bringing into operation of the 1940 Act constituted a violation of the Convention.[37] The Minster for External Affairs read the letter sent to the Council of Europe, the first time it had been made public, and stated that he had not been advised that the Act constituted a violation of the Convention. He was reminded that the Consultative Assembly of the Council of Europe had reported that the letter in fact announced that there had been derogation from the Convention. The Minister refused to be further drawn because submissions were then being made in the Supreme Court concerning the Convention and he thought it would be undesirable to expand on what he had said. On 6 November 1957, a motion was tabled in Dail Eireann "that the Government should forthwith release from custody...persons who are interned under the Offences Against the State Acts". In speaking against the motion, the Minister for Justice explained that for the first six months of 1957, 103 persons, convicted of offences against the State and firearms offences, had been committed to prison for periods ranging from 14 days to 6 months, 41 of whom had served their sentences.[38] Most were known to be preparing to resume their activities. The 62 remaining in prison were due for release shortly. The 4 July raid in Northern Ireland in which a police officer was killed was referred to. The aborted trial in which persons had been acquitted of an armed raid for explosives, due to the intimidation of witnesses, meant that the ordinary courts were inadequate to secure the due administration of justice. Not surprisingly, the motion was heavily defeated.[39]

A further three months passed before the issue was raised again. On 20 February 1958, the following motion appeared on the order paper: "that Dail Eireann is of opinion that the internment of person without charge or trial, in existing circumstances, is contrary to the spirit of the Convention of Human Rights which was ratified by this country, and calls upon the Government to adhere to the full terms of the Convention by discontinuing the internment of persons without charge or trial."[40] In the preparation of a response within the Department of External Affairs,[41] legal advice was offered that a discussion at that time could be most untimely because of the Lawless application, which at that stage was the subject of an interchange of views between the parties and was due to come before the European Commission of Human Rights in March. Clearly, it would put the Government at a disadvantage if it had to deploy its arguments in public. Arguably the matter was not *sub-judice* since the Commission was not a court though it could be pointed out that the proceedings before the

Commission were private and that it would prejudice that consideration to have the matter debated publicly. As an international instrument, the European Convention provided machinery for considering applications and it did not seem proper for the Government, as a party to proceedings, to make statements on the matter. If the substance of the complaint came to be considered by the Commission, it was presumed that: the Government did not admit that there had been a derogation under Article 15 (1) of the Convention; and, there was no reason to admit this, unless and until the Commission decided otherwise. However, without going into the strictly legal aspects, the Minister might, if the motion was pressed, having initially indicated the undesirability of public discussion, state that the Government's action was within the spirit of the Convention. It was clearly the intention that the Convention could not be used as a protection for those who wished to overthrow the institutions that guaranteed human rights. In an advice to the Minister, the Secretary of the Department referred to the legal advice. He also pointed out that the standing orders of Dail Eireann did not provide for any specific power of the Chairman of Dail Eireann to rule out of order a motion of which proper notice had been given. It was nevertheless accepted that, in certain circumstances, he might do so. It was the recognised practice that a matter, whilst under adjudication by a court of law, should not be brought before the House. A court of law for this purpose would normally mean one of the domestic courts since there was no provision in the Constitution or statute law for the recognition of any other courts. Accordingly, the question that arose was whether the Commission of Human Rights, as the duly appointed body to hear applications in respect of alleged violations of the Convention, could be deemed to be on the same footing as a domestic court. The acceptance of a motion was entirely a matter for the personal and exclusive discretion of the Chairman of Dail Eireann. The matter was then taken up verbally with the Clerk of Dail Eireann, who expressed some doubt as to whether this case could properly be described as coming within the category of *sub-judice.* He adverted to the possible implications of treating it in that manner. By doing so it would imply acceptance by the Government of any decision reached. He undertook to put the matter to the Chairman and in a later communication it was indicated that the Chairman had been in touch with the sponsors of the motion and promised to convey the result to the Department of External Affairs. The motion was not raised again in Dail Eireann until 26 November,[42] some nine months later, and it is unclear whether or not these tactics were responsible for that delay.

The Minister for External Affairs said that the Chairman would not allow a detailed discussion of a case before the domestic courts and that the same procedure should be adopted when there was a case[43] before a European Court,[44] which Dail Eireann had accepted in the same way as it had accepted the domestic courts.[45] When the Minister asked for a chance to persuade the Chairman of that, the proposer of the motion agreed to postpone the discussion provided that time would be guaranteed by the Government to allow a discussion if it was decided that the motion was in order. The Minister agreed to this request. The Minister then wrote to the Chairman enclosing a copy of the memorandum containing the legal advice. When the motion came on 2 December 1958,[46] the Chairman said that he had written to the proposer of the motion stating that the Minister for External Affairs had stated that in the matter of human rights, the jurisdiction of the European Court of Human Rights has been accepted by the State, and that a person had commenced a case bearing on the subject matter of the motion and that in such circumstances a debate in Dail Eireann on the motion should not occur until any judicial hearing and determination of the matter had taken place. For that reason the motion was ruled out of order. When the proposer asked if the Minister's statement meant that should the Court of Human Rights uphold the case, that decision would be accepted by the Government, the Chairman replied that he had nothing to say on that and that he had been given the information that the Court of Human Rights was on "all fours" with the domestic courts on matters within its competency. The Chairman wrote to the Minister stating that he had considered the memorandum forwarded to him, and in view of the position as stated he had informed the members concerned on that date that a debate on the motion should not occur until a judicial hearing and determination of the matter had taken place.

Attention now switched to Seanad Eireann where the motion "that Seanad Eireann is of opinion that all those internees against whom the Government possess sufficient evidence to prefer a charge, should now be charged and tried by the ordinary courts, and that all other internees should now be released" appeared on the order paper. In preparing a response the Department of Justice considered the possible contents of an appropriate answer.[47] Then, the Department of External Affairs intervened by forwarding a copy of the note prepared for the Chairman of Dail Eireann on the question of the Lawless case being *sub-judice* and a copy of the reply from the Chairman, which conveyed his decision. The Department of Justice then decided to follow the lead of External Affairs and attempted to have the motion ruled out of order. This was because it was considered almost impossible to keep the Senators tied down to dealing with internment as an abstract subject and to refrain from debating the merits of internment in the light of the present political situation vis-à-vis the IRA.If the Senators did go into the merits of the situation, the Minister could not justify his exercise of detention powers because to so do would be to cut right across the attitude of the Minister for External Affairs in his approach, which had succeeded, in getting the motion on internment ruled out of order. A discussion in the Seanad would, no doubt, be used to influence the decision of the Commission on Human Rights. At this juncture that body was conducting an enquiry as to whether there was a state of public emergency threatening the life of the nation which warranted derogation from the State's obligation under the Convention. The opinion of the Lord Mayor of Dublin was canvassed and presented to the Commission as indicative of public opinion. A debate that would deal with internment as an abstract subject would serve no useful purpose. It would give the proposer of the motion and others "of that kidney" an opportunity of posing as the friends of freedom and presenting the case for release from detention in an attractive light. It would be well nigh impossible for the Minister to refute, tied as his hands were from referring to the realities of the situation. The Secretary of the Department of Justice wrote to the Clerk of Seanad Eireann drawing the attention of the Chairman of Seanad Eireann to what had happened in Dail Eireann. Notwithstanding that the Seanad motion was in different terms, and made no express mention of the Human Rights Convention, it appeared to call in question the necessity for the measures taken. It invited a debate as to whether these measures were strictly required by the exigencies of the situation, which was one of the questions that arose under Article 15 of the Convention in proceedings to which the State was a party that were going on in the European Commission of Human Rights. That being so, the Minister thought that the Chairman might wish to consider the propriety of allowing these matters to be debated at the present time. Enclosed was the copy of a submission that was made to the Chairman of Dail Eireann on behalf of the Minister for External Affairs together with a copy of the Chairman's decision.

When the motion came on for discussion in Seanad Eireann, on 10 December 1958,[48] the Chairman said that he understood that a process had been commenced as a result of a case, which had a bearing on the subject matter of the motion, and which might come before the Court of Human Rights. As the State had accepted the jurisdiction of that Court he ruled that the matter was *sub-judice* at the moment and could not be debated pending the judicial determination of that case and that the proposer had been notified earlier of his decision. In reply, the proposer of the motion said that while he accepted the ruling, the subject of his motion was not the Human Rights Convention, that had not been mentioned. The State's plea, as he understood it, was to try to prove that the Government had not acted *ultra vires* in interning people. His motion made no such suggestion. His motion dealt explicitly with the internees, whereas the case before the Court of Human Rights dealt solely with a man who had been released and to whom his motion could not apply. The Chairman responded that he had given very careful consideration to this matter and was satisfied that debate could prejudice the fair and impartial hearing of the case. The Court of Human Rights was in a similar position to the domestic courts on matters of competency. The proposer would appreciate that the motion was not ruled out but merely deferred for consideration to a later date.

In an era when executive government conducted its affairs in secret, the ready resort to any justification to stifle debate is hardly surprising. But in this instance it had all the elements of high farce. Even if the matters were debated in the Houses of the Oireachtas in Dublin, those debates would have to be translated into diverse European languages, these reports would then have to be wired to the four corners of Europe, then be published in the media in seventeen European countries that stretched from Norway in the north to Turkey in the south, then be read by the members of the Commission, and the yet unappointed judges to an unestablished court, and then be of a such a nature as to be influential to the detriment of the Irish Government's case. The chances of any matter discussed in the Irish Houses of the Oireachtas being reported abroad must, even in this modern age of communication, be slender but to imagine that could have happened in the 1950s borders on the ludicrous. Leaving that absurd situation aside, what is particularly disappointing and somewhat disturbing about this episode is how extraordinarily easily parliamentarians were dissuaded from debating in the Houses of the Oireachtas matters considered of public importance. In addition, these incidents proved that the supervisory control over detention powers that Dail Eireann possessed under statute were hollow and meaningless. Unfortunately, this point was never fully exploited by Lawless, and consequently by default, the Strasbourg organs were able to hold that effective parliamentary control in some way mitigated the possible abuse of detention powers.

Notes

[1] See generally: *The IRA*. T.P.Coogan. (1972) and *The Secret Army - A History of the IRA 1916-1970*. (1972). J.Bowyer Bell.

[2] The Taoiseach in Dail Eireann on 28 October 1954 (147 DD 160-250) and 30 November 1955. (153 DD 1349-50).

[3] Bowyer Bell refers to this group as the "Lawless column". op.cit. p.331.

[4] Lawless case. ECHR. 1960-61. Series B, p.469.

[5] DJ File S.9/58/1. As late as April 1959, the police claimed that they rechecked this information with their informant.

[6] Lawless Case. op.cit., p.470. Address by Attorney General. 10 April 1961.

[7] Ibid. p. 471.

[8] Ibid. p.472.

[9] MacBride, in April 1959, asked the sub-Commission of Human Rights: "this man [X], whose name you have seen over and over again...who has been referred to day in and day out here, was...never...interned...He is...the employee of a State body...If he was such a dangerous desperado and if the Government really thought that he was so dangerous that anybody seen in his vicinity should be imprisoned without trial, would he not have been interned ?"

[10] Detention without trial had been introduced in Northern Ireland on 27 June 1957.

[11] Government Minute: Item 1. 12 members were present, as was the AG.

[12] For a discussion on a similar undertaking during the 1922-25 period, see *Emergency Law in Ireland. 1918-1925*. op.cit. pp.230-32.

[13] DT File S.16274A.

[14] Lawless Case. ECHR. 1960-61. Series B. p. 459.

[15] Ibid. p.474. 10 April 1961.

[16] In Dail Eireann. 64 DD 197.

[17] Coincidentally, the same day that the Supreme Court dismissed Lawless's *habeas corpus* application and two days before Lawless lodged his complaint with the Council of Europe, which the Government must have known was certain to happen.

[18] The single proven incident of such support was by District Justice Michael Lennon when he remarked, after a copy of Iris Oifigiuil was handed into court showing that Part V of the Offences Against the State Act 1939 had been brought into force, that "this proclamation does not end with God save the King". The Government later requested, and received, the judge's resignation because his conduct was calculated to bring the law into contempt and was inconsistent with the obligation to uphold the Constitution and the law, which the judge assumed when making the declaration on his appointment, and warranted his removal in the event of his being unwilling to tender his resignation: 62 DD 566: 12 June 1957.

[19] DJ File 9/58/2. District Justice Fitzpatrick sentenced 15 men on 14 January 1957 and heard no further subversion cases until 12 February 1959.

[20] 1956 Report of the Commissioner of the Garda Siochana [police force] on Crime.

[21] Ibid for 1957, p. 27.

[22] Offences Against the State Act 1939, section 21. £50 fine and/or not exceeding 3 months' imprisonment on summary conviction and on indictment not exceeding 2 years'.

[23] Ibid. Section 52. Imprisonment not exceeding 6 months.

[24] Ibid. Section 12. Fine up to £50 and/or imprisonment not exceeding 3 months.

[25] DJ File S.9/58/2.

[26] The Criminal Law (Jurisdiction) Act 1976 provides such a mechanism in certain cases.

[27] DT File S.13706B.

[28] Affidavit of James Carroll TD, sworn for the Strasbourg proceedings.

[29] *Ireland 1912-1985. Politics and Society*. J.J. Lee. (1989). p.329.

[30] *de Valera. Long Fellow, Long Shadow*. T.P. Coogan. (1993). pp.669-690.

[31] *Lawless Case.* P.O'Higgins. Cambridge Law Journal. (1962) pp.234-251 at p.249.

[32] Offences Against the State (Amendment) Act 1940 (Commission for Inquiring into Detention) Order 1957. (S.I.157 of 1957).

[33] A British newspaper, when reporting on the Detention Commission described him as "Col. Hanger-Joyce" because of his membership of the Military Tribunal (which had operated during the war years) and which had sentenced persons to death. He sued for libel claiming that the innuendo meant that he had lightly awarded the death sentence without due regard to the principles of justice. Despite the newspaper having admitted the libel and publishing an apology, a jury awarded Joyce £2,000 damages.

[34] See Appendix 1 for articles of the Convention.

[35] Offences Against the State (Amendment) Act 1940, section 3 (4).

[36]

1953.	Dail Eireann adjourned	5 August	- resumed	20 October.
1954.	" " "	15 July		27 October.
1955.	" " "	14 July		26 October.
1956.	" " "	26 July		24 October.
1957.	" " "	4 July		23 October.
1958.	" " "	17 July		27 October.

[37] 164 DD 31-34. The member asking the question was one of Ireland's parliamentary representatives in the Consultative Assembly of the Council of Europe.

[38] 164 DD 608-660; and 20 November 1957: 167 DD 827-834. The proposer of the motion, complained (624) that the usual practice of sending copies of all regulations to members of Dail Eireann, when the House was in recess, as a matter of courtesy, had not been observed.

[39] 103 votes against to 5 votes in favour.

[40] By three members of the opposition Labour Party.

[41] DFA File 417/39/19/4/2.

[42] 171 DD 1113-1119. 26 November 1958.

[43] Lawless's case had been declared admissible in August 1958: see pp.82-84.

[44] The European Court of Human Rights was not formally established until 20 April 1959 (see p. 10), a point not taken in the debate.

[45] Dail Eireann never approved the Convention: see p. 6.

[46] 171 DD 1562-1565. 3 December 1958.

[47] DJ File S.85/58.

[48] 50 SD 145-146.

4 Lawless's Detention and his Pursuit of Domestic Remedies and Release

Introduction

Within days of the introduction of internment, Gerard Lawless was arrested and detained without trial. When two months had passed, Lawless considered making a complaint to the European Commission of Human Rights that his detention without trial infringed the European Convention of Human Rights. A condition precedent of lodging such complaint was that domestic remedies must be exhausted. This chapter deals with the three issues that might fall within the category of domestic remedies and were highly relevant when the jurisdiction of the Strasbourg system was subsequently invoked. First, there was Lawless's application to the Detention Commission, the statutory body established to review individual detentions; secondly, there was his *habeas corpus* proceedings in the domestic courts; and, thirdly, there was his undertaking not to engage in future subversive activities, which resulted in his release.

Lawless's Arrest and Detention without Trial

Lawless was unemployed and decided to travel to England to find work.[1] On the evening of 11 July he purchased a boat ticket to London via Holyhead. When about to board the boat, at about 8 o'clock in the evening, he was arrested by the police on suspicion of being a member of an illegal organisation, pursuant to section 30 of the Offences Against the State Act 1939.[2]

What began as a very casual event was to culminate five years later in the making of legal history before the European Court of Human Rights. Those involved in the saga must, as it meandered through the labyrinthine process, have occasionally wished that the police on that fateful summer's evening had literally missed the boat!

Lawless was conveyed to a police station and interviewed by Insp. Philip McMahon who informed him that if he gave information about the IRA he would be paid well and would be fixed up with a good job. Lawless greatly resented being considered a potential informer. Insp. McMahon was to say in evidence, before the European sub-Commission of Human Rights, that he asked Lawless to sign an undertaking, which was in "a rather simplified form and only required him to uphold the Constitution and its laws and to dissociate himself from illegal organisations". Lawless refused, though when McMahon was asked whether the undertaking was in written form, he answered that it was not and the reason it was not was because he wanted to find out whether Lawless would sign any form of undertaking. McMahon then said he next asked Lawless whether he "would give even a verbal undertaking to sever his connection with the [illegal] association". Lawless said he would not. McMahon claimed that he "had considerable discussion with [Lawless] on the verbal undertaking" and eventually accepted "that [Lawless] would not give any form of undertaking whatever".[3]

At the same hearing, Lawless stated that he did not at any time refuse to give an undertaking in the form that was eventually tendered to him. He said that at the time of his arrest he was willing to give such an undertaking, and that before the date on which he gave an undertaking, he was not given any opportunity by the authorities to give an undertaking in that form. At that hearing, while the Attorney General cross-examined Lawless on other matters, he refrained from cross-examining Lawless on the form and content of the undertaking suggested by McMahon. The Attorney General was later to claim before the European Court of Human Rights, accurately though somewhat disingenuously, that Lawless "did not say...what the precise form" was of the undertaking that was suggested to him on the night of his arrest.[4] Lawless was detained overnight and on the next day, he was informed that he was to be detained in custody for a further twenty-four hours.

Meanwhile the police, who regarded Lawless "as skilled in the use of firearms and an active, energetic and dangerous member" of the IRA splinter group, applied to the Minister for Justice for a warrant for Lawless's detention. The Minister had regard to Lawless's previous history and to the fact that Lawless was unwilling to give an undertaking as to his future conduct.

Consequently, on 12 July 1957, the Minister for Justice issued a warrant in the following terms:

> OFFENCES AGAINST THE STATE (AMENDMENT)
> ACT, 1940 - Section 4
>
> In exercise of the powers conferred on me by section 4 of the Offences Against the State (Amendment) Act 1940 (No.2),[5] I, Oscar Traynor, Minister for Justice, being of opinion that Gerard Richard Lawless, of No.2 Larkin Flats, Ballybough, Dublin, is engaged in activities which, in my opinion, are prejudicial to the security of the State, do by this warrant order the arrest and detention of the said Gerard Richard Lawless under the said section 4.
>
> Given under my Official Seal this 12th day of July, 1957.
> Oscar Traynor - Minister for Justice

Lawless was conveyed by military vehicle to a military detention barracks and some days later he was transferred to the Curragh Internment Camp in County Kildare, which was operated by the military. He was detained there until he was released. On 1 August 1957, Lawless applied for legal access[6] and stated that the business for which he requested the visit was his detention.[7] There can be no doubt but that from the outset Lawless intended to seek redress under the European Convention of Human Rights and not in a domestic forum but to do so he had first to exhaust domestic remedies.

Proceedings before the Detention Commission

The first possible domestic remedy was to have recourse to the Detention Commission. Whether this was a domestic remedy and whether the Detention Commission was a safeguard against the abuse of the exercise of the powers of detention were recurring themes later in the Strasbourg system. On 8 September 1957, Lawless applied to the Government[8] to have his detention considered by the Detention Commission, established under section 8 of the Offences Against the State (Amendment) Act 1940. In a covering letter, his solicitor wrote that the application was put forward on the understanding that Lawless would be legally represented at the inquiry by solicitor and counsel and that the usual rights as regards the production of documents, the right to *subpoena* and cross-examine witnesses, and all other rights and privileges enjoyed in a court of law would be accorded. He also requested a summary of the evidence that it was proposed to adduce at the hearing.[9] In response, the Government[10] referred the continuation of Lawless's detention to the Detention Commission.[11] In a reply to Lawless's solicitor, approved by the Taoiseach, it was stated that there was no provision in the 1940 Act for entertaining applications subject to conditions imposed by the applicant. While the manner of conducting the inquiry was for the Detention Commission to settle, it seemed that parts of the letter were based on a mistaken view of the statutory position. The Detention Commission informed the Department of Justice that Lawless's application would be considered on Tuesday, 17 September. Lawless's solicitor had been informed that he was at liberty to be represented by solicitor and counsel. The Commission noted that there was some doubt as to its powers to administer an oath and to take evidence on oath and that it would be glad of any assistance which counsel could give on the point. Finally, it requested the furnishing of such information and documents, relevant to the subject matter of the inquiry, which was in the possession or procurement of the Government or of any Minister of State.

Approval was given by the Minister for Justice to supply the Detention Commission with a dossier in triplicate which contained (i) a police list, in chronological order, which showed IRA outrages committed in 1957, (ii) a copy of a police report, dated 12 September 1957, as to Lawless's IRA history, (iii) a copy of police reports in relation to Lawless's conviction for possession of incriminating documents, (iv) a copy of police reports in relation to charges preferred against Lawless for illegal possession of firearms in September 1956, (v) a departmental note which stated (a) that Lawless was informed after his arrest, and before a request was made by the police for a detention warrant, that he would be released on giving an undertaking that henceforth he would not be a member of any unlawful organisation, and (b) that Lawless was informed in writing on 16 August 1957 that he would be released on signing an undertaking to respect the Constitution of Ireland and the laws, and to declare that he would not be a member of or assist any organisation which was an unlawful organisation, and (vi) a copy of the detention warrant. The Detention Commission was informed that the Minister for Justice would not be represented but that the Attorney General would instruct counsel to assist on questions of procedure but would have no instructions in relation to the facts.

The Detention Commission sat, for the first time, on 17 September 1957, in the Courts' Martial Room, Connolly Barracks, Curragh Camp in County Kildare.[12] Counsel and solicitor represented Lawless, with Sean MacBride SC leading the legal team. Brian Walsh SC represented the Attorney General. Opening the public hearing, Judge O Briain stated that the Commission had no chairman and no president and that it was in doubt as to (a) the power to administer an oath, and (b) the right to sit *in camera*. Counsel then addressed these points, and, following an adjournment, Judge O Briain announced that the Detention Commission had the discretion to sit in public or *in camera*, or partly in public and partly *in camera*, as it thought fit. Counsel then addressed the issue regarding the power to administer an oath. Following a further adjournment, Judge O Briain stated that the Detention Commission was not satisfied it had power to administer an oath. A ruling was then made that the remainder of the proceedings would be *in camera* and all persons then present, including the press, other than Lawless, his two military guards, counsel and solicitors left the room.

Judge O Briain then stated that in a response by the Department of Justice to a request for information and documents, three copies of a file of documents had been handed to the Detention Commission that morning. From a cursory examination, the files appeared to contain a number of reports by police officers who were anonymous and whose standing in the force was not apparent. The members of the Detention Commission had read some of these documents, though there had not been time for all the documents to be read. The Commission further ruled, after hearing argument on the matter, (a) that it was not bound by the rules of evidence; (b) that while bound to act in a judicial spirit, it was not a judicial body; (c) that it would not divest itself of the 'secret and confidential' file and would in all probability read it; and (d) that it reserved the right: (i) to hear and receive evidence and documents without disclosing such evidence or the contents of such documents to Lawless or his legal advisers, and, (ii) to act on evidence which was undisclosed to Lawless or his legal advisers. The Detention Commission also ruled that the onus of justifying the continued detention of Lawless rested on the Minister for Justice who could discharge that onus only through an officer of his Department, or of the police who would give the necessary evidence and produce the relevant documents. The Detention Commission would not embarrass the executive in preserving the security of the State. When appropriate it would interview officials or police officers in the absence of Lawless. Before doing so substantial grounds for that course must be advanced. Substantial grounds must also be advanced for the proposition that any information should not be disclosed to Lawless.

The Detention Commission suggested, but did not rule, that a *précis* of the grounds for Lawless's detention (without any indication of the supporting evidence) should be given to him. The Detention Commission expressed some dissatisfaction at the manner in which the Minister for Justice had behaved in that there had been a failure to tender any responsible witness to justify Lawless's detention. Counsel for the Attorney

General made clear that he had no instructions of any kind in regard to the application. His instructions were limited to procedural matters, but he agreed to convey the views of the Detention Commission to the proper quarters. When, at the end of the day, and after further legal argument, the Commission proposed to adjourn, counsel for Lawless protested against any adjournment beyond the next day on the ground that Lawless should not be penalised because of the executive's failure to produce proper and adequate evidence.

The following day, Lawless applied to the High Court for *habeas corpus*. When the Detention Commission sat again, on 20 September, in public, it took the view that, pending the determination of the High Court proceedings, it should not proceed further with the inquiry into Lawless's detention.

Habeas Corpus Proceedings in the Domestic Courts

The second possible domestic remedy was an action by Lawless in the national courts to challenge his continued detention. On 18 September 1957, Lawless made an *ex parte* application to the High Court for a conditional order of *habeas corpus*, which was granted.

Three days of legal argument, on a range of issues, followed before a divisional High Court.[13] Sean MacBride SC argued that because the State had ratified the European Convention of Human Rights the Government could not rely on powers that violated the Convention. In the alternative, the domestic law of the State must be construed in a manner that would avoid violating the Convention. The powers of detention for an indefinite period without charge or trial were clear violations of the United Nations Declaration of Human Rights, which, being a codification of individual human rights, civilised states were expected to observe. This code formed part of the law of nations or of international law which itself formed part of the common law, and, as such, was incorporated into the domestic law without legislative intervention. The Convention of Human Rights created common international obligations that conferred enforceable rights on individuals, limited the action which governments may take, and had the effect of incorporating the rules of international law for the safeguarding of personal liberty, and conferring rights on individuals which were enforceable against governments. Arbitrary arrest and indeterminate detention conflicted with the Convention. The Constitution provided that the State in its international relations accepted international justice and morality and the generally recognised principles of international law and a breach of an international convention, such as the Convention of Human Rights, constituted a breach of both those provisions.

Brian Walsh SC, for the Attorney General, argued that domestic law was, in all respects, paramount in internal affairs and no rule of international law could be allowed to derogate from it. If there was a conflict between international law and the domestic law, then the domestic law must prevail in internal matters. Customary international law formed no part of domestic law save in so far as it was adopted into it: so far as it did not conflict with domestic law, it may be enforced with it. The Convention of Human Rights had no effect on domestic law. The Oireachtas, by the ratification of the Convention,[14] did not intend to make it part of the domestic law or to give it any supreme position in the State. It was merely an international agreement to which the State had given its approval through the Oireachtas.

The High Court, in a reserved decision,[15] dismissed the application in a judgment that was delivered by the President of that court. As to the status of the Convention of Human Rights in Irish law, the court noted that it was an agreement by contracting states with one another. The principle was accepted that every domestic law was to be so interpreted and applied, as far as its language admitted, as not to be inconsistent with the comity of nations or with the established rules of international law. Accepting the submission that the Convention did not sanction preventative detention, the language of the 1940 Act did not admit of an interpretation that would prevent a conflict with its provisions. Therefore the matter must be dealt with on the basis that such a conflict did exist. Were the law and the Convention irreconcilable? These were points on which the court had not heard counsel.

Apart from the Constitution, the position appeared to be that rules of international law were not part of the domestic law, except in so far as they have been made so by legislation, judicial decision, or established usage. To that extent the courts may apply its rules so long as they were not in conflict with an enactment of the legislature or a rule of the common law. The court noted that the effect and scope of the provisions of the Convention as to personal liberty were not absolute in that it recognised as possible the existence of conditions and circumstances in which temporary and exceptional restrictions on personal liberty may be legitimate. It may be possible to equate the condition of public emergency threatening the life of the State with the necessity to secure the preservation of public peace and order and the security of the State contemplated by the 1940 Act. The court did not pursue any inquiry whether the executive had informed the Council of Europe of their action in bringing into operation the 1940 Act because the failure to furnish such information could give Lawless no enforceable right in the domestic courts.

The executive was entitled to rely on the 1940 Act as part of the domestic law that had been expressly declared to be constitutional.[16] Consequently, the grounds based upon the Convention of Human Rights had not been established. Davitt P concluded:

> ...Where there is an irreconcilable conflict between a domestic statute and the principles of international law or the provisions of an international convention, the courts administering the domestic law must give effect to the statute... If this principle were not to be observed it would follow, that the executive government by means of an international agreement might, in certain circumstances, be able to exercise powers of legislation contrary to the letter and spirit of the Constitution. The right of the citizens of this State to be bound by no other laws than those enacted by their elected representatives in the Oireachtas assembled is one to be carefully preserved and jealously guarded.

Lawless appealed to the Supreme Court, and after four days of legal argument, very similar to that presented in the High Court, the Supreme Court held unanimously that the appeal failed.[17] The Chief Justice read the reserved judgment of the court. The court noted[18] that the insuperable obstacle to importing the European Convention into the domestic law, if it was at variance with that law, was that the Oireachtas had not determined that the Convention was part of the domestic law. Nor were rights granted or obligations imposed in addition to those of domestic law.[19] No argument could prevail against the express command of the Constitution, before judges whose declared duty it was to uphold the Constitution and the laws. Maguire CJ added:

> ...The court accordingly cannot accept...that the primacy of domestic legislation is displaced by the State becoming a party to the Convention...nor...that in the domestic forum the executive is in any way estopped from relying on the domestic law. Nor can the court accept the contention that the 1940 Act is to be construed in the light of, and so as to produce conformity with, a Convention entered into ten years afterwards. The intention of the Oireachtas must be sought in the conditions which existed when it became law...the court does not find it necessary to express any opinion on the question whether the provisions of the 1940 Act are in violation of the Convention.

Resumed Proceedings before the Detention Commission

Following the Supreme Court dismissal, the Detention Commission resumed its hearing on 6 December 1957. At that *in camera* hearing the Chief State Solicitor attended and stated that he represented the Attorney General. Before he withdrew, he read from the judgment of the Supreme Court, and then said that he would be available at his office to assist in any way as to procedure, but that he did not propose being present at the continued hearing. The Attorney General was thus not represented at the hearing though a senior police officer represented the Minister for Justice. The police officer was requested to have available for the Detention Commission, at the next hearing, the reports from the several police officers which formed the basis for the accusations made against Lawless relating to two armed raids carried out in 1957. The police officer undertook to do so. Lawless's counsel requested a copy of the police report, dated 12 September 1957, which had been presented to the Detention Commission that day, as setting out the grounds of Lawless's detention. It should be made available to his legal advisers before the resumed hearing, except those portions that had not been read out for alleged security reasons. The police officer stated that he would consult his superiors on the matter. The Detention Commission then adjourned.

At the resumed *in camera* hearing, on 10 December, the Minister for Justice was represented by the Attorney General, Andrias O Caoimh SC, who made submissions on what he perceived to be a misunderstanding in relation to the previous sitting of the Detention Commission. Judge O Briain informed the Attorney General that when the matter was adjourned, counsel for Lawless was cross-examining a senior police officer on a report which he had handed to the Detention Commission as setting out the grounds of Lawless's detention. He had read out that report with the exception of two paragraphs. The Attorney General objected to this cross-examination because Lawless's legal advisers were treating the Detention Commission as a court of law which it was not - it was merely an administrative body and had been so regarded by the Supreme Court. Judge O Briain stated that at the previous day's hearing counsel for Lawless had, in cross-examination, elicited that the report had been compiled from a number of written police reports and that counsel had asked that these other reports be furnished, not to him, but to the Detention Commission. The Attorney General said that it was intolerable that the Detention Commission should have allowed the police officer to be subjected to a very searching enquiry. The production of reports involved risks of a very high order in case the name of any informer might be disclosed.

Accordingly, the Attorney General said that while he did not object to furnishing these reports to the Detention Commission in private session, he objected to any further information or document being given in the presence of either Lawless or his legal advisers. He asked that the police officer be heard in closed session. In reply, Judge O Briain said that the executive should have furnished, as was incumbent on it, all the documents relating to Lawless in the first instance. How could counsel for Lawless test the case put forward if cross-examination was not allowed? Could the Attorney General show how the Detention Commission could reconcile the Government's difficulty with counsel's duty to present Lawless's case? It was a pity that the Attorney General was not present at the previous sitting to object, as the police officer had not objected to being cross-examined. The Detention Commission must deal with the questions referred to it without bias and must give each party an opportunity to present a case. How could this be done if no testing of the State case was to be allowed by cross-examination? The Attorney General replied that if any cross-examination was necessary, it should be done in the absence of Lawless and his legal advisers. The Chief State Solicitor noted that it appeared "that Judge O Briain was constitutionally incapable of conducting an inquiry of this nature divorced from the trappings of court procedure". Counsel for Lawless said that he had elicited at a previous hearing that while in police custody, on 14 May 1957, Lawless had given a full account of his movements for the date on which it was alleged he had taken part in an armed raid. Although this account had been taken down in writing, it had not been made available in compliance with the request of the Detention Commission to the Government for all documents relating to Lawless's case. It would be wrong and unjust to accede to the request to receive evidence in private session though the Commission had already ruled that it reserved the right to do this. It was very difficult to deal with the charges made without having a copy of the police report that the Detention Commission had already agreed should be furnished.

The Detention Commission adjourned and on its resumption, Judge O Briain announced that the Detention Commission was of opinion that it was a fundamental consideration governing its inquiries that it should act judicially and without bias, and give all parties a fair opportunity of presenting their case. The adequate presentation of a party's case involved not merely the affirmative statement of that case but the reasonable testing of the case by relevant cross-examination. On application being made, the Detention Commission would disallow any question, otherwise relevant and proper, the answering of which might involve any danger to any person or to the State. Nor would the Detention Commission disclose to Lawless, or his legal advisers, any document furnished by the authorities if the Detention Commission was satisfied that the objection to such disclosure was well grounded. The Detention Commission declined to go into private session, with Lawless and his legal advisers excluded, and ordered that the cross-examination of the police officer should be resumed. After these rulings were announced, the Attorney General renewed his application and Judge O Briain, after consulting the other members, refused to change this decision. The Attorney General then requested an adjournment until the following day to afford an opportunity of consulting with the Government. When Judge O Briain indicated that the application could not be refused, counsel for Lawless stated that to avoid an adjournment, he would open Lawless's case after lunch.

When the hearing resumed, counsel said that Lawless had sworn an affidavit that he proposed to put in evidence. In the affidavit Lawless denied that he had taken part in either of the two armed raids mentioned in the previous chapter. At the conclusion of the reading of the affidavit, a member of the Detention Commission asked counsel if Lawless was going to say when he had ceased membership of an illegal organisation and why he would not give assurances for his future behaviour. Counsel contended that was unnecessary in view of the averments in the affidavit. Judge O Briain then pressed counsel on the desirability of Lawless informing the Detention Commission when he had ceased to be a member of an illegal organisation. Counsel replied that the Detention Commission would have to investigate the charges in detail as the affidavit was a complete denial of the truth of very serious allegations made. The Attorney General informed the Detention Commission that if Lawless gave a solemn undertaking that he would not in future be a member of an illegal organisation, or assist it, he (Attorney General) would recommend to the Minister for Justice his immediate release. The Detention Commission then adjourned to enable each side to consider the position and to consult with each other.

Accordingly, when the Detention Commission resumed, Lawless gave a verbal undertaking that he would not "engage in any illegal activities under the Offences Against the State Acts 1939 and 1940". Judge O Briain said that the Attorney General could endeavour to contact the Minister for Justice or some other member of the Government to have an order made for the release of Lawless. If there were any hitch in the arrangement the Detention Commission would resume its hearing on 13 December. The Detention Commission then adjourned.[20] On the following day, the 11 December, the Minister for Justice made an order for Lawless's release. Following his release, in a statement to the newspapers, Lawless said that his complaint before the Commission of Human Rights would proceed.

It was very understandable that Lawless would accept liberty, even when it was offered conditionally. Facing the indefinite loss of liberty, isolated from family and friends and ostracised from the main IRA group of detainees and lodged in a heavily fortified army camp which was set in a bleak landscape, was obviously difficult to bear. The onset of winter with short days and long hours of darkness and the nearing Christmas season would have heightened the desire to be free. Being housed in huts in dormitory accommodation which was devoid of privacy and with poor recreational and vocational facilities were obviously aggravating features. Finally, having to face the reality that the general population, while sympathetic to the cause, were opposed to the methods, and, apart from some opposition to detention without trial, the widespread indifference of the community would understandably have militated in favour of freedom. Admittedly, some detainees remained in custody for almost two years. Had Lawless remained in custody, the conduct of his application to Strasbourg might have been decidedly different. The immediacy of the alleged injustice done to Lawless was considerably diminished by his release. Had he refused freedom, his application would have merited a higher priority,[21] with the likelihood of a speedier investigation,[22] and, most importantly, would probably have attracted a fact-finding visit to Ireland by the Commission of Human Rights. The willingness of Lawless to give any form of undertaking must have come as a relief to the Government. It was probably hoped that his application to Strasbourg would not proceed further, or might be peremptorily rejected by the Commission since Lawless was then free. It is interesting to note that the form of undertaking given by Lawless was not offered to other detainees and it is indicative of the keenness of the Government to be rid of Lawless from custody once he invoked the European Convention. His application to Strasbourg must have caused embarrassment and created an element of trepidation in Government circles because of the uncharted waters of the Convention. Had Lawless remained in detention it would have placed the Government in a more precarious position. The release of Lawless, without giving an undertaking, during the pendency of his application would have led, on the one hand, to the accusation of preferential treatment and, on the other hand, to the accusation that the Government was fearful of being indicted for breach of the Convention. Had Lawless been kept in custody it would have increased the scrutiny from Strasbourg not merely with regard to his case but with regard to the general application of detention without trial in the circumstances then pertaining in Ireland.

Notes

[1] DJ File S.9/58/6.(1993 Release). Facts taken from affidavits which Lawless and police officers swore for the High Court proceedings.

[2] "S.30.- (1) A [police officer] ...may without warrant stop, search, interrogate, and arrest any person...whom he suspects of having committed or being about to commit or being or having been concerned in the commission of an offence under...this Act or an offence which is for the time being a scheduled offence....

(3) Whenever a person is arrested under this section, he may be removed to and detained in custody...for a period of twenty-four hours from the time of his arrest and may, if a [police] officer... not below the rank of Chief Superintendent so directs, be so detained for a further period of twenty-four hours."

[3] DJ File S.9/58/18. (1993 Release) CE. Marked secret. DH/ Misc (59) 27, p.47.

[4] Lawless Case. ECHR. 1960-61. Series B, p.474.

[5] "4.- (1)Whenever a Minister of State is of opinion that any particular person is engaged in activities which, in his opinion, are prejudicial to the preservation of public peace and order or to the security of the State, such Minister may by warrant...order the arrest and detention of such person under this section."

[6] Offences Against the State (Amendment) Act 1940 (Detention) Regulations 1957. (S.I.146 of 1957). Paragraph 26 (3).

[7] DJ File S.9/58/6. (1993 Release). Affidavit of Ciaran McAnally, solicitor for Lawless.

[8] "8.- (1) As soon as conveniently may be after this...Act comes into force, the Government shall set up a Commission....

(3) Any person who is detained...may apply in writing to the Government to have the continuation of his said detention considered by the Commission, and upon such application being so made the following provisions shall have effect, that is to say:-

(a) the Government shall, with all convenient speed, refer the matter of the continuance of such person's detention to the Commission;

(b) the Commission shall inquire into the grounds of such person's detention and shall, with all convenient speed, report thereon to the Government;

(c) the Minister for Justice shall furnish to the Commission such information and documents (relevant to the subject-matter of such inquiry) in the possession or procurement of the Government...as shall be called for by the Commission;

(d) if the Commission reports that no reasonable grounds exist for the continued detention of such person, such person shall, with all convenient speed, be released."

[9] DT File S.1627A.

[10] Government Minute. 10 September 1957. Item 7.

[11] AG File SR 54/38.

[12] Facts taken from affidavit of Ciaran McAnally (DJ File S.9/58/8), and the memorandum of Chief State Solicitor (AG File SR 54/38) and newspapers reports which, according to the Chief State Solicitor, "were a fair synopsis of the proceeding".

[13] Davitt P., Dixon and Teevan JJ.

[14] Dail Eireann had never approved the Convention. See p. 6.

[15] Cited in the law reports, and known in Irish law, as In re O Laighleis (the Irish form for the surname Lawless)[1960] IR 93; 95 ILTR 92.

[16] Both courts noted the decision of the former Supreme Court in Article 26 and the Offences Against the State (Amendment) Bill, 1940: see pp. 20-21.

[17] 6 November 1957. Lawless lodged his claim with the Council of Europe two days later.

[18] Lavery, Kingsmill Moore, O'Daly and Maguire JJ concurred.

[19] Article 29.6 of the Constitution: "No international agreement shall be part of the domestic law of the State save as may be determined by the Oireachtas."

[20] This was the sole case heard by the Detention Commission.

[21] e.g. in the Simon-Herold v Germany case, a claim was made by an applicant in custody that he had been ill-treated (a claim never made by Lawless). The President ordered that the application be treated as a priority. YBECHR. 14. 1972 pp. 352-398.

[22] The application was first considered a little over a month after its lodgement. Once Lawless was released the process slowed down with an admissibility hearing in June 1958 and a decision in August 1958 despite the fact that other persons continued to be detained.

5 European Commission of Human Rights Admits the Lawless Application

Introduction

The dismissal of the proceedings in the domestic courts cleared the way for Lawless to initiate a complaint to the European Commission of Human Rights that his detention without trial breached the European Convention of Human Rights. His immediate task was to secure the admissibility of the application to guarantee that a full investigation would be subsequently made. This chapter deals with the admissibility process, and concentrates on whether Lawless had exhausted domestic remedies, a condition precedent to invoking the jurisdiction of the Commission. The Commission had existed for three years. Its tardiness in developing a body of jurisprudence must have raised concern that the Convention of Human Rights was in real jeopardy of being rendered worthless because of the Commission's inability to admit some cases of substance even if the generality of applications were unmeritorious. Both parties anticipated that the Commission would admit the application. The pleadings and the record of a hearing on the admissibility issue are disclosed for the first time. The archival material reveals that the re-internment of Lawless was considered and that the Irish Government was aware of the Commission's private deliberations. Both the United Kingdom and Northern Ireland Governments took an understandably keen interest in the case.

Jurisdiction of the European Commission of Human Rights

The European Commission of Human Rights may only deal with the matter after all domestic remedies had been exhausted, according to the generally recognised rules of international law, and within a period of six months from the date on which the final decision was taken. It cannot deal with any petition which: (a) is anonymous, or (b) is substantially the same as a matter which had already been examined or had already been submitted to another procedure of international investigation or settlement and if it contained no relevant new information, or (c) is incompatible with the provisions of the Convention, or (d) is manifestly ill-founded, or (e) is an abuse of the right of petition.[1] While the activities of the Council of Europe continued at a regular and increasing pace, in which Ireland played its part, the implementation of the European Convention of Human Rights was slower and gradual. The Commission was only established in 1953, from which time inter-state applications could be brought. It only became competent to hear individual petitions in 1955; five years after the founding states signed the Convention. When the events the subject of this work occurred, even the European Court remained as yet an aspiration. The President of the Commission,[2] in 1958, said, "no doubt, some will be found to regret that the number of positive decisions by the Commission has not been higher. I venture to think that the number may increase a little when the significance of the Convention as a legal instrument and of individual remedy before the Commission is more generally appreciated by the legal profession in member countries. I have the impression that very few lawyers...have any awareness of the Convention". Many individual applications were lodged by the end of 1957, by "numerous persons, who believe themselves to be the victims of erroneous judgements in a civil or criminal case".[3] Two notable exceptions were the *German Communist Party* case,[4] and the first inter-state application, *Greece v United Kingdom*, concerned with events on the island of Cyprus and commenced as late as 1956.[5] Both applications were to have relevance to the Lawless case.

Lawless Lodges his Application

While still detained without trial and in exercise of the right of individual petition, a complaint and claim,[6] entitled "Gearoid O Laighleis v The Government of the Republic of Ireland" was filed, on 8 November 1957, with the Council of Europe.[7] The lodgement of this claim could not have taken the Government by surprise because the relevancy of the Convention had been raised in the domestic courts and in parliament. There is no evidence to suggest that Lawless, or other detainees, or any other person, corresponded with other Council of Europe states with the aim of canvassing the initiation of an inter-state application against Ireland. Nor is there any evidence to suggest that other member states, on their own initiative, considered making such an application. It is interesting to note that when, over the years, derogation was made by a state with regard to territories within Europe, which has only occurred a handful of times, there was a very strong likelihood that another state would instigate a complaint. Accordingly, when the UK derogated with regard to the island of Cyprus, Greece made a complaint. When derogation was made, after a coup by the Greek colonels, Denmark, Norway, Sweden and the Netherlands made complaints. When the UK derogated with regard to Northern Ireland, Ireland made a complaint, and when Turkey derogated, after an army coup, France, Norway, Denmark, Sweden and the Netherlands made complaints. The only occasions when inter-state applications were not made following derogation were when both the UK and Ireland derogated in 1957.

Lawless claimed that his detention without trial constituted a flagrant violation of Articles 5 and 6[8] of the Convention. He requested the Commission of Human Rights to take all steps within its competence to secure (a) his immediate release from detention; and (b) the payment of compensation and damages for his detention; and (c) the payment of the costs and expenses incurred in attempting to secure his release. His complaint alleged that if the Government pleaded that the arbitrary powers of detention were justified, it would be contended: (a) that there was no war or other public emergency threatening the life of the nation which would justify a valid derogation; and (b) that no valid notice of derogation had been communicated to the Council of Europe; and (c) that the measures taken were not strictly required by the exigencies of the situation. On the 16 December 1957, Lawless's solicitor sent a notification that while Lawless had been released from detention he maintained his claim for compensation and costs.

Consideration by Group of Three Commission Members

Under the rules of procedure, as they then stood, the Commission appointed three of its members[9] to carry out a preliminary examination as to a claim's admissibility. If these members unanimously reported that the application appeared to be admissible, notice had to be given to the State concerned, which was then invited to submit its written observations. If the group were not unanimous the Commission had to consider the application, and had to (a) either declare at once that the application was inadmissible, or (b) give notice of such application to the State concerned which was invited to submit written observations on the admissibility of such application.[10] As soon as Ireland's Permanent Representative to the Council of Europe received information on the lodgement of Lawless's complaint he reported that a large file had already been assembled and was formally in order and ready to go to the three-man group. The decision on *prima facie* admissibility would not take long.[11] The three-member group consisting of Faber, Crosbie and Erim[12] considered Lawless's application on 16 December 1957 and reported to the Commission. Two days later the Commission considered that report,[13] and decided to invite the Government to submit its written observations, before 30 January 1958, on the admissibility of the application. It stated that this finding did not prejudice any decision the Commission might take on admissibility.[14]

General Comment on the Pleadings

The pleadings by the parties were voluminous, diffuse and repetitive.[15] The major reason for this appeared to be the vagueness of the procedural rules and an absence of a clear directive as to how facts were to be proved and contentious issues were to be resolved. This lacuna may have arisen because it was expected that the cases lodged would be confined to strictly legal issues and it was probably unforeseen that contentious and complex issues of facts would require resolution. This left the parties, in the early cases at least, in a state of confusion. Lawless initially proved facts by affidavit and while the Government considered that method at an early stage, decided against this as a method of proof. The Commission, and as will be seen later the Court, appeared to adopt the stance that a fact, raised by one party and not expressly denied by the other, was accepted as proven. A further hindrance was the lack of precedent in that Lawless's application was one of the few serious cases to proceed beyond the initial stages. A final reason may have been that the procedure of the Strasbourg system was based on continental jurisprudence that may adopt a more flexible approach to proving facts than does common law jurisprudence.

Government Lodges Observations on the Complaint

A series of inter-departmental meetings was held with representatives from the Departments of the Taoiseach, External Affairs, Justice and Defence and the office of the Attorney General in early January 1958. It was decided that the observations would be taken care of by the Department of External Affairs,[16] in corroboration with Justice, and with the Attorney General willing to help at any time. It was desirable to plead as many grounds as possible when replying. It was noted that Lawless had not availed of the opportunity to secure his release by giving the undertaking and that the proceedings before the Detention Commission had not been completed at the time he applied to the European Commission. Lawless had indicated that he was engaged in military activities. The fact that the Government had derogated from the Convention was relevant to the admissibility issue. It was necessary to consider whether such a plea might cause Lawless to press the European Commission to investigate whether the measures taken in derogation were greater than were strictly required by the exigencies of the situation. External Affairs thought that, apart from the derogation effected under Article 15, the powers of detention were likely to be contrary to Article 5 (1) (c) and 5 (3). That was so unless it could be said that persons had been detained "in order to secure the fulfilment of any obligation prescribed by law", such as the constitutional obligation of loyalty.[17] The Permanent Representative, reporting from Strasbourg, confirmed that a historical statement would be useful because it could not be assumed that the Commission members would have any real knowledge of the situation and that derogation did not arise on the admissibility issue. That had been decided in the Cyprus case. It was difficult, because of reticence, to illicit any further information on the arguments raised by the British on the admissibility issue in that case, though a further effort, under more social conditions, would be attempted. On the domestic remedies issue, the view of the Commission was that this meant "remedies in the normal procedure" and that exceptional, administrative measures were likely to be ruled out, and this might mean the Detention Commission. It would be worthwhile to ask Ireland's Embassy in Brussels to inquire from the Belgians about a man called De Becker,[18] who was released from prison on signing an undertaking that he would leave Belgium and never return. The other side was in constant correspondence with the Commission so, no doubt, were well up on the whole issue. It was desirable that statements made by Lawless should be proved by affidavit and that other evidence should, as far as possible, be supported by affidavit. The Government's observations would be sent to Lawless's solicitor for comments and, if considered necessary, the Government could reply to these. Finally, it was suggested that a stopover in London, on the return to Dublin, to discuss the matter with the Foreign Office might be a good thing but there may be a political angle to this. In a telegram, he was instructed "no need stop London" though, as will be seen later, the British Government did discuss the case with both the Taoiseach and the Department of External Affairs. The Government decided[19] that the Taoiseach and the Ministers for External Affairs and Justice, in consultation with the Attorney General should settle the observations.

In its observations the Government submitted that Lawless's application was inadmissible on two broad grounds.[20] The first ground was that a group, styling itself the "Irish Republican Army", had refused to accept the Irish State, its institutions of government, and the right of the people to decide by majority questions of national policy. The IRA organised as a secret military body, claimed and exercised the power of life and death, carried arms and engaged in activities of a military nature in clear contravention of the Constitution.[21] When the IRA declared war on Britain in 1939 and proceeded to acts of violence both in Britain and in Ireland[22] the Government was obliged to take effective action to deal with that growing threat. Accordingly, the Offences Against the State Acts 1939 and 1940 were enacted. Under these laws the IRA was declared an unlawful organisation. Further measures were necessary under the Emergency Powers Acts during the 1939-1945 war, when, in spite of a neutrality policy supported by all parliamentary parties, the IRA attempted to embroil the State in the conflict by seeking the support of one of the belligerents. The effect of the measures taken led to a reduction in IRA activities. The professed objective of IRA activities was to end the partition of the island of Ireland. The Constitution declared that "the national territory consists of the whole island of Ireland, its islands and the territorial seas". It recognised, however, that pending the re-integration of the national territory *de facto* jurisdiction could not be exercised in a part of that territory (viz. the 6 north-eastern counties known in British law as Northern Ireland and treated under that law as forming part of the "United Kingdom of Great Britain and Northern Ireland"). The application of its laws was limited accordingly.[23] A substantial minority in these 6 Counties desired integration with the area under the jurisdiction of the Government and successive Governments had endeavoured to secure this by peaceful means. The IRA endeavoured to usurp the authority and functions of the legitimate organs of the State and disregarded the pledge of loyalty to the State. It persisted in maintaining within the State a military force not authorised by the Constitution that had as one of its objects the establishment by force of a government other than the constitutional government responsible to the elected parliament. This constituted an armed attack on freedom and democracy. The IRA renewed its acts of violence in 1954. Successive Governments made repeated appeals and warnings for the ending of these illegal activities. The effectiveness of the 1939 and 1940 Acts were essential for the protection of the democratic institutions that existed for the safeguard of individual rights and freedoms. The decision to bring detention into force was to deal with a situation that was fraught with danger for the peaceful existence of the State and for her relations with a neighbouring State. Any activity that prevented such effectiveness would be incompatible with the basic purpose of the European Convention of Human Rights. Notice of the measures taken was given to the Council of Europe on 20 July 1957.

The second broad ground raised was that Lawless was an IRA member. It would be intolerable if those who openly flouted the Constitution and the laws and who refused to recognise its democratically elected government and lawfully constituted courts, and who endeavoured to embroil the State in war were to be afforded *locus standi* before a body set up under a Convention, signed and ratified by the Government, and drawn up by the Council of Europe, of which Ireland was a founder member. The Government was deeply conscious of its obligation and it would be an abuse if a Convention established to safeguard democratic freedoms served the purpose of an organisation whose methods were negations of democracy. Lawless had engaged in activities aimed at the freedoms safeguarded by the Convention. When before the domestic courts on criminal charges he refused to recognise the authority of those courts. Lawless was informed on his arrest, and while detained, that he would be released on giving an undertaking not be a member of any unlawful organisation, but he refused. Lawless was released by ministerial order when he gave a solemn undertaking not to engage in any illegal activities contrary to the 1939 and 1940 Acts.

The Government's observations were sent to Lawless's solicitor with the invitation to reply, if possible, before 25 February 1958. The Permanent Representative reported that two submissions on each side were normal. The Commission did not consider itself a court of law but a "watchdog to ensure that human rights were respected, and it did not demand the same kind of procedure as a court". On the whole he got the impression that the going was not going to be easy.[24]

British and Northern Ireland Governments' Interest in the Case

British embassy officials in Dublin had regular meetings with officials in the Department of External Affairs, a usual practice in diplomatic relations, and reported on these to the Commonwealth Relations Office in London. This office dealt with Irish affairs because of the historical fact that the Irish Free State had once dominion status within the British Empire. As the Lawless case progressed it became a regular topic for report. The first account[25] noted that the Human Rights Commission was considering whether "the appeal of Gerard Lawless is admissible" and that the "Irish

Republican Government" had been asked to give its written observations upon the application. The next report, which recorded a series of meetings, noted that the Irish Government "expected UK support when the matter came up to the Commission. They were so confident that they would receive our support that they did not think it necessary to seek it. Perhaps it would be more right to say that they would have found it embarrassing to seek it, particularly if by any chance the fact that they had done so leaked out". A copy of the Government's reply was requested and it was agreed to furnish this. Subsequently, it was not furnished because "unexpected difficulties had arisen". The Irish official claimed, acting on information from Strasbourg, that the President of the Commission, Waldock, the UK representative, "had taken a very firm line to the effect that all documents...were secret and that there could be no question of their being handed around anywhere. In the circumstances...it was clear that anything said to Waldock could only be unhelpful." The report ended by saying, "the Irish delegate...is James Crosbie, until recently a Senator. He is well known to us and none of us have any doubt that he will treat Lawless the right way". A copy of this report was sent to the Foreign Office and the Home Office. The Home Office dismissed the reasons given by the Department of External Affairs for not furnishing a copy of its observations as "obviously inadequate". Waldock's remarks clearly related to Commission policy and were not concerned with the question whether a government showed elsewhere a document prepared by that government for the Commission. "Probably the Irish Government dislike letting the UK in on a political question...whether the emergency powers were enacted because of 'a public emergency threatening the life of the nation.' " Since that was the point that the Commission would have to consider there was no action which the British Government could take at that stage. Waldock was there as an independent person and in no sense as a representative of the British Government. It would clearly be improper to approach him and equally improper to approach the Secretariat, for a copy of the Irish Government's case. The Commission was an independent quasi-judicial body and the British Government had no right to see any document submitted to it, unless other parties showed them. "We must leave it to Waldock to come to his own decision as to what view he will take of the dispute: if there is to be any influencing of him at all it should be left to his fellow member of the Commission, Crosbie...to do it." The Foreign Office noted this was the first it had heard of this affair, apart from a brief mention in a previous report from Dublin. The Northern Ireland Government queried the British Home Office as to whether the text of the "Irish Republican Government's" answer to Lawless's petition was available. This prompted a query to

Strasbourg on the Foreign Office's understanding that these documents would only be available if the Committee of Ministers had to pronounce on the case but that otherwise they would not be made available to other governments. The working documents would not become available but their contents would probably be included in the Commission's report. The progress of the case was that the "Irish Republican Government" had sent in its reply that had been copied to Lawless. It was hoped that pleadings would be finished before the plenary meeting of the Commission in the beginning of June because the Commission wanted, if possible, to decide the case during that meeting.

The UK Government must have been both pleased and relieved that the Irish Government introduced detention without trial, since there had been discussions on the security issue at different levels between the two Governments. Apart from any influencing which the British did, it was obviously beneficial because of the probability that similar measures on both sides of the border were bound to squeeze the IRA. The UK Government must also have been relieved because the most likely source of complaint that its actions in Northern Ireland were in breach of the Convention[26] would be the Irish Government, since the right of individual petition was not available to those living within the jurisdiction of the UK. When the UK Government, then the colonial ruler, had introduced similar measures in Cyprus, Greece, which had deep historical connections with Cyprus, lodged a complaint. By introducing similar measures, and likewise derogating from the Convention, the Irish Government had, to use a sporting metaphor, snookered itself in this regard.[27]

Exchange of Further Pleadings

In his reply to the Government's observations Lawless's noted[28] that his detention without charge was not denied. Nor was it contended that there existed a state of "war or other public emergency threatening the life of the nation", or that Ireland was entitled to derogate. These matters were premature and irrelevant to the issue of admissibility. Since the restraint of IRA activities was essential for the protection of democratic institutions, the Government had not introduced any legislation under the emergency provisions of the Constitution.[29] Nor had it sought to avail of the powers conferred by the Constitution[30] and the law[31] for the establishment of special courts, nor availed of the powers conferred by the Constitution[32] for the establishment of military tribunals, nor had any person been tried for treason.[33] Lawless had exhausted all domestic remedies but failed to secure his release. He was ultimately released by ministerial order without the intervention of any legal process and during the pendency of his complaint to the European Commission. Lawless had declined to sign an undertaking because he could not reasonably respect the Constitution without reservation so long as it permitted detention and he had conscientious objection on religious grounds to some of its articles. The verbal undertaking he eventually gave was different to that which had been earlier presented to him and did not require a declaration in writing to respect the Constitution and the laws. The obligatory signing of such an undertaking was not a domestic remedy.

Lawless's reply was forwarded to the Government, and the Commission requested that any further written observations should be made before 27 March 1958 because the members intended to continue their examination of Lawless's application during its April session. In the preparation of a reply, consideration was given to compiling a list of violent IRA activities in Northern Ireland in recent times. This prompted a query from the Department of External Affairs to the Department of Justice for an authoritative statement, if necessary in co-operation with the police force of Northern Ireland, unofficially if this was considered a political necessity. The position was explained by the Department of Justice that the Commissioner of the police force of the Irish Republic had issued a definite instruction not to engage in any form of co-operation with the Northern Ireland police. This had followed a direction of the Minister for Justice in the previous Government and had not been amended by the present Government. The police in the border area in the Republic, which had been reinforced at considerable expense, patrolled that area as effectively as possible with a view (1) to preventing IRA incursions from the Republic into Northern Ireland, and (2) to apprehend returning raiders. There had been, in fact, a form of co-operation between the two police forces, but it was strictly a one-way traffic. The Northern Ireland police had, from time to time, conveyed information as to contemplated IRA raids, with the idea that the police of the Republic would take the necessary preventative action. The police had no objection to receiving such information and acted on it as they though fit. There was no question of any reciprocal supply of information. The Northern Ireland police conviction that the vast majority of IRA activities in Northern Ireland emanated from the Republic were not founded on fact. There was probably a hard core of IRA in the Northern Ireland who operated without any assistance from the Republic. The Department of Justice concluded that there would be no change in that policy, unless and until the Government issued a direction. It was noted that the Department would not seek such a direction. Consequently, a list of incidents, month by month, in Northern Ireland between December 1956 and February 1958 was sent to the Department of External Affairs which had been compiled by the police from press reports and no responsibility for their truth or accuracy could be taken. The Secretary of the Department of External Affairs, in a brief to the Minister on the draft reply, said that this list was an impressive one, running to several pages, which by its baldness would be more eloquent than a detailed recital in the body of the reply. It had been agreed that a complete draft of the proposed reply would be submitted to the Taoiseach, the Ministers for External Affairs and Justice and the Attorney General. The Attorney General had taken the preparatory consultation and supplied additional paragraphs on the events before the Detention Commission.[34] In addition, he had supplied the questionnaire addressed though the European Commission to Lawless, discussed later in the chapter. The Department of Justice noted that the Attorney General had taken a foremost part in the discussions and had vetted the final draft, and that some minor changes had been made at the instance of the Taoiseach. The Government decided that the Taoiseach and the Ministers for External Affairs and Justice should settle the observations on the reply in consultation with the Attorney General.[35]

The Attorney General, in a note,[36] observed that there was a strong case for holding that the European Convention did not contemplate detention without trial, though Article 5 was not clear in this regard. The question of derogation then arose and the notice given to the Council of Europe was likely to be questioned by Lawless's counsel on the grounds that it did not purport to be a notice of derogation in unqualified terms. Also it did not specifically state that there was such an emergency, though it was improbable that the notice would be held to be ineffective on either of these grounds. If a factual investigation of the same kind was undertaken here, as had been taken in the Cyprus case, by persons having little or no knowledge of Irish political events, "it would be rash to forecast the result likely to be arrived at, and one must envisage the possibility that they would hold that the circumstances did not justify derogation". In that event, the Council of Europe would be asked to take action and while this might be of a diplomatic nature only it would certainly cause embarrassment and might lead to the withdrawal of Ireland from the Council of Europe.

As part of the preparation of the Government's observations, the Attorney General contributed a memorandum of the events before the Detention Commission. In the ultimate paragraph of the final draft, which was later deleted, it was stated that there had been good grounds for suspecting that Lawless, since his release, had engaged in subversive activity. If these were persisted in, it may necessitate his renewed detention before the European Commission had disposed of the present application. It was noted that the object of these activities might be to force the authorities to detain him again.

The Government's observations on Lawless's reply[37] repeated that Lawless, at the material times, had been a member of an unlawful organisation, that his detention was justified and not in violation of the European Convention. For convenience, Lawless's history, such as his IRA membership, his arrest and trial on firearm offences, his arrest and conviction for possessing incriminating documents, the events before the Detention Commission and his release were recapitulated, with additional material, in view of Lawless's persistence in misleading the Commission. Lawless had not exhausted domestic remedies in that he had failed to give an undertaking that was at all material times available to him and the reasons advanced for not availing of it were obviously specious. This undertaking was clearly to be read in a reasonable sense, with the signatory being asked to undertake to respect the Constitution and the laws, in the sense that ordinary, law-abiding persons do so. The right of citizens to hold opinions about the desirability of particular provisions of the Constitution and the laws was not questioned, and the right to attempt to change such provisions provided he did so in a constitutional and legal manner was the very basis of democratic government. It would be absurd to suppose that any democratic government would, or could, exact from any citizen an undertaking to regard every constitutional or legislative enactment as sound. What was expected of citizens was that they would obey the Constitution and the laws and, when the public interest required, give an express undertaking to do so. It was in this sense that the undertaking must be construed and no other construction was reasonable. To decline to sign such an undertaking disclosed an unreasonable refusal to accept the authority of the democratic organs of the State. The reasons advanced by Lawless were not in his mind when he refused to sign the undertaking. His advancing them for the first time in his reply supported the view that the application was vexatious, an abuse of the right of recourse and was made for publicity and propaganda purposes. The activities of the organisation of which Lawless was a member would undermine the institutions that were designed to protect the rights and liberties set out in the Constitution. The list of incidents in Northern Ireland proved the seriousness and persistency of the IRA campaign which could, if continued, have created a state of civil war within the island of Ireland and, further, risked causing war with Great Britain. The reintegration of the national territory was a fundamental aim of national policy to be secured by peaceful means. The Government had a duty to ensure that the people's purpose would not be defeated and that the area within their *de facto* jurisdiction would not be used for acts of violence directed against Northern Ireland.

With the despatch of these observations, and noting that derogation was not relevant at that stage, the Government drew the attention of the Commission to the letter sent to the Council of Europe on 20 July 1957. The Commission acknowledged receipt and added that these would be brought to the attention of the Commission before their next session in June. The Department of External Affairs circulated, for information, these observations to the heads of Irish missions abroad, because it gave a succinct account of illegal activities and of the Government's attitude to the whole question.

In a further reply to the Government's second set of observations Lawless alleged[38] that the main purpose of the Government's observations was to prove that his arbitrary imprisonment without trial was justified on the grounds that he had committed various offences and was a member of some illegal organisation. All these allegations, which were denied, if true, would constitute criminal offences under domestic law and would be cognisable by the courts that were functioning normally. There was an underlying suggestion that the domestic courts were biased, or that domestic law was unsatisfactory, and that the Detention Commission presided over by a judge was wrong in its decision. The Commission should reject such suggestions. The legal system and courts were regarded as highly competent and the Government has voiced no complaint against it.[39] The Government appointed the judges and the Detention Commission. The laws were enacted by parliament, which could amend the law or enact new legislation. Numerous special laws existed which gave the governmental authorities wider powers than those normally found in democratic states. The domestic rules of evidence, similar to those in countries with the common law system such as Britain, the United States, Canada, and Australia were not particularly stringent. The difficulties of dealing with conspiracies were confronted by many states but did not justify the arbitrary detention without trial of "suspects". Likewise, the concealment of secret sources of information was a problem that confronted every state administration. Authorities who choose to act on anonymous or secret information were often guilty of grave injustices, as in the present case. The Government suggested that a state of "war or other emergency threatening the life of the nation" had existed but had not specifically relied on derogation. Did it or did it not rely on derogation to justify detention without trial? If it did rely on derogation that issue did not arise on admissibility. If it did not rely on derogation, the recital of alleged armed activities in territory under its jurisdiction and in that portion of Ireland ruled by Great Britain, was irrelevant and intended to distract the Commission from the issue involved, namely, the right to detain Lawless arbitrarily and without trial.

In the observations of the Government of 23 March 1958, it was claimed that Lawless's membership of an unlawful organisation should be regarded as established unless he satisfied the Commission to the contrary by express and explicit answers to a number of questions posed. Lawless, in his reply of 12 May 1958, said that it was solely out of deference to the Commission that the questions posed by the Government were answered as follows:

Question:	Whether Lawless admitted to having been at some time a member of: (a) the IRA, or (b) some other organisation unlawful under Section 18 of the 1939 Act.
Answer:	Yes.
Question:	When Lawless became a member of any such organisation, with dates in respect of each such organisation of which he was a member.
Answer:	Became a member of the IRA in January 1956 and ceased to be a member in the following June. Was a member of a minority group that had been associated with the IRA from June 1956 to towards the end of 1956.
Question:	Whether he has ceased to be a member of the organisation referred to at 1(a), if he was at one time a member.
Answer:	Yes, as and from the month of June 1956 (see below).
Question:	If so, when and how he ceased to be so.
Answer:	Withdrew support therefrom and severed all connection therewith.
Question:	Whether he has ceased to be a member of every other such organisation to which he at any time belonged.
Answer:	Yes (see answer to Question 2 above).
Question:	If so, when and how he ceased to be so.
Answer:	Withdrew support and severed all connection towards the end of 1956.
Question:	Whether he had at any time since cessor of membership of all such organisation: (a) engaged in training, drilling or military manoeuvres, and (b) if so when he last so engaged.
Answer:	No.

Question:	Whether he had at any time since cessor of membership of all such organisation: (a) carried or had in his possession arms, explosives or ammunition: (b) if so, the purpose for which and the last date on which he had same.
Answer:	No.
Question:	(a) Whether he had in the 1957 or 1958 acted in concert with any other persons in the State in the planning, directions or performance of any military activities either within or without the State, and (b) if so, the nature and date of such activities.
Answer:	No.

Hearing of Sub-Commission of Human Rights at Strasbourg

The European Commission invited both the Government and Lawless to make an oral explanation on admissibility[40] at a hearing fixed for 19 June 1958. The Minister for External Affairs was of the view that the Government should be strongly represented. The Attorney General was prepared to go and proposed to bring Brian Walsh SC with him, together with the Legal Adviser to the Department of External Affairs and a Department of Justice official. After consultation with the Taoiseach this proposal was agreed to. It was noted that Lawless's representatives had requested an adjournment for three or four weeks because the date fixed was inconvenient to counsel. The President of the Commission did not agree to this request. Yet again, the preparation of the Attorney General's submission was a collegiate affair. The Department of External Affairs sent a draft of some general remarks that could be used in the Attorney General's opening statement. He in turn said that "a first reading of this draft [was] excellent".[41]

The European Commission composed of Waldock (President), Eustathiades (Vice-President), Berg, Faber, Beaufort, Susterhenn, Petren, Sorensen, Crosbie and Erim sat formally[42] on 19 June 1958. After opening the hearing and welcoming the legal representatives,[43] the President noted that the Republic of Ireland had accepted the right of individual petition.[44] In recognising the representatives of the Republic, the Commission paid tribute to the enlightened action in assuming this obligation. The President emphasised that the Commission was only concerned with admissibility. It met *in camera* and any report that might ultimately be submitted to the Committee of Ministers was not to be published by the parties. This was because the Commission was entrusted with seeking a friendly settlement on the basis of respect for human rights[45] and attached the highest importance to maintaining the secrecy of its proceedings. Lawless did not attend on the advice of MacBride. The hearing, which lasted one-and-a-half-days, was taken up by the submissions of leading counsel for both parties. Counsel for Lawless took up the first morning with counsel for the Government occupying the afternoon session. The second morning was subsumed with the replies. Simultaneous translations in French and English were available. The transcript shows that counsel only interrupted each other once or twice. The few questions that came from the members of the Commission came, with one exception, from or through the President. The difference between the common law and continental legal systems was again highlighted by the necessity to explain some aspects of Irish procedural law.[46] The only piece of drama in what appeared to have been an otherwise rather staid proceeding was the attempted introduction by MacBride of an affidavit by the Lord Mayor of Dublin[47] to counter the possible raising of the derogation issue by the Government. From contacts within Strasbourg, Lawless's legal team proceeded on the basis that the Commission was more than anxious to admit the case to a full hearing because of the urgent necessity felt to establish itself as a meaningful, credible and influential human rights institution.

This hearing brought together, for the first time, the three personalities who dominated the case. Sean MacBride[48] had, as Minister for External Affairs, signed the Convention on Ireland's behalf. As an advocate he had steered the case in the domestic fora and through the admissibility and investigation stages before the Commission. Although Lawless was to be excluded from the subsequent Court hearing, MacBride by his persistence continued to exert some influence to the end, as shall be noted later. The burden of leading the case for the Government, over the four years, fell on the Attorney General, Andrias O Caoimh. This task he more than adequately fulfilled and, though he had the support of a highly competent administration, much of the credit for defeating the claim rests with him. In particular, his performances before the Court, though somewhat pedantic and ponderous, were effective and at times exacting. Humphrey Waldock, as President of the Commission, and later as chief delegate of the Commission before the Court, stamped his singular authority on the case. His support for admitting the application, and, later, his *volte face* in holding that there was no breach of the Convention, must have heavily influenced the continental Commission members both because of his common law background and his command of the language in which the proceedings were conducted. His greatest contribution was to come, when by persistence and persuasion, he successfully gained some limited role for Lawless, and all subsequent applicants, before the European Court of Human Rights.

Lawless Argues his Application is Admissible

In his submission, MacBride said that the case was simple: it was that Lawless's detention without trial for an indefinite period of time constituted a violation of Articles 5 and 6. In considering these provisions it was convenient, for a proper perspective of the circumstances which prompted European states to enter into the Convention of Human Rights, to examine the Declaration of Human Rights adopted by the United Nations Assembly in December 1948. When the Statute of the Council of Europe was adopted, specific reference was made to this Declaration in its Preamble and it should be used as one of the canons of constructions when interpreting the European Convention. Lawless had taken steps to secure his release. He had availed of the right of recourse to the Detention Commission. Following this, he brought *habeas corpus* proceedings in which the domestic final court of appeal found that the Convention could not be reconciled with the 1940 Act, and that it must apply domestic law by reason of the Constitution. Lawless had thus exhausted all domestic remedies.

It was suggested that Lawless should have signed an undertaking. This was not a domestic remedy: there was no legal sanction which entitled the executive to make any person's liberty conditional upon the signing of any undertaking of any kind. The guarantee to life, to personal liberty, to the right of private property would all become practically meaningless if they became subject to the imposition of conditions not provided by law but arbitrarily imposed by a government. Obviously, the domestic remedies referred to in the Convention were those which were provided by law and recognised as proper remedies by international law. Lawless had political and religious objections to signing an undertaking to "respect" the Constitution and the laws though had no objection to abide by them. In the light of international law and in what was regarded as the normal "domestic remedies", it could not be concluded that the signing of a political undertaking was a valid "domestic remedy",[49] The right to personal liberty could not be conditional upon the signing of undertakings or of political conditions. Otherwise, that would create an imbalance between the right to personal liberty and the rights of governments. It was suggested that Lawless's detention was necessary to secure the fulfilment of an obligation prescribed by law. The obligation must be one "prescribed by law". There was no law that made liberty conditional upon the signing of some undertaking. There was no evidence that Lawless failed to comply with any obligation imposed by law. True, he was charged with some offences but he was either convicted or acquitted. In so far as he was convicted, he purged his offence by serving the sentence the domestic courts imposed. In so far as he was acquitted, the acquittal of the competent domestic courts was conclusive. The Commission was being asked to reverse the findings of the domestic courts and to do so without evidence. Article 5 (1) (b) related to the securing of some positive act by law such as, for instance, the payment of a tax, not an indefinite or vague obligation. If Article 5 (1) (b) was wide enough in scope to encompass the commission of offences at large, it would make complete nonsense of Articles 5 and 6. The "obligation" referred to must be the fulfilment of some positive clear-cut legal obligation cast upon a citizen by his domestic law. If Lawless failed to comply with any such obligation, the domestic courts were the place to deal with any alleged breach of such legal obligations in the due process of law.

There was no parallel with the *German Communist Party* case.[50] There the articles of the Convention related to the right to form associations, a right subject to limitations of a completely different nature to those under Articles 5 and 6. The German Communist Party was found to be unconstitutional by the German Federal Constitutional Court after a hearing lasting some ten months. The European Commission had based its decision on the findings of that court, which had been arrived at in due process of law after hearing all the parties. To relate Article 17 to the Lawless case would involve a finding of facts by the Commission that: (a) Lawless was a member of the IRA or some cognate group, which he denied vehemently, and that (b) the IRA, or other cognate group, was an organisation which came within Article 17. The Commission could not, at this stage, make a finding of facts adverse to Lawless. This case was of considerable importance in determining an individual's rights vis-à-vis the state. It would form an important precedent under the jurisprudence which was being established. The Commission must guard sternly the rights guaranteed against encroachment.

Government Argues the Application is Inadmissible

The Attorney General opened his submission by acknowledging that the Convention had, since signing, been regarded as a considerable and significant advance in international law by embracing the rights of the individual as against the state. The Convention was unique: whereas heretofore international law had dealt with states and their mutual relations, this Convention gave a new status to the individual as a subject of international law, an advance made in a certain context. If rights were to be recognised in international law, so also must duties. It was not the intention of those who drew up the first effective charter of rights for the individual vis-à-vis the state that the individual should be exempted from obligations to the organised community in which the individual lived. This Convention could be interpreted only within the framework of the Statute of the Council of Europe, from which it flowed. Accordingly, the Convention reiterated these principles and in particular stressed that peace in the world was best maintained, on the one hand, by an effective political democracy and, on the other, by a common understanding and observance of human rights on which they depended. The importance of preserving democratic institutions as the only framework within which individual rights could flourish were stressed throughout the debate in the Consultative Assembly which led to the elaboration of the Convention. It was against this background and in this context that the Commission should consider the admissibility of this case. If this application was treated as admissible it would enable the Convention to be availed of for the purpose of undermining democratic institutions and the form of society and civilisation which the Convention was designed to protect. The Constitution of Ireland guaranteed the rights of individuals but subject to their observing their political duties as citizens of a State that was thoroughly democratic.

After the Constitution was enacted a small group styling itself "the Irish Republican Army" refused to accept the State and the right of the people to decide by majority questions of national policy. Lawless was at one time a member of the legitimate army of the State and when joining took an oath of loyalty and declared that he would not join or be a member of or subscribe to any secret society. The IRA was a secret society. On his own admission he became an IRA member while still bound by that oath. In September 1956 he was found in possession of firearms and was acquitted of the charge. Then he was found in possession of documents that indicated the type of activity in which he was engaged. He made no explanation to the trial court and he was convicted and sentenced.[51] No reasonable person could believe that there was a wholly innocent explanation for the possession of these documents. When Lawless appeared before any court, where he was liable to cross-examination, he never volunteered to give evidence. Instead he refused to recognise their authority.

When dealing with persons engaged in an armed conspiracy it was impossible to adduce evidence which would satisfy a court in any civilised society, without endangering the lives of those who had given the authorities the evidence, a feature not peculiar to our system of courts. This was common in all countries where armed secret societies engaged in activities that the lawful powers of those communities endeavoured to suppress. The Government had to choose between two evils. It could allow these unlawful activities to continue because the persons so engaged could not be put on trial without danger to the lives of others. Or it could detain the persons engaged in these activities without calling witnesses to establish by proper legal evidence the fact that they were engaged in these unlawful activities. It was only with the greatest reluctance that detention without trial was brought into operation. A Detention Commission had to be established. It was true there was no law that required that the Government should release from detention an individual who signed an undertaking to respect the Constitution and the laws and not to engage in illegal activities. But there was no other country in which the executive had such powers of detention and which had voluntarily indicated that on signing a simple form agreeing to obey the law those persons detained would be immediately released.

Article 5 (1) (c) enabled persons to be deprived of their liberty in cases of lawful arrest or detention. "Lawful" meant under the law when it was reasonably considered necessary to prevent the commission of offences. The Government felt that it was reasonably necessary to detain persons to prevent them committing violent offences. In our system of jurisprudence there was no offence known to the law of "tending" to commit an offence. One must go beyond the stage of "mere intention" to do something. Once the first positive step was taken, an offence or at least an attempt was committed. In that sense, when Article 5 (3) spoke of trial, it could not be referring to the trial of a person who was arrested when it was reasonably considered necessary to prevent him committing an offence. The arrest of persons of the type mentioned was not a breach of Article 5 of the Convention.

Domestic remedies had not been exhausted when Lawless lodged his application. His case was still pending before the Detention Commission. The matter ultimately came to a conclusion when he gave an undertaking as to his future conduct before the Detention Commission. He had not exhausted a very valuable right of release, not enshrined in any law, but stated clearly and explicitly to him after his arrest. Lawless was not asked to respect the Constitution; he was asked to comply with it and the laws although the word used was respect. "To respect the law" meant that a person, who said, "I will respect the law" meant "I will show respect for the law". He may hold his own opinion about it, provided he complied with it.

Article 17 had been interpreted by the Commission to exclude from consideration any application brought by a person or a body which had as one of its objects the destruction of any of the rights guaranteed by the Convention. Article 17 was material to this case. The Commission decided, in the *German Communist Party* case, that the body putting forward the claim was destructive of the rights guaranteed by the Convention. Lawless and his associates had engaged in activities which, apart from the many other attacks on democracy, included the right to take human life in the exercise of activities aimed at securing their objectives. A body of that kind, or a person engaging in such activities, whether a member of a body or not, was not entitled to place any reliance on the Convention by reason of Article 17.

Brian Walsh SC submitted that the jurisprudence that governed this hearing required that the burden of proof must be discharged by Lawless. He must prove that all the domestic remedies had been exhausted. Proceedings had never been instituted either against the Irish State as a juridical body, or against the Government. An action for damages had not been instituted. The only proceedings instituted were for *habeas corpus*. The remedies available under the Convention should only be available to those who had shown, not merely before this Commission, but before the domestic courts, that they had always acted in good faith. The admitted facts indicated a juggling of the various procedures by Lawless which could not be deemed a pursuance in good faith of the available remedies. This application has now proceeded as one for damages. The domestic courts had made clear that if Lawless had been removed from the police station without the production of a warrant or without being informed or being made aware to whence he was being brought, then until the moment he was actually lodged in the Internment Camp his arrest was illegal. That in total may be a comparatively small period of time, but nonetheless it was a period of time in respect of which this application was brought. Lawless had an action for damages for false imprisonment in respect of that interval of time. Because no such action had been instituted it indicated that damages for false imprisonment was not the motive uppermost in Lawless's mind. Lawless had shown a consistent and a persistent contempt for the Constitution and a cynicism that enabled him to make use of it when it suited him, namely in the *habeas corpus* proceedings. But when he was charged and appeared in court, he either refused to take part in the proceedings or refused to recognise the authority of the court. That coupled with his other activities indicated the degree of cynicism and disrespect for the organs of law and authority and for the Constitution that enshrined ordinary democratic rights. This threw sufficient light on his motives as to lead a reasonable person to conclude that this was not a *bona fide* application. It was beyond doubt that Ireland was a democratic State with all the democratic freedoms carefully enshrined in its Constitution. It was beyond doubt as a juridical concept that no international body could acquiesce in, or approve of, any form of proceedings which showed that the very freedoms which were thus enshrined were to be used as the instrument of its own destruction. The concept of preventative justice was one recognised in Irish law by the 1940 Act and the contents of which had been found by the Irish courts not to be repugnant to the Constitution. It was, under the Irish system of jurisprudence, based on the fact that as yet no offence had been committed. Its object was to prevent its commission. It would be impossible under the Irish system to bring to trial a person who had not, in fact, committed an offence. Every person deprived of liberty by arrest was entitled to challenge the legality of it by way of *habeas corpus* procedure. It had been held under Irish law that a person detained in accordance with the 1940 Act was not detained on a criminal charge. Insofar as anything had to be determined it was not the determination of a criminal charge, and insofar as it was a right, it was a civil right. It was a principle of Irish law that no person could be arrested and incarcerated without knowing the reason why and without having an opportunity of testing the validity of that in the courts. So far as *habeas corpus* was concerned that was a procedure which was confined to the superior courts. The Detention Commission worked on a slightly different aspect in that it had to enquire into the reasonableness of the detention. It was prevented from reaching that conclusion rapidly, in this case, because of the intervention of the legal proceedings. But even in the end, it still did not have to reach it, because Lawless elected to give the undertaking that was necessary to secure his release. If a strict construction were applied, the Detention Commission would be considered a domestic remedy within the meaning of this Commission's jurisprudence. Lawless had invoked the Commission's assistance before he had concluded his other proceedings. The only remedy now sought was for damages that had never been explored in any domestic court.

Conclusion of the Hearing

At the conclusion of the submissions, the President asked if the parties could remain behind in case the Commission had any oral questions. The Commission reserved the right to send the parties written questions. When the Commission returned, the President said that a final statement as to

Lawless's claim should be filed. When the hearing concluded, in a report to Dublin it was noted that the Commission had rejected the affidavit of the Lord Mayor of Dublin and the derogation issue was not developed. It was felt that MacBride was more effective in the reply that he had been on the previous day, although the last part of his intervention dragged. The Commission was to meet ten days later and it might be possible to obtain some indication of how the Commission's opinion was likely to go. Without venturing any forecast as to the probable findings it was felt that the Government team had made a good impression, though the Commission was not at full strength with only ten of the fourteen members present.

In compliance with the Commission's request, Lawless's representatives, before leaving Strasbourg, filed an amended statement of complaint. The material difference from the original statement was that, because Lawless was at liberty by ministerial order, the request to secure his release no longer arose. Instead a claim for compensation and the costs and expenses incidental to the proceedings both in the domestic courts and before the Commission of Human Rights was substituted.

On 17 July 1958, the most senior officials within the Department of Justice recorded their impressions on the likely outcome of the case at that stage in an interchange of written comments. The Assistant-Secretary wrote that reading the file from "stem to stern" it was "anybody's bet which way the cat would jump". The Secretary replied that "we had none of the law but all of the merits" and he believed that it is on the merits that a decision would be taken. If the first leg was lost the second might easily be lost to the extent of having the justification for derogation called in question. "Should this happen it will serve us right for having signed the Convention and what is worse ratified it. Did Justice have an opportunity of expressing an opinion on ratification?" Back came the comment that the Department of Justice "expressed fears of the effects of [individual petition] but External Affairs, the experts in international procedure, assured Government that our fears were groundless and that we had adequate protection against complaints such as Lawless has since brought". The final words came from the Secretary who commented: "Good! We may have the melancholy satisfaction of being able to say - we told you so."

European Commission of Human Rights Admits the Application

During the ceremonies celebrating Europe Day, on 3 September 1958, in Brussels, the Secretary of the Department of External Affairs had conversations with Crosbie, the Irish member of the Commission and

Waldock, President of the Commission. Crosbie told him, in confidence, that the Lawless application was found to be admissible, information that was subsequently confirmed by Waldock.[52] According to Crosbie, the Commission had not been very impressed by the actual merits of the Lawless application: their decision was based on what they considered to be the arbitrary powers of arrest and detention. Waldock said that he himself would probably draw up the detailed reasons for the Commission's decision, that he might be able to clear the draft quickly and informally with some of his colleagues or he might have to clear it formally with the whole Commission. In view of a leakage of information, Waldock proposed to have a brief communiqué issued merely stating that the application had been declared admissible. Subsequently, the Government were formally notified, on 8 September 1958, that the Commission of Human Rights had, in private session on 30 August 1958, declared the Lawless application admissible. A certified copy was forwarded in due course.[53] The decision to admit could not have come as a surprise to either party. Despite the Government's pessimism, it must have been a disappointment that the case was to progress to a full hearing, while Lawless and his legal team must have been delighted that the first obstacle had been successfully overcome.

The Commission decided that the contention that the application was inadmissible for alleged failure to exhaust domestic remedies must be rejected for the following reasons. Under Irish law a person claiming to be illegally detained had proceedings for *habeas corpus* and an action for false imprisonment available as remedies before the ordinary courts. Lawless had sought his release in *habeas corpus* proceedings that had been dismissed. The grounds that led to this dismissal would have equal force in proceedings for false imprisonment, in the ordinary courts, with respect to detention. Further proceedings did not offer a reasonable prospect of success and must be regarded as an ineffectual remedy. It followed that under the generally recognised rules of international law it was not necessary for Lawless to have recourse to such further domestic remedies before submitting his case to the Commission. Lawless was detained over 153 days and whatever action for false imprisonment was open to him with respect to the brief period of two hours related to an infinitesimal part of the period of detention. A judgment in his favour in such an action could not have altered his position with respect to his subsequent detention, though it remained a question whether the failure to institute such an action had the consequence that Lawless's claim to compensation with respect to that period must be excluded from consideration. Since facts relating to this question formed an integral link on which the whole claim was based, the

Commission deferred its decision on this question until after the investigation of the facts, and accordingly reserved its decision until a later stage in the proceedings.

The question arose whether what was required was the exhaustion of remedies in the whole system of legal remedies and in particular whether recourse to the Detention Commission was a domestic remedy the exhaustion of which was required. It was unnecessary to pronounce upon this question because Lawless was no longer in detention. This application was confined to a demand for compensation, and it clearly appeared and was not disputed, that the Detention Commission was confined to recommending release and did not extend to recommending compensation. This right of recourse was not therefore an effective remedy for the purpose of securing the redress that formed the subject of this application. Account had to be taken of the fact that Lawless obtained his release from detention and amended his claim to one for compensation. The Commission, as an international tribunal, was not bound to treat questions of form with the same degree of strictness as municipal law. It followed that, even if the original application was regarded as being defective in that it was filed without first exhausting the remedy before the Detention Commission, the application was not subject to that defect in the form in which it was presented later.

Since the signing of an undertaking to respect the Constitution and the laws and agreeing not to be a member of any unlawful organisation was not a legal provision, that procedure could not be considered a domestic remedy within the meaning of the generally recognised rules of international law.

The Commission in the *German Communist Party* case held that members of an organisation found to be engaged in activities aimed at the destruction of the rights and freedoms set forth in the Convention, were debarred by Article 17 from invoking in their own favour the provisions concerning freedom of association. The possibility that that principle might be applicable in the Lawless case was not excluded by a *prima facie* consideration of the statements of the parties and the evidence submitted. However, there was a direct conflict between the parties on a crucial point of fact, namely, whether Lawless had or had not ceased to be a member of an illegal organisation or group, which engaged in activities of the kind covered by Article 17, when he was arrested and detained. Because the Commission was not possessed of sufficient evidence to enable it to pronounce upon that fact, which was closely connected with matters arising upon the merits of the claim, the Commission decided to join to the merits the Government's preliminary objection founded upon Article 17.

The Commission's task, in deciding whether the application was inadmissible as manifestly ill-founded, was limited to determining whether a *prima facie* examination of the facts and the statements did or did not disclose any possible ground on which a breach of the Convention could ultimately be found to be established. It could not be concluded from a *prima facie* examination of the facts and the statements that there was no possible ground on which a breach of the Convention could ultimately be found to be established. Whether the application constituted an abuse of the right of petition depended on the outcome of the issue whether or not Lawless had been the victim of a breach of the Convention, which issue essentially belonged to the merits and could not be decided at this stage.

Private Deliberations of the Commission Disclosed to the Government

In a further recorded conversation, Crosbie offered "information and comment on the Lawless case" to the Secretary of the Department of External Affairs. The Commission had voted eight to four in favour of admissibility. Waldock, Eustathiades, Faber, Erim, Dominedo, Susterhenn, Janssen-Pevtschin and Skarpedinsson voted in favour. The members opposing were himself, Berg the Dane, Petren the Norwegian and Sorensen the Swede. Generally speaking, the vote reflected a post-war "hangover" of opposition to "strong" government. No one had much sympathy with the case but there was a substantial feeling that the relevant law was inconsistent with democratic government. In his opinion, Waldock's vote in favour of admissibility was to be ascribed to his sharing, on balance, the sentiment just mentioned, and was not attributed to a desire to put us in the same boat as Northern Ireland as regards the observance of human rights. One of the strongest advocates of admissibility was the German, Susterhenn. Crosbie said that, prior to the vote, which was taken on the principles of *juriores priores* with him therefore the first to vote, he made a statement in which he endeavoured to paint the *psychological-political* background[54] to the situation. He laid stress on the fact that Lawless could have found the key to his release by making a declaration. This led to a strong outburst by Susterhenn who described the method as "blackmail". It would seem that the Government could meet the preoccupation of those who voted in favour of admissibility by instituting some court procedure, such as re-establishing special courts. Crosbie thought that the Commission would hardly have disposed of the case for perhaps another twelve months because the procedures were slow and the Commission was over-burdened. It must have been extremely advantageous for the Government to have knowledge of the private deliberations of Commission. In the preparation of the next stage of the proceedings, it must have been useful to have known the attitudes of the various members, the issues of particular concern and the standing and numerical strength of those who favoured upholding the complaint and those who opposed it. The propriety of Crosbie divulging the internal considerations of the Commission is highly questionable. In his favour it should be noted that the relationship between a Commission member and the Government of the state of which is a national was, and remains, unclear. The Convention merely states that "the members of the Commission shall sit...in their individual capacity".[55] While it might not be correct to expect from Commission members the traditional impartiality and confidentiality demanded of domestic judges, it is somewhat of a surprise to discover how detailed the information Crosbie supplied to the Government was. In addition, the admonition given by the President of the Commission to the parties that the Commission met *in camera* and attached the highest importance to maintaining the secrecy of its proceedings must have rang very hollow indeed when the person divulging the private deliberations of the Commission was one of its members. How Crosbie's actions hindered the settlement of the Lawless case on friendly terms will never be known.

Government Expresses Concern at the Decision

Because of the lack of archival material for this period it is impossible to say with certainty how the Government viewed the decision to admit the application but it must have been with considerable disappointment and some alarm. The only recorded view of the Government's reaction comes from British sources. The Commonwealth Relations Office relayed to the Foreign Office reports from Dublin. The first,[56] having noted that the English press had not mentioned the Commission's decision, stated that an official in External Affairs had told the writer "some time ago that he had advised the Government that their...derogation should refer to the existence of a state of emergency. The Taoiseach, however, overruled this advice on the ground that there was no such state of emergency. They are now suffering from this decision." A second report stated that "...our Ambassador in Dublin [said] that Mr. de Valera [the Taoiseach], who had a long discussion with him on the subject, is very worried about the implication of the decision...our Ambassador suggested that the difficulty...could easily be overcome by declaring a state of emergency.

This, however, de Valera is very loath to do as he estimates that there would be great political difficulties in this course."

During the month of August highly inaccurate speculation on the progress of the case appeared in the Irish newspapers. For example, one newspaper carried a report that "the Commission found that Lawless is entitled to a judicial trial before a court constituted under the aegis of the Commission". The Secretariat of the Commission, in early September 1958, issued a public communiqué[57] which, after setting out the facts, merely stated that the Commission had declared the application admissible and, without disclosing any detailed reasons, noted that this decision concerned the application's admissibility and not its merits. The statement explained the next stage of the procedure, which was the establishment of a sub-Commission to ascertain the facts and to attempt to secure a friendly settlement. Failure to secure a settlement would lead to the Commission stating its opinion on the merits of the case and the present ruling did not pre-judge in any way such opinion.

Notes

[1] Articles 26 and 27 of the Convention.

[2] On Europe Day, 3 September, printed 34 BYIL pp.356-363 at p.361.

[3] 34 BYIL at p.360.

[4] YBECHR 1955-56-57, pp.222-225.

[5] YBECHR 1955-56-57, pp.132-134. The report of the Commission was adopted on 26 September 1958 and remained confidential for 39 years until it was made public on 17 September 1997 and is now published in Human Rights Law Journal, vol.18, No.9-12.

[6] DJ File S.9/58/6.(1993 Release). 30 paragraphs with schedules.

[7] The application was registered under file number 332/57 on 12 November 1957.

[8] See Appendix 1 for articles of the Convention.

[9] Rules of Procedure, Rule 34, as it was then.

[10] Ibid. Rule 45, as it was then.

[11] AG File SR 54/38.

[12] See Appendix 2 for biographical notes on members of the Commission.

[13] At the 11th Session of the Commission: 16-20 December 1957.

[14] The information in this section is contained in DFA File 417/39/19/4/2 Parts 1 & 2.

[15] Truncated versions of these pleadings are printed in the Lawless case. ECHR. 1960-61. Series B. pp.23-34.

[16] The pleadings on the Government side were drafted by the Permanent Representative to the Council of Europe (with no legal background) within the Department of External Affairs and not by the Legal Adviser in that Department or in the office of the Attorney General.

[17] DJ File S9/58/1.

[18] ECHR. 1962. Series B. De Becker was a Belgian journalist who served the policies of the occupying German power from 1940-45. In 1946 he was sentenced to death for collaboration but this was later commuted to life imprisonment. He was released on condition that he would not engage in political activities and that he would take up residence abroad. He claimed that these restrictions breached the Convention. For later developments see p.174, footnote 8.

[19] Cabinet Minute. Item 2. 24 January 1958.

[20] DJ File S.9/58/7. (1993 Release). Contains 25 paragraphs.

[21] Article 15.6.1° provides that "the right to raise and maintain military or armed forces is vested exclusively in the Oireachtas".

[22] *The IRA*. T.P.Coogan. op.cit. Chapter 5: *The Bombing Campaign*. The British Parliament enacted, the Prevention of Violence (Temporary Provisions) Act 1939. During the debate, an explosion, at King's Cross Station, killed one man and injured 15 others: see in general *Emergency Powers in Peacetime.* D.Bonner. 1985. For the preparation of this Act see: O.Lomas. [1980] Public Law 16.

[23] Articles 2 and 3 of the Constitution, as they were then.

[24] Hand-written letter ended with "Urgent representation for an allowance to cover supply Chateau Latour to McNulty [Secretary to the Commission] would be in order".

[25] BPRO. FO 371/137788/1733/10 & 12.

[26] YBECHR 1955-56-57, p.50. The UK Government notified the Secretary General of the Council of Europe that "a public emergency...exists in...Northern Ireland" which led the Northern Ireland Government to bring emergency measures into force on 27 June 1957.

[27] In 1971 when internment was introduced in Northern Ireland, the Irish Government did not follow suit, and initiated complaints against the UK.

[28] DJ File S.9/58/8. (1993 Release). 21 February 1958.

[29] Article 28.3.3°. See p. 17.

[30] Article 38.3.1° provides that "special courts may be established by law for the trial of offences in cases where...the ordinary courts are inadequate to secure the effective administration of justice, and the preservation of public peace and order".

[31] Part V of the1939 Act contains the current law with regard to special courts.

[32] Article 38.4.1° provides that "military tribunals may be established...to deal with a state or war or armed rebellion".

[33] Article 39 of the Constitution and the Treason Act 1939 provides that "treason shall consist only in levying war against the State, or assisting any State or person or inciting or conspiring with any person to levy war against the State, or attempting by force of arms or other violent means to overthrow the organs of government established by this Constitution, or taking part or being concerned in or inciting or conspiring with any person to take part or be concerned in any such attempt".

[34] DJ File S.9/58/1.

[35] Cabinet Minute. Item 2. 2 March 1958.

[36] AG File SR 54/38. 27 February 1958.

[37] DJ File S.9/58/9. (1993 Release). 23 March 1958. 22 pages with schedules.

[38] DJ File S.9/58/10. (1993 Release). 12 May 1958.

[39] A judge was requested to resign: see p.45, footnote 18.

[40] Rules of Procedure, Rule 46 (1), as it was then.

[41] AG File SR 54/38.

[42] Rules of Procedure, Rule 25, as amended in June 1958 read: "a quorum of the Commission shall be two-thirds of its members. However, a majority of the members shall constitute a quorum when the Commission considers the admissibility of an application".

[43] S.McBride SC, T.J.Connolly SC and S.Sorahan BL instructed by C.McAnally of P.C.Moore & Co. Solicitors appeared for Lawless. The AG., B.Walsh SC and A.Hederman BL instructed by the Chief State Solicitor appeared for the Government.

[44] Waldock (UK), Eustathiades (Greece) and Erim (Turkey) represented countries that, at that time, did not recognise the right of individual petition. Thus these members could adjudicate on complaints coming from within states which had recognised the right of individual petition and members from states which had recognised the right of individual petition could not adjudicate on complaints from individuals within the UK, Greece and Turkey, though they could hear inter-states applications involving those countries.

[45] Articles 28 (b), 31(2) and 33 of the Convention.

[46] Sorensen said, "although most members understand English they may not be entirely familiar with the technical terms of the English law."

[47] For an extract from this affidavit, see p. 38.

[48] BPRO. DO 35/7943/88/13. On 23 July 1959, the British Embassy in Dublin noted that "Sean MacBride, is one of the stormier petrels of Irish politics and a former Adj.-General of the pre-war IRA...MacBride, who is a barrister...has done his utmost to make things difficult internationally for the [Irish] Government by personally taking a test appeal...to the Human Rights Commission in Strasbourg."

[49] In Kent v Dulles (1958) 353 US 116 where the US Supreme Court held that the Secretary of State had no authority to deny passports on the basis of Communist Party membership.

[50] YBECHR 1955-57, pp.222-225. The decision is printed only in French.

[51] AG did not mention Lawless's acquittal on an IRA membership charge: see pp. 32-33.

[52] At which Waldock presented an address: see footnote 2, supra.

[53] DJ File S.9/58/12 (1993 Release). Printed in Lawless case. ECHR. 1960-61. Series B. pp.35-51. The decision contains no indication as to whether the decision was unanimous or not but see p.86 for revelation of the Commission's private discussions.

[54] This may have influenced Waldock who used this expression in his opinion when deciding on the merits of the case, see p. 144.

[55] Article 23 of the Convention.

[56] BPRO. FO 371/1377/1733.

[57] DJ File S.9/58/1.

6 European Sub-Commission of Human Rights Investigates the Application

Introduction

The next stage in the process, as it was then structured, was the establishment of a sub-Commission. The parties were invited to submit pleadings that concentrated on a new set of issues. These were whether detention without trial breached the Convention, and if it did, had the Government effectively derogated, which it was entitled to do when a public emergency threatened the life of the nation, though only to the extent strictly required by the exigencies of the situation. The Irish Government justified the introduction of detention powers on the ground that failure to curb IRA activities could result, *inter alia,* in war between Ireland and the UK. This extraordinary claim was made in private and was later suppressed and expunged from the official publication of the case and is made public here for the first time. The decision by the sub-Commission not to make a fact-finding visit to Ireland is severely criticised. Instead, a private hearing in Strasbourg was held at which evidence was heard, the first case in which this course of action was taken. A central issue was the role that Lawless played in the material events. The *de facto* ending of detention without trial occurred prior to this sub-Commission hearing. Formal contact between the Governments of the Irish Republic and Northern Ireland is revealed for the first time. The conciliation role of the sub-Commission was greatly emphasised though the efforts made to achieve a friendly settlement ended in failure.

Establishment of Sub-Commission

Once the Commission accepted a petition, it had, with a view to ascertaining the facts, to undertake with the parties an examination of the petition and, if need be, an investigation, for the effective conduct of which the State concerned had to furnish all necessary facilities. The Commission at the same time placed itself at the disposal of the parties with a view to securing a friendly settlement on the basis of respect for human rights as defined in the Convention.[1] The Commission performed these functions by means of a sub-Commission, which consisted of seven members, with each party appointing a member of their choice, and the remaining members chosen by lot.[2] Presumably the purpose of permitting each party to nominate a member to the sub-Commission was to demonstrate the fairness of the proceedings by insuring that the interest of each party would be adequately protected. Having declared the application admissible, the President laid down 22 September 1958 as the time limit[3] before which the parties should state whether they wished to avail of the right to appoint a person of their choice to membership of the sub-Commission.[4]

The first issue for the Government was their nomination to the sub-Commission and this was given a great deal of consideration. Within the Department of External Affairs it seemed that the choice must necessarily fall on James Crosbie because, although he acted in a purely personal capacity, he "owed his appointment" to the Government. He was personally sympathetic and it would be extremely useful to have someone familiar with the situation and fully aware of the difficulties that confronted the Government. So far as the other Commission members were concerned, the point was raised as to whether it was out of the question to nominate Waldock, a distinguished lawyer and more fully conversant with the situation in Ireland than the other members, except Crosbie. The Government might choose Sorensen of Denmark or Petren of Sweden, probably the two most distinguished international lawyers and it was known that "they sided with us on the admissibility question". Of the others, except Berg of Norway, it was known that they were unsympathetic on the admissibility issue, particularly the German, Sustenhenn, "who was very strongly" against the Government and they were hardly of such distinction as to justify being chosen on their merits. "The other side may well choose the Greek, Eustathiades, which whom MacBride [was] very friendly." Crosbie may prefer not to be nominated lest he should be made appear to be "our man". There was much to be said for "waiving our right and as a gesture, it would show our confidence in the merits of our case to withstand any objective examination". The Minister for External Affairs took the view that Crosbie should be designated. It "would be invidious and indeed an unwarranted reflection on him, not to [be] asked to so act, and further, that it would be highly desirable that he should be, as it were, our advocate in the Commission". Accordingly, the Taoiseach, the Minister for Justice and the Attorney General agreed to this suggestion. Crosbie was asked to, and agreed to act as the Government's nomination to the sub-Commission.

It has already been noted, with that great wisdom which hindsight bestows, that had some events in the course of the case been handled in a different manner the final outcome might well have been different. The first fault, very understandable and easily forgiven, was the giving by Lawless of an undertaking which resulted in his release from detention. But the next mistake, the nomination of Waldock to the sub-Commission by Lawless's legal representatives, can neither be as easily understood nor forgiven, and which, as we shall see in a later paragraph, came even as a surprise to the British authorities. The blame for this blunder, for that is what it turned out to be, must lie with MacBride. The nomination of Waldock was made to demonstrate to the Commission that Lawless's activities were not anti-British, nor were they aimed at the British people. What more real way of showing the genuineness of these sentiments than to nominate the United Kingdom member of the Commission to the body which was to investigate a complaint made by an Irish national relating to matters of a highly sensitive political nature between the Governments of the United Kingdom and Ireland? Lawless thus said to the Commission that he had implicit confidence in Waldock's impartiality. While the motivation underlying this decision was laudable, it was a strategy fraught with danger, as subsequent events very evidently proved. Having regard to Waldock's nationality, and the pivotal position he held within the Commission as President, it seemed an extraordinary risk for MacBride to have taken. It might have been a reasonable assumption that members of the Commission would be very slow to condemn their own governments. This would happen, not because their impartiality was suspect, but because their particular knowledge of the facts would have given them a deeper insight into the underlying events raised in the particular case. Applying this rule of thumb, Waldock's nationality was only incidental because, after all, the complaint was made against the Irish Government and not against the United Kingdom Government. But events were taking place in Northern Ireland, which *de facto* was part of the United Kingdom, that had repercussions on relations between the United Kingdom and Irish Governments, and on community relations within Northern Ireland. These events were going to be crucial ingredients in the future management of the case by the Irish Government. The United Kingdom and Northern Ireland Governments were grappling with precisely the same IRA threats as the Irish Government and indeed had responded in the same way with the introduction of detention without trial. Waldock had exceptional knowledge regarding such events and, as already stated, would have been sympathetic to his own Government's predicament. It would be only in the most extraordinary circumstances that Waldock would have publicly made a condemnation of his own government, a factor which must have been appreciated by MacBride. Waldock was thus placed in a most invidious position in that a conflict of interest clearly existed. To expressly condemn the Irish Government would be an implicit condemnation of the United Kingdom Government, and, in circumstances in which that Government was not a party and had not been granted a hearing. Conversely, to expressly exonerate the Irish Government would have been an implicit exoneration of the United Kingdom Government. Incidentally, this is yet another unique feature of the Lawless case. As far as this author can ascertain, the Lawless case is the only case taken under the European Convention of Human Rights where the conduct of a government which was not a respondent and accordingly was not represented at the hearing was under scrutiny. There is no evidence to suggest that Waldock attempted to excuse himself from accepting Lawless's nomination.[5] An essential ingredient under the Convention, that of fairness and even-handedness, expressed in the notion that the applicant would have a "friend" at the investigatory stage, was absent and thus rendered the entire process suspect. As President of the Commission, Waldock was in a position of particular influence. Add to this the fact that the continental members of the Commission would have been aware of the commonality of language and legal systems between the United Kingdom and Ireland,[6] which sprung from a common political, constitutional and legal history. And given the part-time nature of the Commission and its workload, the natural inclination of those members would have been to rely on the opinions and conclusions of Waldock on the issues. That is precisely what had happened on the admissibility issue: Waldock dominated the oral hearing and, it seemed, wrote the decision of the Commission. In deference to MacBride, it may well be that he was very aware of Waldock's influence and that he deliberately nominated him knowing the dilemma it would pose. Hopefully, Waldock in attempting to resolve that conflict would put his sense of fairness and his obligation to the Convention before his loyalty to his country. It may well have been a clever and subtle device to neutralise the most potent member of the Commission. But as already noted, it was a very precarious strategy and with hindsight was a mistake. A more straightforward tactic would have been to nominate a more sympathetic member, such as Eusthatiades or Susterhenn, to the sub-Commission and hope that Waldock would not be drawn by lot. If that had happened, his influence would have been very reduced because he would not have been a member of the investigatory body. Had Waldock been drawn by lot, the only hope then would have been that Lawless's nominated member would, as Lawless's "friend", been able to exert sufficient influence over the other members of the sub-Commission and subsequently the remaining members of the plenary Commission to sway them in favour of Lawless.

The Government was informed that Lawless had nominated Waldock, who accepted the nomination, and failing him, Susterhenn or Eustathiades. Following the nominations of Crosbie and Waldock, the Commission President drew by lot[7] the remaining five sub-Commission members, Dominedo, Eustathiades, Faber, Berg and Erim. Sorensen, Susterhenn and Beaufort, were the substitutes.[8]

British Government Supportive of Irish Government

The United Kingdom's Permanent Representative to the Council of Europe reported[9] to the Foreign Office that the Lawless case had been declared admissible and that both sides had time to prepare a case as it seemed unlikely that it would come before the sub-Commission until the following February. The Irish Government had designated ex-Senator James Crosbie as its representative on the sub-Commission. "It is interesting to note that Lawless, who is accused of activities in connection with the IRA should have chosen Professor Waldock as his representative on the sub-Commission." Much of the case would rest on the allegation that Lawless was an IRA member at the time. The IRA, like the Communist Party, was an organisation dedicated to the overthrow of the established form of government by violence and *ipso facto* not entitled to the protection of the Convention of Human Rights. It was on these grounds that the German Communist Party's application was "thrown out". Lawless strongly denied that he was an IRA member at the time of his arrest. The Irish Government contended that it was entitled to arrest him and others under the "special 1939 legislation" which had been brought into force. The Council of Europe had been informed that these emergency measures had been reintroduced. The Irish Government had not maintained that this constituted derogation to the Convention. In fact, the Irish Foreign Minister publicly stated that there had been no derogation when questioned. "He was no doubt compelled to do so as he could hardly argue that the life of the nation was in danger." The Irish Government had, however, let it be known that if the sub-Commission felt that the emergency measures should have been communicated as derogation to certain articles of the Convention it would make derogation. As a final remark the official added "as you will see, this case seems hopelessly involved". Some days later, the

Commonwealth Relations Office reported to the Foreign Office that the Lawless case had been ruled admissible, relaying a conversation that an official of the Dublin Embassy had with de Valera, discussed in the previous chapter. It was noted that the British Government's interest in this matter was the same as those of the Irish Republic. "It would be politically most undesirable were there to be a decision at Strasbourg which would place the Republic in such a position that they might have to release all those now in detention. This would give a tremendous boost to the IRA and might well result in a widespread increase in acts of terrorism on the border of Northern Ireland. Naturally the British Government wanted to avoid this at all costs." Then the question was posed: "was there any way in which the British Government could assist?" The answer depended largely on the form of the sub-Commission: for instance, was its composition known and was the United Kingdom representative on it? Or was it an *ad-hoc* body set up to deal with a particular issue? Had it a political complexion or had it a judicial character? If the former, was there any opportunity of lobbying and would the Irish Republic and the United Kingdom be able to argue as to the political implications of a decision involving the release of those now detained? The Foreign Office replied that it was only in the event of the Committee of Ministers being brought into the case that any opportunity of expressing a view would occur. While the case was in the hands of the sub-Commission, the Commission or the European Court, the first two quasi-judicial bodies and the last a judicial body, there would be no opportunity for the British Government to intervene in any way.

Parties Invited to Submit Pleadings

Lawless had six weeks, extended by four weeks, from the date his solicitor received the full text of the admissibility decision, to submit his arguments and conclusions. These were filed on 20 November 1958 and a copy forwarded to the Government. Once again the pleadings submitted were voluminous, diffuse and repetitive, despite the fact that considerable pleadings had already been filed and a hearing had already taken place. Though it must be said, in fairness to the parties, that while the material facts remained the same, the legal issues had changed. Attention now turned to the central issue. That was whether detention without trial breached the Convention, and if it did, had the Irish Government been entitled to derogate from its obligations because of circumstances which pertained at the time.

Lawless's Arguments and Conclusions

In his arguments and conclusions[10] Lawless claimed that his detention without charge, trial or the intervention of the due process of law constituted a violation of Articles 5 and 6, by reason of which he was entitled to compensation, damages, costs and expenses. With regards to Article 17, the *German Communist Party* case[11] was not applicable because, notwithstanding the Commission decision, the German Government could not have arrested and detained without charge or trial those it merely alleged were party members. Also, that case was grounded on Articles 9, 10, and 11 which were subject to specific limitations, not applicable to Articles 5 and 6. The onus of establishing that Article 15 (1)[12] applied was on the Government, which had failed to clearly plead derogation. Instead, there was merely an indication that in the event of an adverse Commission finding, the Government *may* then plead derogation. Since derogation may never be pleaded it did not arise. The letter of 20 July 1957 was not a valid compliance with Article 15 (3) in that it had not given any reason for the measures taken which would permit derogation, namely, the existence of a "time of war or other public emergency threatening the life of the nation". On the contrary, the grounds given were (i) "to prevent the commission of offences against public peace and order", and (ii) "to prevent the maintaining of military or armed forces other than those authorised by the Constitution". These did not connote that the life of the nation had been threatened. Offences against public peace and order arose daily in most states. The existence of an unauthorised armed group may not, dependent upon its size, purpose and activity necessarily constitute an actual threat to "the life of a nation". The failure to rely on the existence of "a state of public emergency threatening the life of the nation" (i) in the letter of 20 July 1957 and (ii) in its written and oral submissions, were indicative that the Government did not seriously believe and was not prepared to state that such an emergency existed. If satisfactory proofs established that a situation existed that warranted derogation, then detention without trial had been grossly in excess of any measures "strictly required by the exigencies of the situation". The ordinary courts were functioning normally without let or hindrance. In 1957, 122 persons were charged with offences under the 1939 Act; of these 109 were convicted and 13 acquitted. Most were charged before detention was brought into force; since then such suspected persons were in the main detained and not brought before the courts. Statutory provisions existed which enabled offences to be tried by (a) military tribunals which may deal with a "state of war or armed rebellion", and (b) special courts which required no special legislation, consisting of military officers, and (c) military courts which may try civilians on any charge whenever a state of emergency existed.[13] Laws enacted under a state of emergency had the effect of suspending the operation of all constitutional safeguards and could, with regard to the trial of offences, have altered, relaxed, or suspended the rules of evidence and procedure. Although the Government had not asked parliament to pass any such legislation it was obliquely asking the Commission to declare that an emergency existed. Accordingly, ample powers were available to bring offenders to trial. Arbitrary indefinite detention without trial was a manifestly excessive measure.

In correspondence with the Secretary General of the Council of Europe, Lawless's solicitor confirmed that he had received the Government's letter of 20 July 1957 and assumed that this letter had been regarded as a notice of derogation both by the Government and the Council of Europe.[14] A reply stated that it was merely intended to communicate a copy of the letter and that its terms could not possibly support any assumption that it constituted a notice of derogation. The Secretary General, as depository of all formal acts concerning the Convention, communicated the letter to all contracting states and had no competence to decide, or even to state an opinion, as to the legal effect of such communication.

Government's Counter-Memorial

With the enclosure of Lawless's arguments and conclusions, the Government was informed that it had six weeks to submit its counter-memorial. The Government inquired whether evidence was accepted on affidavit and, if so, at what stage of the proceedings. A reply stated that, while the rules of procedure[15] referred to "evidence and arguments", it did not specify the nature and form of evidence and it rested with the sub-Commission to determine, in each case, how much weight should be given to documentary evidence. Without prejudicing the opinion of the sub-Commission, the Government were entitled to present evidence on affidavit though such production did not affect the Commission's right to ordain, if need be, an inquiry. Yet again, it seems that the bulk of the drafting was done within the Department of External Affairs[16] with additional material supplied by the Department of Justice, though with the Attorney General having the final say, after counsel had considered the draft. The police authorities were consulted on a wide range of issues. They were requested to supply statistical information such as a summary since 1940 of incidents in which members of unlawful organisations were involved that featured force, intimidation, or interference against legal institutions or individuals. Also a summary from 1940 of arms, ammunition and explosives secured by the police from unlawful organisations and their adherents was needed. In addition a report giving an up-to-date full account of Lawless's history and associations with subversive organisations was requested.[17] Finally, the police authorities were asked to comment on the statement that of the 122 members of unlawful organisations charged under the Offences Against the State Act 1939 in 1957, 119 refused to recognise the court, and, in 1958, of 15 charged, 13 refused to recognise the court. The police reported that it would be impossible to state whether each of the individuals remained mute in court or whether each stated that he would not recognise the court. It would also be impossible to state whether a person as one of a group had it stated on his behalf by somebody else that he refused to recognise the court.[18] The Attorney General met with Insp. Philip McMahon to discuss the 11 to 13 July 1957 period. A copy of the draft was sent to the Commissioner of the police. The Governor of Mountjoy Prison gave a report on Lawless's associations when in prison. The Government decided that the Taoiseach and the Ministers for External Affairs and Justice, in consultation with the Attorney General, should settle the terms of the counter-memorial.[19] A memo to the Minister for Justice noted[20] that some weeks previously, the Secretary of the Department had expressed the view that the Government had no more than a sporting chance of winning; and a very pessimistic view was taken. As a result, however, of the inter-departmental discussions, and of additional knowledge gained of the circumstances, and of the way in which the case was being argued, there was no longer a feeling of despondency. There remained a feeling that the Government may lose if the Commission followed the pattern it adopted in the Cyprus hearings. There they held, unchallenged, that it was within its competence to judge (1) whether a public emergency threatening the life of the nation existed and (2) whether the measures derogating from the obligations under the Convention were taken only to the extent strictly required by the exigencies of the situation. In the Cyprus case, a sub-Commission made an investigation on the spot, they were on the island for 12 days, during which they questioned many persons, mayors of towns etc., and asked for police files, which were given and examined.[21] If a similar sub-Commission were to come here and examine the situation in the same way they would scarcely take the view that a public emergency threatening the life of the nation existed here at any time in the period since 8 July 1957. It was also felt, from a reading of the Cyprus documents, that the sub-Commission would scarcely report that the Government had not gone beyond the extent strictly required by the exigencies of the situation.

However, the counter-memorial was the best possible one in the circumstances.

The Government in its general observations[22] stated that Lawless's complaint must be rejected because the arguments and conclusions did not disclose any breach of the Convention. Where a country, like Ireland, was governed on democratic principles and respect for human rights, its government should be presumed to have acted accordingly until the contrary was definitely proved. In the past, democratic governments had been overthrown because of their inability or unwillingness to take the steps necessary to stop the growth of armed subversive organisations, which, in some countries, had deliberately and avowedly made use of democratic institutions and liberties in order to destroy them. The Government traced the history of the IRA and its activities during the 1939-45 period and the governmental responses. In September 1958, the IRA Army Council repeated an instruction to avoid "aggressive action within the 26-Counties area". This was based merely on temporary political expediency, and forbade members to "swear or pledge allegiance or recognition to the partition institutions of Government of the 6-Counties or 26-Counties States" or to "swear or pledge recognition of their legitimacy as sovereign governing bodies for the Irish people". The document included the 26-Counties "institutions of Government" and was an assertion that "in effect they are still imposed on the Irish people by the British Imperial Government". This denial of the legitimacy of the institutions of the State was reflected in the attitude of the Sinn Fein organisation, the IRA political wing, which included leading IRA members in its controlling and executive body. Although four Sinn Fein members were elected to Dail Eireann in March 1957, they had refused to take their seats.[23] In the past few years the IRA had declared war on, and carried out war-like operations against, the police force of the 6-Counties and the military forces of Great Britain stationed there, in defiance of the rightful authority of the parliament, government and people of the Irish State. These activities were still continuing, although they had considerably decreased since the IRA leaders and more active members were placed in detention. These steps were taken because the ordinary methods that had been previously relied on of enforcing the law and preventing unlawful activities had not succeeded in keeping IRA activities in check. There was no lack of will on the part of the IRA to keep up its campaign as actively as possible as was evidenced from IRA claims to have carried out "widespread operations".

The ordinary methods of enforcing the law, under which persons had been tried and sentenced, had not proved effective to prevent violent IRA activities. The decision to introduce detention was taken immediately after a particularly grave incident in Northern Ireland in which a police officer was shot dead and another wounded. In that week, too, men on trial for the armed robbery of explosives were acquitted in the domestic courts because witnesses had gone back on their identification during the trial because of intimidation. The Government concluded that the situation constituted a public emergency threatening the life of the nation and that failure to take immediate and effective steps to check IRA activities would have resulted in efforts to maintain order being defeated and civil war possibly provoked. From their special knowledge of the circumstances, the Government was satisfied that the exigencies of the situation required the introduction of preventative detention and that no other measure could deal rapidly and effectively with the situation. Lawless had been detained because it was reasonably necessary to prevent him committing offences against public order and security, as was contemplated by Article 5 (1) (c).

The argument that this paragraph was subject to sub-paragraph (3), and that Lawless should have been "tried", was a strained construction. The intention to commit a crime was not an offence until some overt act with criminal intent was done. Accordingly, Article 5 (3) could not be held to apply to Lawless, because his detention was reasonably considered necessary to prevent him committing an offence. The domestic courts had held that a person so detained was not detained on a criminal charge and a "trial" would therefore be inappropriate. Detention, when reasonably considered necessary to prevent the commission of offences, need not be followed by a "trial" and this was authorised by Article 5 (1) (c). If any action had been taken contrary to Article 5 then this was in exercise of the right of derogation under Article 15, a right not a privilege. Article 15 did not provide for the giving of any form of "notice of derogation" nor was derogation conditional on the giving of such information. The communication must be subsequent to the taking of the measures, the purpose of which was to keep the other Convention parties informed. The Government, at the earliest opportunity, gave that information in the most comprehensive terms of the measures taken and of the reasons therefor. It was for the government taking the action alone to determine when such a state of emergency existed and what measures were required by the exigencies of the situation.

Such a construction of the Convention was supported, though it was recognised that the Commission had the competence and the duty of inquiring into a government's appreciation of the extent of an emergency and of the measures required to meet it.[24] It was beyond contemplation that a government acting in good faith should be held to have breached its Convention obligations unless its appreciation of the situation was manifestly unreasonable. A dispute between an individual and a government was materially different from a dispute between two governments. In the latter case the Commission may not lean in favour of either party and would not raise any presumption in favour of one such party. In the former type of dispute, a presumption existed in favour of the legality of the acts of the government, a presumption that should be applied by the Commission. A government could not be in breach of the Convention if it took measures that it considered necessary, even though some other measure, also in derogation of rights guaranteed, might have been adopted as an alternative. To protect the community and its liberties detention without trial was adopted as the least oppressive measure.

Experience had shown that the IRA could not be successfully dealt with in ordinary courts. Evidence sufficient to satisfy a court could not easily be obtained and even when it was obtained, witnesses were afraid to give evidence, judges and jurors were threatened and on occasion witnesses and jurors had been shot. Of 122 cases of persons charged under the 1939 Act in 1957, the accused in 119 cases did not recognise the established ordinary courts, whose judges were independent and not subject to removal by the Government.[25] Lawless refused to recognise the courts, although he claimed that he should have been tried by such a court in July 1957 rather than being detained. Special courts could not deal with the problem because such courts, which had functioned in the past, adhered to the ordinary laws of evidence, and the same problem would have been met, the inability to produce witnesses to give evidence, which the mere change of venue would not have solved. There could be no reasonable objection, during a public emergency, of requiring a citizen to give an undertaking not to be a member of, or assist, any unlawful organisation. A detainee giving such an undertaking was released. Apart from that, the detainee had the legal right to apply to the Detention Commission and once it reported that no reasonable grounds existed for his continued detention, the person must be released. Detention under these circumstances, even if in conflict with Article 5, was not an unwarranted derogation from the rights guaranteed by the Convention. Detention permitted by law was carefully defined and subject to legal and constitutional provisions.

The Commission, in the *German Communist Party* case, decided that this fundamental provision was designed to safeguard the rights listed in the Convention by protecting the free operations of democratic institutions. The application of Article 17 would not make Lawless an outlaw. All the ordinary resources of law had been open to him. The Convention was not an instrument which individuals or groups, opposed to orderly government, could use to assert their alleged right to engage in activities that denied the rights of other members of the community, including the basic right to life. The Convention was designed with the very opposite intent. Lawless had not been deprived of his rights under domestic law, but he was debarred from being heard by the Commission since he refused, when charged, to recognise the lawfully established domestic courts, and had by his actions aimed at the destruction of those very rights which the Convention protected. The Government did not accept that Lawless had desisted from such activities. Instead, he sought to avail of the Convention to facilitate the continuance of subversive activities. The Commission would have no difficulty in determining that the IRA was a body contemplated by Article 17 and that any persons who pursued the same kind of unlawful activities were debarred from availing of the Convention. When Lawless was committed to prison he requested to be put in a separate part of the prison in association with two other remanded men. One of these men was the leader of the splinter group of which Lawless was a member and was later convicted of membership of an unlawful organisation and possession of incriminating documents. The other man was later convicted of the unlawful possession of firearms though acquitted of membership of an unlawful organisation charge. When both of these men were tried on an armed robbery charge, they refused to recognise the court and were acquitted because witnesses who had earlier identified them went back on their identification at the trial. Lawless continued to associate with them until his discharge from prison. The Government did not accept Lawless's assertion that he was not at the time of his detention a member of an unlawful organisation or group. On the contrary, on the day of his arrest, the police received confidential information which confirmed that Lawless was still an active member of the IRA splinter group and the indications were that he intended leaving temporarily for England to avoid detention. This information came from a source which for security reasons could not be disclosed, and caused his arrest. After his arrest an interview with police officers proceeded on the basis that he was still a member of the IRA splinter group and during the course of which he refused to dissociate himself from this group.[26]

De facto Ending of Detention without Trial

In the last months of 1958, a large number of detainees, about 50 to 60 in all, were released without the insistence on an undertaking as to future conduct when the Government was "satisfied by its own observations and judgement on whether certain men should be released". Further detainees were released in ones and two over the following weeks. In response to condemnations of detention without trial, the Taoiseach, de Valera, said that the detainees would be released immediately if the Government had some assurance that they would adhere to democratic methods. The Government decided, on 17 February 1959, that the persons remaining in detention should be released in batches within the following month or so, for example, by Easter 1959.[27] The remaining detainees were released on 15 March 1959,[28] though the Taoiseach warned that the Government would use all available means to retain authority following an ambush in which four police officers were injured in Northern Ireland. There had undoubtedly been a reduction in subversive violence. The pending investigations by the sub-Commission, a sensitive time for the Government having regard to the known views of the majority of the Commission, must have had a bearing on the decision to release all detained persons at that time. This must remain speculative because the archival material is closed.[29] Evidence to support this contention is found in British records. The Dublin Embassy reported[30] "that re-opening the [internment camp] would risk a rebuff in the Human Rights Commission where MacBride and others would use all possible legal means to frustrate [the Government], and to have to face, as they did in the past, severe criticism...from respectable local persons and organisations". When the British Prime Minister, Harold Macmillan, on a visit to Belfast, on 6 March 1959, criticised the releases, de Valera replied[31] that this statement was ill-advised, uncalled for and harmful. The Government's decision was based on the knowledge of the needs of the situation and that judgement was what was best calculated to serve the interest of peace and order.[32]

Invitation to Sub-Commission Hearing

The sub-Commission[33] decided in private session,[34] to invite the parties to appear on 17 and 18 April 1959. This was to obtain further information and explanation[35] and to hear statements from Lawless and the police officer who had interviewed Lawless on the night of his arrest. Two broad issues concerned the Commission. The first, directed at the Government, was whether, with regard to Article 15, the detention of persons without trial was strictly required by the exigencies of the situation. The second, directed at Lawless, concerned his relations with the IRA at the time when detention without trial had been introduced. The precise questions posed are detailed later. They illustrate how the sub-Commission had narrowed the matters it considered contentious. The parties were also invited to clarify or amplify other points, bearing in mind, however, the considerable amount of argument already submitted. Finally, it was pointed out, that hearings were secret and that failure to observe this requirement might compromise the satisfactory working of the sub-Commission.[36]

No Fact-finding Visit to Ireland by Sub-Commission

We have already noted features in the progress of the case that militated against success by Lawless. The first was his release from detention, and the second was Lawless's nomination of Waldock to the sub-Commission, noted earlier in this chapter. The third such factor was the failure by the sub-Commission to adequately investigate the facts of the case, which will be a recurring criticism in this and later chapters. That very instrument of investigation, the fact-finding visit, which could have been undertaken,[37] was the device that the Government feared most. It was admitted, at every level within the Government, that the case was lost if such an investigatory visit occurred, which proves how illusory, and in a sense fraudulent, the claim that an emergency which threatened the nation had actually existed. The Lawless case was the second occasion in which derogation from the Convention was pleaded on the public emergency ground. In the first case, *Greece v United Kingdom*, the sub-Commission made a fact-finding visit to Cyprus. In subsequent cases in which derogation was a contentious issue,[38] it became the norm to instigate fact-finding missions While it is difficult to understand why some fact-finding investigation was not instigated, there are superficial distinctions between these later cases and the Lawless case. First, all these other cases were inter-state applications which may tend to suggest that allegations made by one state against another rank in higher priority, and are more thoroughly investigated, than individual applications. But as the practice of the Commission developed, fact-finding visits were made following the lodgement of certain individual complaints.[39] Secondly, the events being investigated were current and continuing, which is a more acceptable reason why fact-finding missions were undertaken. Unfortunately, in the Lawless case, some nineteen months elapsed between the introduction of detention without trial, in July 1957, and the first meeting of the sub-Commission in late March 1959. In the meantime circumstances in Ireland, in particular the fact that Lawless was then free, had obviously changed and, more importantly, detention without trial had, as already been noted, factually ended though the legal basis for the measure remained in force. Of necessity, the events and material facts had to be understood and appreciated in a historical perspective. That element of urgency so necessary in the investigation of breaches of human rights was unfortunately missing. Nevertheless, the failure of the sub-Commission to instigate a fact-finding visit to Ireland proved fatal to Lawless's application. The Lawless case is, once again, unique in that it is the sole case in which derogation was a live issue and in which an on-the-spot investigation did not take place. While an on-the-spot investigation might have been pointless, because of the lapse of time and the changed circumstances, it then became absolutely imperative for the sub-Commission to thoroughly investigate all the elements of the case. In particular it was crucial to scrutinise the evidence advanced by the Government to sustain the derogation claim. It could have heard witnesses on the state of affairs that existed in Ireland in July 1957. Deputy James Carroll, TD, the Lord Mayor of Dublin, whose affidavit was the only one filed in this regard, should, at least, have been invited to expand, and to defend, if necessary, the averments he had made.[40] Instead, the sub-Commission invited Lawless and McMahon to address in person very limited and specific matters, and ignored the much wider factual issues. This was a serious dereliction of its functions and the consequences of this failure will be returned to in the next chapter.

Lawless seeks Information from Northern Ireland Government

Because of the absence of material very little is known as to the preparations made at the various stages by Lawless's advisers. But what is known, from State archival material, is that in preparing for this hearing, Lawless's solicitor wrote[41] to the Ministry of Home Affairs for Northern Ireland in Belfast, on 23 March 1959. Information was sought for the years 1956, 1957 and 1958 as to: (a) the number of persons detained without trial in Northern Ireland who were (i) residents of Northern Ireland and (ii) residents of Eire; and (b) the number of persons convicted of offences in connection with violence, by the use of firearms or explosives, to persons or property who were (i) residents of Northern Ireland and (ii) residents of Eire. In a second letter,[42] in probable reply to some query, it was stated that the requested information was required in connection with a hearing that was shortly to take place before a sub-Commission of Human Rights in Strasbourg. It was noted that the entire proceedings were to be *in camera* and that none of the evidence would be made public and all the documents in the case were secret. The Ministry replied on 14 April and supplied the information requested. This correspondence immediately triggered the

Ministry of Home Affairs to inform the Department of Justice in Dublin by letter[43] of this request. This appears to have been done in some unofficial way because after the hearing, at which some of the information was produced by Lawless's counsel, which will be noted later, the Department of Justice wrote two letters, both dated 1 May 1959, and sent them together in the one envelope. The first letter thanked the Ministry for having written on 14 April 1959 and pointed out that, as anticipated, "only *part* of the information given...was passed on and taken out of context it presented an entirely different story from that told in the full...letter of 14 April". It also stated that an official letter was enclosed, asked for a copy of the communication sent to Lawless's solicitor and commented that "we should like to be able to let all concerned know the true position". In the second "official" letter, a request was made that the information in the precise form furnished to Lawless's solicitor be given. It was noted that counsel for Lawless gave in Strasbourg "figures in relation to persons interned and convicted...in the 6-Counties area and those with addresses in the 26-Counties which he stated were obtained though the courtesy of the Belfast Government". The pretence had to be maintained that the Department of Justice had no prior knowledge of these figures. Later in the letter it was recorded that "in the proceedings the Attorney General...informed the sub-Commission that he was quite prepared to accept any written statement by the Belfast Government furnishing those figures".[44] It is not clear whether the Attorney General already knew that this information was in the possession of the Department of Justice. If he did have such knowledge, this statement to the sub-Commission was somewhat misleading. But it is entirely possible that he had not been informed, an extraordinary omission. The Department of Justice may not have wished to make an admission, even in *in camera* proceedings, that the Belfast and Dublin administrations were in contact on sensitive security matters. The Ministry of Home Affairs replied, again using the two-letter practice. In the first letter, the Department of Justice was thanked for explaining the developments in the Lawless case, and the second "official" letter was a covering one which attached a copy of the letter sent to Lawless's solicitor.[45]

Government Preparation for the Hearing

The Department of Justice was informed[46] that Insp. McMahon would be available to attend at Strasbourg and that he had been alerted as to the evidence he may have to give and particularly his long interview with

Lawless on 11 July. The Commissioner of the police force was of opinion that the most important plea in justifying the policy of detention hinged on the ambush of the Northern Ireland police officers on 4 July 1957, when one was killed and another wounded. "This loss of life was the spark which could easily start retaliatory killings in the 6-Counties and result in civil strife and damage to property there which would develop on a religious basis. The 6-Counties authorities have a constant anxiety in this connection and have been apprehensive that the 'Specials' [auxiliary part-time police force] would carry out reprisals. Experience has shown that once this trend started, innocent persons are those who invariably suffer". Yet again, the police were queried on Lawless's participation in the armed raids. The police were satisfied that further investigations made in the matter had been exhaustive and that "under no circumstances could...the source of the information against Lawless [be disclosed] in which very experienced police officers had the fullest confidence. It would be fatal to further work against unlawful organisations...to take any step which might enable persons in such organisations to deduce the identify of the source against Lawless. It would shake the confidence of such persons in the police and their help is vital". The police reported on Lawless's activities since his release from detention. He had been "advised by his counsel to keep away from all subversive activities and meetings of the [IRA] splinter group until such time as his case was finally disposed of by the Commission of Human Rights. In spite of warnings he continued to associate with members of the splinter group and attend meetings of this organisation". Lawless was later to deny any criminal activity at that time. The Department of Justice collated the various items and forwarded these to the Attorney General. It was noted that the police could, in July 1957, have arrested known IRA members under section 30 of the Offences Against the State Act, 1939,[47] questioned them about their movements and searched for incriminating documents. It was probable that convictions would have been secured in many cases, though the sentences would have been short. The police reported that various newspapers, particularly British ones circulating in Ireland, carried reports on the forthcoming sub-Commission hearing. These pieces had been written by a journalist who it was believed had close contacts with the IRA splinter group and received the information on the hearing from one of Lawless's legal representatives. The Government wrote to the Commission on 10 April 1959, a copy of which letter was sent to Lawless's solicitor. On 5 May 1959, on the instructions of the President of the sub-Commission, incidentally after the sub-Commission hearing, a reply which Lawless's solicitor had addressed to the Council of Europe, on 28 April 1959, was forwarded to the Government. The contents of this correspondence had been brought to the attention of the sub-Commission and it was expected that the matters raised would be considered in the course of its next session. In a further letter, in May 1959, the Government acknowledged the letter and stated that it was "at a loss to understand the tone and import of this communication". The initial letter from the Government was intended only to draw the attention of the sub-Commission to the newspaper publicity that the case had received in Ireland and in England. It made no accusation that anyone, either Lawless, or his legal advisers, or any person associated with them, or the Secretariat of the Council of Europe, had been responsible for such publicity. It merely drew attention to the fact and the Government was satisfied that the information in the reports had not emanated from any Government source. That statement was repeated and confirmed and the letter continued that "in this regard it is surely not without significance that all the press reports involved are couched in terms adverse to the Government". The Government was perturbed to learn that in a communication to the editor of an Irish newspaper Lawless's solicitor alleged that "a malicious false statement" was "inspired by an interested party". This was intended to mean that the Government had deliberately given a "malicious false statement" to the press. Not only was this completely false but this letter to an outside party was "a deliberate and calculated perversion" of the Convention and of the method of working of the Commission and proved, as the Government had repeatedly suggested, that this case had been brought for political and propaganda purposes. This was borne out by the fact that the retraction which the newspaper was forced to publish under threat of legal action "actually prejudiced part of the gravamen of the case before the sub-Commission, i.e. whether Lawless was at the relevant times a member of an illegal organisation". The sub-Commission took no action on this matter. There is something hypocritical about the stance taken by the Government in this regard. On the one hand it pretended to be concerned about the leaking of information to the press regarding the workings of the sub-Commission. At the same time the Irish member of the Commission, James Crosbie, was leaking sensitive information on the private deliberations to the Government which, of course, the Government did not refuse and obviously put to good use in the handling of its case.

Hearing by Sub-Commission of Human Rights

The proceedings before the sub-Commission had two distinct segments; the first was the hearing of the witnesses and the second was submissions by the parties on specific issues raised by the sub-Commission. A study of the transcript[48] illustrates obvious differences between how each segment was handled. With regard to hearing the witnesses two obvious difficulties arose; the first was the multiplicity of languages and the second was the collision of two very different legal systems. On the language issue, the President Eusthathiades,[49] and at least two other members of the sub-Commission spoke exclusively in French while other members of Commission, the legal teams and the witnesses, spoke exclusively in English. While translations from both languages took place simultaneously, the witnesses and the lawyers were repeatedly requested to slow down and pause between questions and answers. The President commented upon the quality of the translation, and the transcript contains recorded material that may, charitably, be described as vague. This consequently led to obvious confusion and understandable irritation. The members of the sub-Commission regularly interrupted each other, with the President particularly prone to do so, which resulted in repetition and a disorderly exposition of the evidence. In the question stakes the President and Waldock were to the fore, Crosbie was next, Faber and Erim make the occasional interjection, Susterhenn asked a question or two, and Berg asked none. Questions may have been directed through the President who in turn posed the question and this fact was not recorded in the transcript. It is also obvious that some members, in particular Faber, were confused about some of the facts. Most members of the sub-Commission were academic rather than professional lawyers. The forensic skills used in the examination and cross-examination of witnesses may not have been appreciated by them.

A very different approach, discussed later, was adopted when counsel made submissions. The differences between the common law and continental legal systems were also obvious. The Irish lawyers approached the hearing in an accusatorial manner while sub-Commission members, particularly the President, adopted an inquisitorial approach. The lawyers were constantly reminded of the limited issues to be explored, repeatedly asked to establish the relevance for their questions, and to address their questions to the sub-Commission rather than to the witnesses directly. Counsel was not allowed, though it did happened, to engage in rapid cross-examination.

The hearing lasted three days. On the afternoon and early evening of Friday, 17 April, Lawless and McMahon were heard. Saturday morning was taken up with submissions by Lawless's counsel[50] and the afternoon by the Attorney General.[51] Three hours on Sunday afternoon were given over to the replies. Since this is the first time that these proceedings are published as full an account as possible is given.

After setting out preliminary matters, the President noted that the sub-Commission felt that the most convenient way of conducting these proceedings was first to hear the witnesses that it had invited to appear. The question as to whether the witnesses should be sworn was not addressed at the initial stages and arose later during Lawless's evidence when he was being questioned by Crosbie and only then when the President seemed to confuse the nature of the question. When Lawless was asked whether he took an oath on joining the IRA, the President seemed to appreciate that he was being asked whether he had taken an oath before the sub-Commission. When MacBride intervened to ask whether or not the testimony was being given under oath, the President responded that when he spoke at the outset about a statement he did not mention the word "oath" and that was why Crosbie raised the question.[52] The President concluded, "no statement is made to this sub-Commission under oath". When the Attorney General asked whether evidence must be given on oath,[53] Waldock interjected to say not with Lawless, who was an applicant. The President explained that, as an international body, the sub-Commission took account of the various systems of procedure used in various countries and wanted to bring out that procedure or substance in its own procedure. When faced with a person who was to give evidence before it and that person was at the same time the applicant, the sub-Commission would hear him without an oath and through a statement to which it should attribute such value as may be given before an international body.[54] When MacBride indicated that Lawless was willing to give evidence under oath, the President said that account would not be taken of that remark because a decision had already been taken. When Insp. McMahon came to give evidence he was asked to swear to speak the truth, the whole truth and nothing but the truth.

Issues for and Statement by Lawless

The sub-Commission desired to ascertain from Lawless whether, in July 1957, he had ceased to be a member of, and ceased support for, an illegal organisation. In addition the sub-Commission wanted to ascertain whether he acted unreasonably in refusing, on 11 July 1957, to sign an undertaking to respect the Constitution and the laws, and his continuation until 11 December 1957, to refuse to sign such undertaking. In his short statement,[55] Lawless said that he was not a member of any illegal organisation in any part of 1957, nor did he give any active support to such organisation. He held religious and political convictions that debarred him from respecting his own Constitution because it allowed detention without trial. As a Roman Catholic, he regarded his Church as the one true Church, and he could not respect any Constitution that attempted to put any other Church on equal terms. He did not stand for any intolerance to any individual for his religious convictions, lack of religious convictions or philosophical convictions. He had not refused to give an undertaking not to engage in activities contrary to the Offences Against the State Act 1940: in fact in July 1957 he was willing to give such an undertaking.

Questions from Sub-Commission

The President asked Lawless at what date he ceased IRA membership and what steps he took to show that decision. Lawless stated that he ceased membership towards the end of 1956, and when pressed to identify that more clearly, he replied in December, and to show his decision he dissociated himself from the organisation and ceased all activities in support of it. He was in the IRA on idealistic and patriotic grounds. He ceased membership when he concluded that it was not getting sufficient support from the mass of the Irish people to achieve its aim, and also, that the ending of the partition of Ireland was first and foremost for the Irish Government. When Faber asked why, since Lawless was ready to sign this undertaking, he did not sign it, the President interrupted to say that did not arise because he had not been asked to do so.[56] Crosbie then asked a series of questions about the IRA. Lawless explained that he joined the IRA in early January 1956, it was not a social club, nor was a subscription paid. He joined after taking part in some procedure, that he did not take an oath, nor did he join for a particular period, he joined voluntarily and left voluntarily and he was prepared to state on oath that the IRA was not an oath-bound organisation. The President said that the oath aspect was not one with which the sub-Commission had to deal.[57] Crosbie asked exactly what steps he had taken to sever IRA connections. Lawless said that he ceased to attend parades, he dissociated himself and ceased all activities in support of the IRA. When asked about the charge in May 1957, after he allegedly left the IRA, Lawless agreed that he could have appealed his conviction to a higher court. Was it not a fact, asked Crosbie, that the group to which Lawless belonged felt that the IRA was not sufficiently active and that, bluntly put, his resignation from the IRA was purely fictitious? Lawless acknowledged that he had left the majority IRA in June 1956 because he did not believe them active enough, though when he said he left the IRA in 1956 he meant he left the splinter group to which he had been attached. He had left all illegal groups in late 1956 and had been in none in 1957. Waldock said that frankly what bothered him was the documents in respect of which Lawless had been charged in May 1957. Lawless said they came into his possession in 1956, they related to some projected operation about that time, they had lain in a suitcase on top of his wardrobe and when he saw the police near his home he took them out to dispose of them. Waldock commented that he understood Lawless's religious and political scruples, but when and how did it become clear that he could sign some form of undertaking that would enable his release? Lawless said that he was at all times prepared to give the undertaking which he eventually gave, though he had not told anyone of this because in the internment camp he would not have been taken seriously had he asked to be released by giving that undertaking. It was only before the Detention Commission that this became an actual possibility. When Faber said that what worried him was why Lawless would have carried that document to England,[58] Waldock answered that this document was not found when Lawless was going to England. When Waldock asked what questions were put to him in court about the documents, Lawless replied that he was asked none. Faber asked did the IRA leaders know that he had ceased to be a member. The President said that an answer had been given, it was inactivity, the lack of activity. When the point was pressed as to whether Lawless was considered a traitor, the President said that was a matter of appreciation on the part of the leaders. Faber said he asked this to show that there was scepticism as to the way in which Lawless ceased to be a member. The President said that this was a question of subjective reaction of the leaders and the sub-Commission could take that point up in their own appraisal of the facts. When Faber asked was this way of resignation sufficient, Lawless replied it was the traditional way, to cease activity and to withdraw support. Erim asked whether Lawless went through procedures other than just taking part in parades when joining the IRA. Lawless explained that he was approached in December 1955 by some personal friends and, when he agreed to join, he was brought to a recruit class in which he was told the IRA rules, and when he completed six weeks, he gave a simple pledge to obey lawful orders. There was no oath or any suggestion of oaths.

Questions from Attorney General

In reply to the Attorney General[59] Lawless said that he first took objection to the Constitution on religious grounds in spring 1954. Was there any inconsistency between his religious scruples and the oath he took on joining the Defence Forces? Lawless said that he got his religious objections after he had attended lectures, given by Professor Father Fahey,[60] on Sunday mornings in Dublin, in which Article 44 of the Constitution[61] came under constant abuse. From these lectures the seed was sown in his mind that in following Catholic Church teachings it was impossible to avoid the outlook that he could not respect the Constitution. When he joined the army reserve he joined voluntarily and there was no question of anyone forcing him to take the oath, the main part of which was swearing to be faithful and the other part did not enter his mind. He was 17 years of age at the time, was unaware of Irish history, and was not aware that a man could be interned without trial. The President asked was this a Roman Catholic priest and was it usual for the Constitution to be mentioned in sermons at church. When Lawless said no, the President asked was it by chance that he happened to listen to that sermon. Lawless said there was a misunderstanding, it was not in church. Waldock said it was lectures. Lawless admitted that he and other men broke away from the main IRA body in June 1956. When three named men were mentioned Lawless said that he would prefer not to give any information about his time in the IRA.

Lawless admitted[62] that he took part in a raid in 1956 when guns were stolen. When the Attorney General said that Lawless had been arrested in possession of a considerable quantity of firearms, Lawless commented that the figure of speech "considerable quantity" was not very exact. Lawless said that he was found not guilty of that charge. When asked would Lawless agree that he was acquitted on a technicality, the President asked did this imply a legal appreciation? This prompted Waldock to say that they were interested in whether Lawless was a member of an illegal organisation in July 1957. The Attorney General said that it was essential to give the sub-Commission some idea of Lawless's background during the periods leading up and subsequent to July. The Attorney General then asked that when Lawless was in court did he question the jurisdiction of that court to try him as a republican soldier? Lawless said that was not so. When asked whether he had said: "this court is merely being used to safeguard the last remnants of the British Empire", Lawless replied that what he said was "whether the judge realised it or not but that the Special Branch (the police) were using the process of the court to protect the last remnants of the British Empire in my country", in Ireland.

Waldock then said that what was wanted was evidence of what really was Lawless's position between December 1956, when he said he ceased to be an IRA member, and July 1957 when he was detained. The President said that he had asked Waldock to speak in Anglo-Saxon terms but "he was speaking to be quite clear" that if both sides were carried away from the natural and normal aim, which was fact-finding, then that was not what the sub-Commission was trying to do. Waldock commented that he thought the aim of the Attorney General was to obtain from Lawless a sufficient statement of his attitude of mind towards the court in order to determine whether there was any evidence of his still being an IRA member. The Attorney General said it was a little more than that. Lawless had voluntarily chosen to explain why he intended to destroy the document in his pocket - it was because he thought it was incriminating. Why then did he consider it more desirable to undergo a month in prison than tell the judge that the document was taken out of his home for the purpose of being destroyed? When the President asked Lawless had he any comments to make, Lawless replied he did not like to have to deal with that as the Attorney General had been misquoting him, but, however, he would like an explanation of a point. The President retorted that it was not for Lawless to appreciate this: that was the task of the sub-Commission, but if Lawless had any comments to make to the question put by the Attorney General, either confirmation or otherwise, he could do so, but not criticism. When Lawless apologised, the President said that perhaps the translation was bad. Lawless explained that when he was charged with IRA membership, a police officer gave evidence of what Lawless had told him - that he was not then a member of any organisation, which the court accepted and dismissed the charge. How could he deny that he had possession of incriminating documents? Lawless said that he was technically guilty. When Waldock asked was his answer that it was not any good making an explanation of how the document came into his possession because the charge was that he was in possession, Lawless replied that was correct. The Attorney General asked whether Lawless was aware that the court might have imposed a lighter sentence or no sentence at all, even though he had been convicted of the offence. Lawless said he did not know if he would have been given a lesser sentence. When asked whether since his release he had consistently refrained from all activities in support of illegal organisations or those engaged in illegal activities, Lawless replied that he had.

Following a short adjournment, the President requested the Attorney General to be kind enough to put his questions very clearly, indicating at the same time their relevance in regard to the matters of interest to the sub-Commission. It went without saying that Lawless's legal representatives were not deprived of the possibility, when questions were put, of submitting remarks as to the relevance of the questions. Lawless admitted that since his release from detention he had frequently visited premises used, and had been active in supporting, an organisation for the relief of political prisoners' dependants' and that he was not a member of Fianna Eireann in 1958. When the President inquired what was this organisation and the Attorney General explained that it was a youth organisation which had been associated with Republican activities, Lawless replied that he would like to put on record that he did not agree with that description of

Fianna Eireann. Lawless admitted that he had attended a commemoration ceremony at Bodenstown in June 1958 and that it was organised by the boy scout organisation, Fianna Eireann. He did not march in military formation because he had a bad leg, that it was raining and that he got a lift in a car from a newspaper reporter. Lawless said he was aware of an organisation called Saor Uladh. Ex-Senator [of Seanad Eireann], ex-MP [of the British House of Commons], Mr.Kelly, was certainly a member of that, from what he had read in newspapers in 1958. Kelly went to the USA on behalf of that organisation but he did not know whether he was the leader, but that could possibly be. When asked did he know that members of that organisation met in the same premises as the prisoners' dependants' organisation, Lawless said that he did not. He added that the prisoners' dependants' organisation was a legal organisation, that the courts had decided it was entitled to collect money and there was a provision in its constitution that no member of an illegal organisation could be a member of it.

Lawless admitted that he attended remand hearings of a named person on a charge of intimidating witnesses.[63] Was this charge of intimidation related to another case where firearms were used? Lawless replied that he did not think that was a question for him to answer as he thought he was to be questioned about his movements, not the movements of others. When Susterhenn asked what was the object of that procedure according to the newspapers, Lawless said that it was a report of an appearance of a personal friend, the nature of that friendship was that they had both been courting the same girl. When the Attorney General asked whether he had interfered with the St. Patrick's Day parade in Dublin in 1959, Lawless said no, that protest was organised by unemployed persons. When the Attorney General asked whether Lawless refused to recognise the authority of the court in May 1957, the President interrupted to ask whether Lawless had the assistance of a lawyer? Lawless said he had not, he took part in the proceedings, he cross-examined prosecution witnesses and he did not refuse to recognise the court. Lawless was then asked whether three named men were also in court and were two of them remanded in custody to prison on a charge of armed robbery of explosives and sent forward for jury trial on that charge. Lawless said that he believed so on the basis of newspaper reports. Did Lawless of his own volition occupy with them and another named man, a separate part of the prison? Lawless said that there was no such thing as a separate part of the prison. He and one of the named men occupied a triple cell, having been put there by prison staff, and there was no question of whether they liked it or not. As it happened Lawless did like it. One man was a personal friend, and the other occupied an adjoining cell. Did he associate habitually with these men during exercise and recreation? Lawless said that he associated with these men as he did with two named men who were in for theft, and the manager of a garage in prison for fraud, and an American citizen in for smuggling. He associated with these people, and not with others, because he could talk about current topics, they were not nitwits and their crimes were not revolting, such as sex crimes. Lawless said he objected to answering when asked whether these men were in the splinter group. When the Attorney General asked whether Lawless knew, without mentioning names, who had taken part in the armed raids for explosives, Lawless said the answer was no. The Attorney General asked whether Lawless remembered being asked on the night of his arrest to give information as to the location of arms or ammunition in the conversation with Insp. McMahon. Lawless replied that while he had no such information, he resented being considered an informer. Was he asked questions about the splinter group? No. Was he asked questions about the IRA? Yes. Was he asked to dissociate himself from the splinter group? Lawless replied no, and he informed the police officers that he was not in any illegal organisation.

Questions from his Counsel

Lawless was reminded[64] of the wording of the undertaking which he gave in December 1957 and asked whether he had been given an opportunity by the authorities to give that form of an undertaking, either verbally or written, at any time before that date. Lawless replied no. What was his objection to the written form tendered in August 1957? Lawless replied that he took exception to the word "respect". When asked what meaning did he attach to that word, Lawless said that "respect" was what you gave to your father and your mother, which were love, honour and obedience. This was the meaning he put on "respect" and that was what he was called on to give - love, honour and obedience to the Constitution. Lawless stated when asked, that the Political Prisoners' Dependants' Association had been granted a court licence, that Fianna Eireann was not banned and that it was one of the oldest boy scout organisations. When asked about the Bodenstown ceremony, Lawless explained about Wolfe Tone,[65] and how every political party in the 26-Counties and even the State Army of the 26-Counties claimed, in some degree, to be followers of Tone's teachings. Crosbie interrupted to ask was that the Republican Army. When Lawless said he meant the official army, Crosbie commented - the army of the Irish Republic? Lawless said he was about to say the army of the Irish Republic, the official armed forces of the State. That army had an independent commemoration in Bodenstown. Lawless was questioned about his intention of going to England to seek employment. When released from detention he worked in a Dublin bakery in February 1958, but when the work got slack he went to England in August and got a job in London. A month or so later he returned to Dublin.

Issues for and Statement by Insp. McMahon

The sub-Commission desired to hear Insp. McMahon on the question as to whether Lawless, in July 1957, had ceased to be a member of, and ceased to support, an illegal organisation. Insp.McMahon was sworn. His statement[66] covered the two armed raids on explosive factories, Lawless's arrest in May 1957, the failure of witnesses to these raids to identify him, his conviction for possession of incriminating documents, his association in prison with members of the IRA splinter group, his attendance at classes where instruction was given on the use of explosives, his visits to the Border for observation purposes between his release from prison and his arrest in July 1957. During a conversation on his arrest McMahon asked Lawless if he was willing to hand over the arms in his possession, the property of the splinter group, and to dissociate himself from the IRA and illegal organisations. He attempted to ascertain whether Lawless would sign a form of undertaking, which was in a rather simplified form and only required him to uphold the Constitution and its laws and to dissociate himself from illegal organisations. Lawless refused to do so. The undertaking was not in written form because the witness said that he was attempting to ascertain whether Lawless would sign any form of undertaking. Lawless declined to give even a verbal undertaking. He next asked Lawless would he be willing to pass on information he had on the splinter group in return for money and Lawless's reaction was to have nothing to do with the offer. When McMahon asked could he refer to notes to refresh his memory, the President said he should give his evidence first in a general way.

Questions from Sub-Commission

Erim asked had the witness enquired of Lawless whether he was a member of that illegal organisation and if so what was the reply? McMahon said that he had not asked Lawless that question because his whole discussion was on the basis that Lawless was such a member. That was accepted on Lawless's part in that he did not admit or deny membership. The witness agreed with Crosbie that Lawless was arrested in both instances as a result of information received. Susterhenn asked what did the witness do to check the information that Lawless had been involved in two armed raids. McMahon said that the reliability of the confidential information was based on the fact that, from time to time, before and since, information that came from the same source was very truthful information on other matters. In addition two of the men whom he had received information on were identified and a quantity of stolen ammunition was found in the house of one of those persons. Waldock asked what connection had the witness with the proceedings in May 1957? McMahon said that Lawless was then arrested not because it was suspected he had a document but because of suspected involvement in the two raids that he, McMahon, had positive information about. Did he see Lawless at the time? No, he saw Lawless in court but as he had not found the documents he had not asked Lawless any question about it. He heard it said in court that when Lawless was arrested he said he was in nothing then and he also heard him say that he refused to recognise the court. He was unaware of what, if any, explanation was offered for the possession of the documents. Waldock said it was strange that a prisoner could elect into which part of the prison he could go and asked what evidence there was of this. McMahon intimated that there were no prison records and his information came from the prison staff. When asked by Waldock, with regard to the undertaking, was the witness prepared to swear to the word "uphold" rather than "respect", McMahon said it was his recollection that he used the word "uphold" the Constitution. The witness was satisfied that Lawless, when arrested, was going to England until the heat died down, though he had no indication of this other than circumstantial evidence.

Questions from Lawless's Counsel

MacBride[67] asked McMahon why he had not mentioned in his affidavits that Lawless by his conduct led him to believe that in July 1957 he (Lawless) was a member of an illegal organisation. McMahon replied that he could give no reason. Was not the best evidence an admission by Lawless to him in the presence of other police officers? McMahon admitted that it would be the best evidence but there would not be any likelihood of Lawless admitting membership of any illegal organisation. But had the witness not said that the interview proceeded on the basis that Lawless was a member? Yes, and Lawless did not at any stage deny that he was a member. Lawless was not asked? It would have been ridiculous to ask this of a man whom we knew was a member, said McMahon. The witness admitted that in a report made to his superiors he did not state that Lawless had admitted, directly or indirectly, that he was a member of an illegal organisation. MacBride asked was the witness seriously suggesting that prisoners could elect into what portion of the prison they will go and to select their cellmates or who would be their neighbours? The witness claimed that political prisoners could chose their associates in prison, though he admitted he was acting on hearsay.

Questions from Attorney General

In reply to the Attorney General[68] McMahon handed in a report that dealt with Lawless's associations while in prison.[69] He was then asked could he give information on Lawless since his release from detention? McMahon believed Lawless had continued with the IRA splinter group that had fused with another subversive group known as Saor Uladh, an Ulster organisation under a man named Kelly. Lawless had contacted youths in Dublin and asked them to join. His constant associates were two named men and he had attended political party meetings. In reply to Waldock he admitted that the police had put a watch on Lawless but he took great care that they did not see very much of his activities. The witness said that when Lawless was 16 years old he had joined Fianna Eireann and continued in that for a considerable time and in 1955 he joined the IRA.

Submissions on Particular Issues

As already noted, the witnesses were subjected to questioning, in Lawless's case to intense questioning, not alone from the Attorney General, but by some members of the sub-Commission. In contrast, when counsel came to make submissions, which incidentally consumed the greater time of the hearing, the atmosphere changed completely. What was initially an investigatory event immediately took on the traditional character of a judicial hearing. The sub-Commission members fell silent with the floor left to the advocates. Nothing of substance was challenged; nothing deemed material was sought. Waldock queried MacBride only seven times on matters of little consequence. The Attorney General was occasionally interrupted, mostly by MacBride, once or twice by the President and once or twice by Waldock. The only material question came from Crosbie at the very end of the proceedings. He asked the Attorney General to explain within what period of time a detainee, on his arrival at the camp, was informed of his right to have his case reviewed by the Detention Commission. The Attorney General replied that he was informed as soon as may be and that the Detention Commission had not been set up by 11 July:

it had been set up on 16 July. This was a crucial issue if the Detention Commission was to be considered a real safeguard against abuse but Lawless's counsel did not pursue the point.

Despite the fact that the Government was pleading an emergency, the sub-Commission heard no evidence on this most material and crucial issue. Reliance was placed on the written and oral pleadings of the parties. This was a staggering omission by the sub-Commission. Having failed to instigate a fact-finding mission to Ireland, the sub-Commission then failed miserably to hear credible evidence on the state of affairs in Ireland in July 1957. The Attorney General was to make the staggering claim that these events might have led to war between Ireland and the United Kingdom and might have resulted in serious communal strife in Northern Ireland. These were very serious criticisms of the United Kingdom. Therefore it was beyond comprehension why the sub-Commission did not demand evidence from the Government, particularly about events that it claimed were likely to occur within the jurisdiction of another signatory state of the Council of Europe that was not represented before the sub-Commission. It has been noted that the British Government envisaged that both Governments might be able to argue before the sub-Commission as to the "political implications" of a decision which would result in the release of those detained in the Republic. If a fact-finding visit, or the calling of witness evidence, was not considered necessary, then surely the very least that should have happened, if the sub-Commission was to execute its functions properly, was some very severe and incisive questioning of the Attorney General. Unfortunately, that did not happen and accordingly a question mark must hang over the validity of the report of the Commission.

Issues and Submissions for the Government

The sub-Commission had requested the Government to furnish a full statement on what precise facts justified the contention that detention without trial was a measure strictly required by the exigencies of the situation. In addition, if it was impracticable to deal with members of illegal organisations in the ordinary courts owing to the intimidation of witnesses and the difficulty of obtaining evidence, what was the nature of these cases and by what kind of evidence were the convictions obtained? What response did the Government make to the fact that in 1957, of 122 persons charged under the Offences Against the State Act 1939, no less than 109 were found guilty and only 13 acquitted? Finally, the sub-Commission sought a full statement on what considerations made it necessary to have recourse to detention rather than special courts.

In presenting a response, the Attorney General reviewed, at great length, the history of the partition of Ireland, IRA activities especially during the war years[70] and the measures taken to suppress their activities which included internment without trial. Because of the strong action taken by the Government in 1957, it had since been possible to release all those detained, though the Government had not found it appropriate to determine that the emergency had so clearly passed that it would be justified in revoking the proclamation. Accordingly, the powers of detention were still in force though not being operated. The Government was anxious to revoke the proclamation. When it was thought safe to do so the proclamation would be revoked though he would not like the sub-Commission to feel that because there was no person then in detention the Government was satisfied that the powers taken in 1957 were no longer necessary. Over the years, special courts had always been composed of army personnel because, otherwise, they would not be effective. According to the Attorney General, "...special courts...in the public mind [were] regarded as being something in the nature of courts martial...and the view of a large body of public opinion, if not the majority of public opinion in Ireland, [was] that detention with safeguards [was] regarded as a less onerous method of dealing with the activities of illegal organisations than by having resort to courts other than the ordinary courts...". While special courts composed of army personnel were used during the war years, and most persons brought before them were convicted, it had also been necessary to detain without trial a total of approximately 1,000 persons.[71] Thus, special courts alone had not been sufficient to secure the safety of the State at that time against IRA activities.

The current IRA campaign was then reviewed. As regards the nature of the charges that were dealt with in 1957, there were in fact 129 cases, 69 were for failure to give an account of movements, the remainder for memberships of an illegal organisation and possession of incriminating documents. These convictions were of little value because of the shortness of the sentences. In all these cases there was no evidence other than police evidence. As regards indictable offences, the Attorney General only mentioned Lawless's acquittal on technical grounds and the acquittal of those on trial for the armed raid on an explosives factory. The Government had information that IRA splinter group members had visited the witnesses in this latter case but this could not be proved. In general it could be said that all those who served prison sentences during early 1957 behaved while they were in prison as if they were members of a military force, responding to orders and marching in military formation when on recreation.

There were difficulties in policing the border with Northern Ireland which was 270 miles long with 150 cross-border roads. The Government had endeavoured to the best of its ability to ensure that the territory over which it had *de facto* control was not used as a base from which forays were made into Northern Ireland for the purpose of committing acts of violence.[72] He said that "the Government [was] determined that...no unlawful army would be maintained within our territory for the purpose of engaging in warfare with another nation. The Government...are gravely concerned lest the activities of this unlawful organisation should embroil the citizens of our State in a civil war. The activities of this unlawful organisation are such as would lead to acts of retaliation in [Northern Ireland] against persons there regarded as being of...a nationalist outlook".[73] The Attorney General recalled that there had been very bitter experiences in the past. Many acts of violence were committed around the 12 July and there was reason to think that a single act of violence occurring close to that date would set aflame something that could not be easily extinguished. Such an event occurred on 4 July when a police officer was killed and another injured. This event had to be coupled with the acquittal of the two men on armed raid charges and the imminent release of IRA convicted persons. He then said "it became apparent to the Government that some action must be taken to prevent the spread of these unlawful activities to an even great extent and to prevent the inflammation of the unionist population of the 6 Counties into acts of violence against their nationalist brothers and the possibility, or perhaps the probability, of the outbreak of war between the British forces and ours, a war not sought by either side".[74] A little later the Attorney General added that "if we [had to] take steps to prevent warfare between North and South, and when I say North and South, I mean the British forces in the North and the forces of the Irish Government in the South, or a civil war between citizens of Ireland or citizens of Ireland in the North, the steps which [had to be taken] were to be conditioned by the unusual circumstances...in that the acts of violence for which we were in a sense responsible were being committed outside [the] territory over which we have effective control".[75] Because of the difficulty in producing evidence, the intimidation of witnesses, the statutory duty to apply the ordinary rules of evidence, special courts would have been inadequate.

It was in those circumstances that the Government introduced detention without trial. This was considered a grave step in that it interfered with the normal liberties of citizens, and the Government had at all times been anxious to minimise that inference in any way it could and to ensure that innocent persons would not be detained through some mistake. Hence the

Detention Commission. When the Government realised that there may be some who did not wish to have their cases reviewed, the Government decided that those who gave an undertaking, initially to "uphold the Constitution" but later altered to "respect the Constitution", should be released. Many were released without giving the undertaking. While from July 1957 to March 1959, 206 persons were detained, all have been gradually released on the basis of the Government's considered view that it was safe to do so. He noted that although "the membership of the IRA continued at a pretty high figure during...1957 and 1958, its active membership has declined rapidly in recent months and it is believed that the menace has been overcome."[76] The measures taken were the least onerous that could have effectively dealt with the problem.

Submissions for Lawless

MacBride submitted that the words "strictly required" in the Convention imported an element of caution and stringency when the reasons advanced by a government that invoked Article 15 were being considered. The suspension of the right of trial should only be resorted to in the gravest emergency and only where it has been established that the courts could not function. The figures for subversive crime in 1957 and 1958 indicated that the courts were functioning normally. Leaving aside statistical data, if the situation alleged by the Government did exist, one would have expected that the Commissioner of the Police, in the Annual Crime Report 1957 made to the Government and to Parliament, would have mentioned any abnormal difficulties that confronted the police. There was not a word in support of that suggestion. Surely, before a State could come and argue in favour of detention without trial they must satisfy this sub-Commission that the courts, including special courts, available to them were incapable of functioning by reason of the situation that existed. The Government had failed utterly to do this.[77]

Replies

The replies were taken up with comments by counsel on each other's submissions and on the inferences to be drawn from the facts. The sole novel incident which occurred was when MacBride, in refuting the suggestion that most of those who took part in cross-border raids came from the 26-Counties, produced figures obtained from the Northern Ireland Government, which are given earlier in this chapter. The Attorney General said that while he did not have these figures he "was quite prepared to accept them".

Efforts by Sub-Commission to Effect a Friendly Settlement

The sub-Commission, on 20 April 1959, invited the parties[78] to inform it, before 1 June 1959, "whether they desired to make use of the assistance of the sub-Commission, for the purpose of attempting to reach a friendly settlement, and in that event, to submit their suggestions in regard to that question". Lawless replied that he would be glad to avail of this assistance, that his proposals were without prejudice and that his object was simply to vindicate his personal rights. He was not directly concerned with any issues of general application. While compensation and costs would adequately vindicate his personal rights, Lawless suggested that steps should be taken to give statutory effect in Ireland to the Convention of Human Rights. The Government could take such a step in due course on its own initiative and of its own violation, without compulsion. The Government replied that Lawless, by contending that the Government was not justified in exercising powers that it considered necessary had put in issue the *bona fides* of the Government. A claim so founded could not be the subject of a friendly settlement and the Government could not envisage any settlement of the case, except the withdrawal of the claim. Lawless again wrote that he had at all stages been desirous of reaching a friendly settlement. Finally, the Government stated that its attitude remained unchanged. After a further exchange of letters, the sub-Commission stated that these replies did not appear to provide a basis for a friendly settlement, but the sub-Commission continued to be at the disposal of the parties for that purpose.

Adoption of Sub-Commission Report

The preparation of the report of the sub-Commission continued with meetings on 3 and 4 September 1959 to draft its report. It adopted its report at a meeting in Paris on 14 November 1959.[79]

Notes

1 Article 28 of the Convention.

2 Ibid. Article 29. This article has since been amended: see pp.244-245.

[3] Rules of Procedure, Rule 15, as it was then.

[4] DFA File 417/39/19/4 Part 2.

[5] Rules of Procedure, Rule 32 provided that "if for some reason, a member of the...sub-Commission, considers that he should not take part in the examination of a particular case, he shall so inform the President...". Therefore, Waldock could have withdrawn.

[6] See p.90, footnote 46.

[7] Under Article 29 and Rules of Procedure, Rules 15 and 18, as they were then.

[8] See Appendix 2 for biographical notes on members of the Commission.

[9] BPRO. FO. 371/1377/1733.

[10] DJ File S.9/58/13. (1993 Release). 24 pp. together with affidavits of the Lord Mayor of Dublin and of Gerard Lawless.

[11] YBECHR 1955-56-57, pp.222-225.

[12] See Appendix 1 for articles of the Convention.

[13] Such military courts operated from 1940-1946. See *Fundamental Rights in Irish Law and Constitution*. J.M.Kelly. (1967). Dublin, pp. 274-277.

[14] DFA File 417/39/19/4/2 Part 2.

[15] Rules of Procedure, Rule 47 (3), as it was then.

[16] AG File SR 54/38.

[17] DJ File S.9/58/1.

[18] DJ File.S.9/58/2.

[19] Cabinet Minute. Item 5. 30 December 1958. This was the last set of pleadings in the case to receive formal Government approval.

[20] DJ File S.9/58/1. The AG recorded a similar view a year earlier: see p. 71.

[21] The sub-Commission spent from 13-27 January 1958 in Cyprus. See Human Rights Law Journal. vol 18, No.9-12.

[22] DJ File S.9/58/14.12 January 1959. 23 pages and schedules.

[23] One of those elected, Rory Brady (Ruairi O Bradaigh) was interned: See p.221 for Brady's application to the European Commission.

[24] Relying on Waldock's address: see p. 88, footnote 3.

[25] For forced resignation of a judge: see p.45, footnote 18.

[26] DJ File S.9/58/15. (1993 Release). Lawless lodged a reply on 12 February 1959 and the Government filed a short reply on 12 March 1959.

[27] Cabinet Minute. Item 5.

[28] The powers of detention were revoked on 6 March 1962: see pp. 220-221.

[29] DT File S.16404. Retained under section 8 (4) of the National Archives Act 1986. Letter to author, 15 April 1997.

[30] BPRO. FO. 371/146292/1738.

[31] These exchanges were referred to by the AG when the case came before the Court. Lawless case. Series B. pp. 445-446.

[32] BPRO. DO. 35/7853/20/9/28. When de Valera's successor as Taoiseach, Sean Lemass, met Prime Minister Macmillan, in London on 13 July 1959, the recorded minute made no mention of any discussion concerning IRA activities in any part of Ireland. The only

reference to Northern Ireland was in the context of Lemass saying that he hoped to promote greater co-operation between both parts of Ireland.

[33] Eustathiades, Waldock, Berg, Faber, Susterhenn, Crosbie and Erim.

[34] 24 March1959. The Sub-Commission met six times in 1959: 23-24 March; 17-20 April; 26-27 June; 3-4 July; 3-4 September; 14 November.

[35] Rules of Procedure, Rules 53 and 54, as they were then.

[36] Article 33 of the Convention and Rules 26, as it was then.

[37] Rules of Procedure, Rule 50 (1) provided that "a sub-Commission may take any measures which it considers expedient in order to carry out the duties laid down...[and if]...in order to investigate a case, it is expedient to continue its work in a place other than [Strasbourg] such sub-Commission shall, through the Secretary General of the Council of Europe, request any High Contracting Party to grant it all necessary facilities, as mentioned in Article 28 of the Convention in order that it may carry outs its task".

[38] For the Cyprus case, see footnote 21 supra. In Denmark, Norway, Sweden and the Netherlands v Greece (the seizure of power by the colonels), the sub-Commission visited Greece, heard witnesses, and summoned medical experts to examine witnesses and inspected prisons and camps. The Commission found against Greece, a decision upheld by the Committee of Ministers. Greece renounced the Convention: YBECHR 1969. The Greek Case. In France, Norway, Denmark, Sweden and Netherlands v Turkey (the army had seized power), Commission delegates made a fact-finding visit and met Government ministers, parliamentarians, members of military courts, lawyers, academics, trade unionists and journalists. With the restoration of democracy the parties reached a friendly settlement: YBECHR. 1985. (28). pp.150-156. The single case in which derogation was unchallenged, though whether the measures taken were strictly required by the situation was an issue, was Ireland v UK. While a fact-finding visit to Northern Ireland was not made, Commission delegates heard witnesses in Norway, London and Strasbourg: ECHR 1976-78. (23).

[39] "This year (1968) the whole sub-Commission visited a prison and heard evidence in West Berlin in regard to a case (No.2686/65) where ill-treatment was alleged. In 1966 and 1967, delegated members of two sub-Commissions heard evidence in Austria, and I myself, at the suggestion of the...German Government and with the Commission's approval, visited [an] applicant..in 1966 in order to settle a procedural point..." per A.B.McNulty, Secretary of the Commission, writing in *Practical Application of the European Convention* in *International Protection of Human Rights* (1968).

[40] See p. 38.

[41] DJ File S.9/58/2.

[42] Ibid. 8 April 1959.

[43] Ibid. This letter must have enclosed the copies of Lawless's solicitor's two letters that are on this file.

[44] Unread portion noted: "The figures available show the number apprehended in Northern Ireland, but this is only a small portion of those involved in attacks on persons and property in Northern Ireland who came from and made their way back to Eire. Many of these persons were apprehended in the border counties in Eire while still in possession of firearms, a fact which can be confirmed from contemporary newspaper reports."

[45] A copy was sent to the Attorney General and is the only letter on this subject on AG File SR 34/58 which supports the view that the AG was unaware that the DJ already had this information. The AG later read to the European Court only the portion of the letter given in previous footnote (despite the fact that the opinions therein ran counter to DJ's view formed

a year earlier; see footnote 72 infra.). The AG did not explicitly state that the letter had come directly from the Northern Ireland Government. It may have been intended to create the impression that it had come from Lawless's solicitor: Lawless case.op.cit. pp.465-466.

[46] DJ File S.9/58/2.

[47] See p. 59, footnote 2.

[48] DJ File S.9/58/18. (1993 Release) Doc. DH/Misc (59) 27. 164 pp. .Marked secret. A truncated version is printed in Lawless Case. ECHR 1960-61. Series B.pp.163-178.

[49] Rules of Procedure, Rule 20 (2) provided that "if the President of the sub-Commission for some special reason considers that he should relinquish the office of President in favour of the next senior member". A practice had grown up whereby a member of a sub-Commission, who had been designated by one of the parties, precluded himself from presiding over the work of that sub-Commission: see H.Golsong, Deputy-Registrar of the Court, in *International Protection of Human Rights*. Recueil des Cours (1963) 110. pp.1-151. Since Waldock had been designated by Lawless, the Vice-President took the chair.

[50] S. MacBride, SC, T.J.Connolly, SC, S.Sorahan BL, P.C.Moore and C.McAnally solicitors for Lawless.

[51] AG., B.Walsh, SC, A.Hedermann BL and Chief State Solicitor for the Government. The DEA Legal Adviser and two officials from the DJ also attended.

[52] Which he had not: a prime example of the kind of confusion that reigned.

[53] Rules of Procedure, Rule 55 (1) provided that "after establishing the identity of the witnesses...the President of a sub-Commission...shall request them to take the following oath: 'I swear that I will speak the truth, the whole truth and nothing but the truth.' ". There was also a provision to make a declaration.

[54] [Sic]. Transcript. op.cit. pp. 5/6, an example of the quality of the translation.

[55] Transcript. op.cit. pp.2-14 and Lawless case. op.cit., para.128, pp.164-169.

[56] Ibid. p.3. Lawless, at that stage, had not said that.

[57] Whether testimony should be given on oath arose at this point.

[58] An example of the confusion to which Faber was prone: see p.153, footnote 87.

[59] Transcript. op.cit. pp.15-36 and Lawless case. op.cit. para.129, pp.165-167.

[60] See *Church & State in Modern Ireland 1923-1979.* (2nd edn 1979) J.H.Whyte. pp.163-165 for the Catholic organisation 'Maria Duce' (under Mary's leadership) and pp.72-73 for Father Denis Fahey Cssp. Lawless handed in a booklet entitled "Fiat" published by "Maria Duce" which he had obtained when he attended lectures on Catholic Social Policy. It set out objections to Article 44 and proposed a draft of a better Article 44 (see next footnote).

[61] The relevant portions of Article 44 (deleted in 1972) were: "2. The State recognised the special position of the Holy Catholic Apostolic and Roman Church as the guardian of the Faith professed by the great majority of the citizens. 3. The State also recognises the Church of Ireland, the Presbyterian Church, the Methodist Church, the Religious Society of Friends, as well as the Jewish Congregations and the religious denominations existing...at the date of the coming into operation of this Constitution."

[62] Transcript. op.cit., p.17. Faber asked whether these questions might lead to criminal proceedings against Lawless in Ireland. The President said that anything that came out could not be held against the witness. The AG said that no criminal proceedings would be taken against Lawless by reason of anything he said before the sub-Commission and that he would give such an undertaking if it were required. The AG failed to mention that Lawless could not be tried again on the same charges because of the principle of *autrefois acquit*.

[63] DJ File 9/58/2 noted that this person was acquitted of charges of attempting by threats and persuasion to dissuade two witnesses from giving evidence. A police witness stated that this man was not an active republican.

[64] Transcript. op.cit. pp.37-44 and Lawless case. op.cit., para.130, pp.167-168.

[65] Theobald Wolfe Tone was a United Irishman and one of leaders of the unsuccessful 1798 Rebellion. He died in prison after being captured leading French forces that had come to assist the Rebellion. He is considered by many to be the "Father of Irish Republicanism" and his grave in Bodenstown, County Kildare, has great symbolic importance.

[66] Transcript. op.cit. pp.44-52 and Lawless case. op.cit., para.131, pp.168-169.

[67] Transcript. op.cit. pp.52-61 and Lawless case. op.cit. para.132, p.169.

[68] Transcript. op.cit. pp.62-65 and Lawless case. op.cit. para.133, p.170.

[69] Dated 2 January 1959 and signed by the Governor of Mountjoy Prison.

[70] Transcript. op.cit. pp.97-131 and Lawless case. op.cit. pp. 418-426.

[71] This figure is grossly misleading because it included foreign combatants, including British ones, captured in Ireland and persons detained for political reasons, such as communists, etc.

[72] See p. 70 where DJ noted that "there was probably a hard core of IRA in the 6-Counties who operated without any assistance from the 26-Counties".

[73] Transcript. op.cit. p.109.

[74] Ibid. p.111. For relations between Ireland and UK, see footnote 32, supra.

[75] Ibid. p.112. This melodramatic, though highly effective claim is published here in its original form for the first time. The Government successfully prevented publication of the records of the sub-Commission hearing: see pp. 222-225. In the Commission report (see pp. 138-139), a more sanitised, and highly inaccurate reproduction, was attempted of these remarks. Paragraph 86 noted "that the Government had tried to deal with the matter...as was its duty under international law, to prevent its territory being used for the maintenance of an unlawful army designed to engage in war-fare with another nation". Undoubtedly, the hand of Waldock was at work here. Since he wrote the opinion of the majority on the public emergency issue, it is reasonable to conclude that he wrote the whole section. He obviously appreciated, not alone how exaggerated the AG's claim was, but how embarrassing it was for both the Irish and UK Governments.

[76] *De facto* detention without trial ended 15 March 1959: see pp.220-221.

[77] Transcript.op.cit. pp.84-87.

[78] AG File SR 54/38.

[79] Part IV of the Report of the Commission was omitted from the published report (Lawless Case. op.cit. para.154, p.184) but was printed in the original, which can be seen in DJ File S.9/58/19. (1993 Release).

7 European Commission of Human Rights Reports No Breach of Convention

Introduction

The European Commission of Human Rights made monumental legal history when it concluded its report in the Lawless case. This was the first occasion that an international tribunal had adjudicated upon an alleged breach of human rights instigated by an individual against a state that had voluntarily submitted to its jurisdiction. The completion of the report proved that, despite many obstacles, the Strasbourg system, in particular the Commission of Human Rights, was a workable institution. The report unanimously found that detention without trial, as sanctioned by Irish law, breached the Convention. This was a victory for Lawless. But the Commission also found, though only by the slimmest of margins, that Ireland had validly derogated from the Convention. This was a victory for the Government. In this chapter, the report of the Commission is analysed in great detail and the majority finding is severely criticised. These criticisms are a natural consequence, which flow from the conclusion, highlighted in the previous chapter, that the investigation made by the sub-Commission was flawed and completely inadequate.

Adoption of Commission Report

The Commission, where no friendly settlement has been reached, must draw up a report, and must state an opinion as to whether the facts found disclosed a breach of the Convention. The individual opinions of Commission members may be stated.[1] The sub-Commission, on 14 November 1959, adopted its report for the plenary Commission. The published records do not disclose the form which this sub-Commission report took, though it is most likely that those members who wrote opinions eventually incorporated these into the plenary Commission report. Those who did not write individual opinions expressly joined with one or other of the written opinions. The remaining members of the Commission formed opinions from the written material and from listening and participating in discussions and being influenced by the conclusions of the members of the sub-Commission. The various parts were voted on in detail and the report was adopted on 19 December 1959, some eight months after the sub-Commission hearing. Had the formal vote been delayed until clean copies were prepared, the report would not have been adopted until March 1960, a delay of a further three months, which the Commission was unwilling to allow.[2] The published material leaves this long delay unexplained. In the different but related context of an alleged delay in referring the case to the Court, organisational reasons, such as the part-time nature of the Commission, the working in two languages, and the heavy workload, were offered by the Commission as reasons for the delay. The complexities of the issues, particularly the aspects relating to public order and state security and the fairly evenly balanced views of the members, probably necessitated more prolonged discussions than in an instance where an overwhelming majority clearly favoured a particular result. A consciousness that this first report would offer some opportunity to evaluate whether the Convention was an effective charter of human rights must have contributed in some way to the delay in the adoption of the report.

The conclusion of the British Embassy in Dublin tends to support the suggestion that it was the complexity of the issues that caused delay in producing a conclusion. In a report it was stated[3] that the case had to go to the whole Commission because no agreement between the Government and Lawless had been reached. This bore out the previous view about the difficulty that the Government would face if it tried to re-open the internment camp. The Government got itself into trouble because it was not prepared to admit that there was a state of emergency. Information from an Irish official who went over to Strasbourg was that MacBride produced statements from various public figures to the effect that everything was perfectly quiet and that there was in fact no state of emergency. While it was not known whether it would be necessary for a government to justify its claim that a state of emergency did exist, MacBride's action seemed significant.

The Commission, on 21 December 1959, issued a public communiqué to the effect that, during its 20th Plenary Session, it adopted its report which would shortly be transmitted to the Committee of Ministers. This statement gave no indication of the contents of the report, a failure that was to have repercussions later.

Opinion of the Commission

The Commission was of opinion that the facts did not disclose any violation of the Convention. Although detention without trial breached the Convention, the Irish Government had been entitled to derogate because a public emergency had existed and the measures taken were strictly required by the exigencies of the situation.

The Commission report, considerable in length and detail, was unanimous on some issues and divided on other issues.[4] The information possessed by the Government outlining the attitudes of individual Commission members on the issues proved extraordinarily accurate, and confirmed that the views formed at the relatively early stage of admissibility were simply reinforced by the later arguments and hearings.

The Unanimous Commission

No Basis for Friendly Settlement The Commission confirmed the view of the sub-Commission that there was not a sufficient basis for a friendly settlement between the parties.[5]

Sufficiency of Notification of Derogation Because the jurisdiction of the Commission could be directly affected by derogation it was necessary to examine whether the notice of derogation was in conformity with Article 15 (3). Although drafted in general terms, the Commission considered that certain particulars were required, that notification should be made without any unavoidable delay, and that sufficient information must be furnished to enable the other contracting states and the Commission to appreciate the nature and extent of the derogation. Though no special form was prescribed, the official character and the terms of the letter of 20 July 1957 left no doubt as to the real intentions of the Government. It was addressed with the purpose of complying with Article 15 (3), there was no delay, and its terms were sufficient to indicate the nature of the measures taken. Nevertheless, the Commission noted that the letter was open to criticism in that it did not indicate with sufficient clearness the reasons that led to derogation. The measures taken could not be invalidated merely by the inadequacy of the reasons given for bringing them into force. In stating this opinion, it was not to be understood that in no circumstances whatever might a failure to comply with Article 15 (3) attract the sanction of nullity of the derogation.[6]

Articles 5 and 6 An arrest and detention under the Offences Against the State (Amendment) Act 1940 was not authorised by Article 5, which provided "clearly and categorically that under the Convention a state may not arrest and detain a person upon those grounds except upon the conditions that he is brought promptly before a judicial officer and that he has the right to trial within a reasonable time or to release pending trial".[7] Susterhenn felt this article was one of the "most fundamental of all the rights, apart from life itself, which authorised state interference only by virtue of a judicial decision. These fundamental precepts were the essence of law among all peoples of the free world...[and its] suspension...was the first step, by a state governed by free and democratic law, towards a totalitarian state...".[8] Waldock said that "the right to liberty...was a fundamental right and, without it, many of the other rights...could either not be enjoyed at all or only in a very restricted measure".[9] Eustathiades likewise thought that a defiance of these articles was an extremely serious measure since it infringed that personal freedom on which the exercise of other rights depended.[10]

Article 7 Article 7 did not apply because Lawless had not been detained as a result of a conviction on a criminal charge.[11]

Article 17 Article 17 did not deprive those who sought to destroy the rights in the Convention of the general protection of the rights guaranteed therein. It merely precluded such persons from deriving a right to engage in any activity aimed at the destruction of any of the rights set forth in the Convention. Accordingly, the rights to freedoms of thought, of the press, or of assembly and association may not be invoked for the purpose of destroying the free, democratic order protected by the Convention. The rights in Articles 5 and 6 were in no way diminished by Article 17. An agitator who pursued communist, fascist, national, socialist or generally totalitarian aims was entitled to their benefit because these provisions were concerned with the duties of public authorities towards all individuals. The Article was concerned solely with those who made use of positive rights for the purpose of destroying the free, democratic order. Thus, Article 17 could not deprive Lawless of the rights guaranteed by Articles 5 and 6, even if he had admitted that he acted with revolutionary intent, or with an intent incompatible with the Convention.[12]

Conduct of Lawless Because of his general conduct, Lawless drew upon himself the gravest suspicion that, whether or not he was an IRA member, he was still concerned with IRA activities at the material time. This finding was expressly made in the context of Article 17.

Comment The fact that the Commission found it necessary to make such a finding added a further dimension to the case. It appears that it was not sufficient for the Government to prove that an actual emergency existed in Ireland in July 1957, which justified derogation. It seems that it was imperative to prove that Lawless had, in some real and material way, created or assisted in the creation of the climate which necessitated the advent of the emergency. It must be presumed that the conclusion of the Commission would have been different had this finding with regard to Lawless not been made. The Commission, despite the conclusion that an actual emergency existed and the measures taken were necessary, would have been compelled to conclude that the Government had failed to honour its engagements under the Convention if there had been an absence of evidence which linked Lawless in some real and cogent way to the circumstances which caused the emergency. To hold otherwise would have led to the paradoxical result that, while the existence of an actual emergency had been established, and the measures taken were necessary, it was beyond the jurisdiction of the Commission to enquire whether the measures were correctly directed and applied against Lawless. In other words, once it was held that an emergency existed, a government could behave as it pleased and the affected individuals of the state in question were devoid of the protections offered by the Convention. As a general principle this interpretation has little to recommend it because it would open the Convention to abuse by governments, who could disregard its provisions with impunity once an actual emergency existed.

The Divided Commission

A. Existence of Public Emergency

Opinion The Commission was of opinion,[13] by nine[14] members to five[15] that a public emergency, which threatened the life of the nation, had existed in Ireland in July 1957. The facts and considerations on which this conclusion was based did not materially change during the period in which Lawless was detained.

Jurisprudential Issues

Derogation reviewable Citing the authority of *Greece v United Kingdom*,[16] Waldock emphasised[17] that when any exercise of the right to derogate was challenged, the Commission had the competence and the duty to examine and pronounce upon a government's determination of the existence of a public emergency. Eustathiades declared[18] that it was for each government to judge, when faced with an emergency, whether that situation warranted the exercise of the right to derogate. In the event of disagreement and where a case was brought, the Commission was called upon to express an opinion on the use made of this right. Ermacora said[19] that the Commission was competent to judge whether the emergency was so serious as to necessitate the taking of the measures in question.

Governments possess margin of appreciation Waldock stated[20] that a government had the responsibility to its people to protect them against any threat to the life of the nation. In those circumstances a certain discretion, a margin of appreciation, must be left to a government in determining whether the exceptional measures derogating from its obligation under the Convention were necessary. This principle was first recognised in *Greece v United Kingdom.*[21] Susterhenn expressly supported this proposition.[22]

Definition of time of war or other public emergency There was a divergence of opinion on the interpretation to be accorded to this expression. Writing for the majority,[23] Waldock was of opinion that the words "time of war" should not be restricted "only to a conflict having the character of a total war". The expression "other public emergency threatening the life of the nation" related "to a situation of exceptional and imminent danger or crisis affecting the general public, as distinct from particular groups, which constituted a threat to the organised life of the community". Eustathiades thought[24] that the expression referred to a "situation much more serious than any state of affairs threatening public order or national security, but implied an emergency of such magnitude that affected not one section of the population, but the nation as a whole...[and] that the threat to the existence of the nation must be of as exceptional a nature as war...". Susterhenn defined war[25] as "a fundamental threat to the very existence of a state.... and took on the character of total war [which] threatened the life of the nation itself, its frontiers and internal order, its economy and culture, as well as the life and liberty of its citizens...which must be so intensive and extensive as to represent a real threat to the existence of the state...[and]

that events which were not acts of force *between states* may nevertheless represent a threat, tantamount to war, to the life of a nation". Dominedo said[26] that the expression meant "an extremely grave emergency which must threaten *the very life* of the nation, i.e. its *existence*...".

Definition of nation In *Greece v United Kingdom* the parties and the Commission had agreed that "nation" meant "the people and its institution...the organised society, including the authorities responsible both under domestic and international law for the maintenance of law and order".[27] The question might then be raised which "nation" was threatened in the circumstances then pertaining in Ireland in 1957. Was it the "nation" contained within the borders of the Republic, or was it the "nation" within the whole island of Ireland, despite the political division of the territory? Or was it the "nation" solely within the borders of Northern Ireland, which was not a state in the international sense, or was it the "nation" consisting of the United Kingdom of Great Britain and Northern Ireland? Bearing in mind that a breach of the Convention was being justified, *inter alia*, on the ground that civil strife might possibly occur in a territory outside the jurisdiction of the Irish Government, it is therefore somewhat surprising that the Commission did not attempt a redefinition of "nation". Since the parties studiously avoided dealing with this issue, the Commission wisely ignored the question.

Factual Issues

The threat the IRA's existence posed Waldock and the majority accepted[28] that the IRA had existed in Ireland for a long time. After years of comparatively quiescence a new campaign of violence began in December 1956. This assumed considerable proportions and it continued without interruption throughout 1957, and until 1959. The IRA repudiated the Constitution, with members explicitly forbidden to recognise the authority of the institutions of government and members had consistently refused to recognise the authority and jurisdiction of the courts. It had to be concluded, on these undisputed facts, that in July 1957, there existed an illegal underground organisation which was dedicated to the ending of the partition of Ireland by the use of armed force. The mere existence within a state of such an illegal organisation represented in some degree a threat to the life of a democratically organised state. Susterhenn, while dissenting on other issues, did agree[29] that the existence of a secret, illegal, paramilitary organisation, provided with arms, constituted a *potential* threat to constitutional order which could, at any time, be used for revolutionary purposes. On the other hand, Dominedo noted[30] that the will to achieve the ethnic unity of one's own nation, whatever else it meant, could not mean a will to harm that nation's life; any such proposition would be a contradiction in terms.

Activities of the IRA The appreciation of this second factual issue highlighted the first major difference of opinion within the Commission. Waldock and the majority held[31] that an IRA splinter group was responsible for scattered incidents prior to December 1956, when the main IRA body started a general campaign of violence against targets in Northern Ireland, with heavy damage to property and with IRA volunteers and police killed or wounded. While IRA activity within the Republic made comparatively little impact on daily life, except in the border areas, the chief manifestation of such activity was the illegal recruiting, drilling and arming of commando-type volunteers for operations over the border and the planning and launching of those operations from that territory. The strength of IRA active commando-type elements rose from December 1956 to July 1957 despite the frequent arrest and prosecution of IRA members on such charges as could be formulated, and two successful armed raids were made to steal explosives for sabotage operations. While the ordinary courts continued without interruption as in normal times, it was contended that in IRA cases there were attempts to obstruct the administration of criminal justice by the intimidation of judges and witnesses. Though there had been some cases in which civilian witnesses had given prosecution evidence at IRA trials, these cases had been few. The specific information concerning these threats did not enable the drawing of any decisive conclusion as to the extent of IRA attempts to pervert the administration of criminal justice. While it was clear that the IRA in some measure attempted to obstruct the administration of justice in cases concerning its members, the application of the criminal law in this regard was not rendered wholly impossible. Drawing a contrary conclusion, Eustathiades noted[32] that the number of IRA victims was not large and that there was no abnormal increase in crime. The general picture showed at most a risk of localised disturbances, whereas the problem created by the partition of Ireland had existed ever since that partition came about. Drawing a similar conclusion, Susterhenn[33] said that while the Government maintained that judicial safeguards were lacking in certain political trials, which was disputed, it appeared on the whole that there was no interference with public order and security. For ten years not a single shot had been fired in the Irish Republic for political reasons. For many years there had existed an illegal, oath-bound, paramilitary organisation under severe discipline and equipped with arms, which took part in paramilitary manoeuvres and attacks with the objective to unite Ireland. While combating the IRA and abjuring the use of force to bring about the end of partition, the Government was regarded by the IRA as traitors to national unity. This was why the IRA refused to recognise the institutions of government, the practical consequences of which were that the IRA ignored the laws passed to suppress its campaign. Those members who had been convicted of offences denied that those courts had any jurisdiction over them. But no act of IRA violence had ever been attempted against the Government, army or police of the Irish Republic. Ermacora[34] noted that the main IRA activities were carried out in Northern Ireland which the Government did not sanction and which were not such as to have aggravated the situation in the Republic where life was normal.

Possibility of war between Ireland and the United Kingdom This third factual issue again illustrated the diametrically opposite views of the Commission members. As a starting point, Waldock and the majority, concluded[35] "acts of sufficient gravity, which endangered the external relations of a state, may constitute a threat to the life of the nation no less than acts endangering its internal order". The IRA made active preparations within the Republic for guerrilla attacks on Northern Ireland and committed armed robberies to obtain explosives for their operations. In defiance of the laws and the repeated injunctions of the lawful Government, the IRA launched attacks in neighbouring Northern Ireland with reckless disregard of the grave consequence that might follow. The Government could not have assumed that these attacks would not have produced "serious reactions" from the United Kingdom and the Northern Ireland Governments. "These were matters which any government would be bound to react to most strongly. The Government of the Republic could only expect to avoid serious repercussions from the other governments if it was able to satisfy them that it was using to the full the means at its disposal to suppress guerrilla warfare within its own territory." These were risks which could not be treated lightly and the Government was entitled to give substantial weight to its obligation under international law to prevent completely its territory from being used as a base for attacks upon a neighbouring territory. If it failed to discharge this duty, the continuance of the attacks would engage it in international responsibility to the United Kingdom. Reaching a different appreciation, Susterhenn, while accepting that the activities of the IRA were calculated to embitter the friendly relations between the Republic and the United Kingdom, stated[36] that it could not be maintained that a real danger of war between them had arisen. The United Kingdom Government was fully aware that the Irish

Government had done all it could to suppress IRA activities, although without success. The United Kingdom Government was in just as delicate a position, since some of its own nationals living in Northern Ireland took part in these acts of violence. And it had been unable to stop IRA infiltration into its territory or the commission of acts of violence, still less to prevent its citizens with IRA sympathies from taking part in acts of violence. Considering that both Governments were confronted by the same difficulty, it would be unreasonable to contemplate the possibility of an armed conflict between them. Concurring, Janssen-Pevtschin held[37] that the repercussions of IRA activities upon the relations of the Irish Republic with the United Kingdom were "essentially conjectural and hypothetical and were not backed by any evidence of protests or intervention from outside". Equally, Ermacora said[38] that relations between the Republic of Ireland and the United Kingdom had not become such as to cause a threat to the life of the Irish nation. It had not been proved that any official diplomatic approach was made, nor indeed did the Government advance that argument, although it would have supported its thesis. Dominedo said[39] that it was far-fetched to talk seriously of a danger of war when everyone knew that the true relations between Ireland and the United Kingdom had assuredly grown more settled over the years.

Possibility of communal strife in Northern Ireland This final factual issue again highlighted a radical divergence of opinions. Waldock and the majority[40] felt that the Government was influenced by the fear that, if IRA attacks were not promptly stopped, Protestant groups in Northern Ireland might take reprisals against the Catholic element, which was most in sympathy with the idea of union with the Republic. These fears were based on bitter past experience of such happenings and the danger of their repetition was very real. Despite the existing political division between the two territories, the Government felt a certain responsibility with respect to the peoples of Northern Ireland to prevent them from being exposed to the horrors of civil strife. The maintenance of law and order in Northern Ireland was the responsibility of the United Kingdom and Northern Ireland Governments. Despite that fact the Government was both entitled and bound to have regard to the possible consequences in Northern Ireland of the continuance of IRA attacks launched upon that territory from the territory of the Republic. It certainly could not dissociate itself altogether from the possible consequences of the continuance of these attacks. It would also accord with the spirit of European co-operation, which had inspired the establishment of the Convention, to recognise that members of the Council of Europe had a special responsibility towards each other in regard to unlawful activities in their territory which threatened human rights in the territory of another member. The serious possibility could not be overlooked that, if the fears of reprisals in Northern Ireland had been realised, bitter resentment would have been aroused in the Republic with the risk of a general deterioration in the whole dangerous situation. Dissenting, Susterhenn noted[41] that past experiences had shown that it was not easy to find a cure for this dangerous situation though it was the function of the United Kingdom Government to preserve order between religious groups in Northern Ireland.

Conclusions The Commission majority concluded,[42] that in making a determination on 5 July 1957 that there existed in the Republic of Ireland a public emergency threatening the life of the nation the Government did not go beyond the proper margin of discretion allowed under Article 15 (1) of the Convention. Dissenting, Eustathiades held[43] that the threat to public order and security could scarcely be described as a threat to the life of the nation. Any investigation of the situation must be based on existing facts only and could not take account of subjective predictions as to future developments or unilateral fears that the situation may degenerate and the threat increased, these fears being equated in advance with an exceptional emergency. Such fears had little foundation since no intensification of IRA activities was apparent. Susterhenn concluded[44] that life in all sectors, political, economic, transport, education and the press and the administration of justice, went on as usual. That being so the emergency could only be regarded as *potential.* It had persisted in virtually unchanged form for years and since it had not led to any serious disturbance of general public order or of external relations, it could not be regarded as exceptionally grave. It was only a *latent emergency* of a minor degree. Although it had been in existence for many years it had not developed into an actual emergency and since it had not interfered with normal life it could not be considered a public emergency threatening the life of the nation, analogous to war. It was more of a danger against public order. Dominedo held[45] that while it may have been possible to infer the existence of a danger to public order, it was not possible, keeping within the bounds of reality, to say Ireland's very life was at stake, both that of the *State* and the *Nation*. An ordinary person of responsibility who regarded the conditions of life objectively was bound to reach this fundamental conclusion. There was not an *explosive* situation: the threat was not immediate, serious and persistent and a comparison with historical examples of threats to the life of a nation impelled the same conclusion. There was only a question of danger to public order. The acts regarded as threats to the public order of the nation were not after all meant to *threaten* that nation but rather, ultimately, to unite and hence, *strengthen* it by the accession of elements alleged to be irredentist. In the eyes of Lawless, the acts committed were not against Ireland but for Ireland. Janssen-Pevtschin[46] agreed that the emergency had not been actual but only potential. Ermacora held[47] that the emergency had not been so serious or exceptional in that IRA action upset neither ordinary life nor the life of the state, according to the principles of public municipal law. A 'notstand' (state of emergency) existed if constitutional rules could no longer be applied and the institutions of government no longer functioned.

Comment Some remarks are called for on the majority conclusion that a public emergency, which threatened the life of the nation, actually existed in Ireland at the material time. The first, was whether the Commission was competent to consider matters and facts which had occurred in a state which was not the respondent in the case? Put another way, to whom and by whom were the engagements enumerated in the Convention owed? Ireland undertook, as did all the other signatories, to "secure to everyone within their jurisdiction the rights and freedoms defined in this Convention".[48] Ireland did not, under this Convention, undertake any obligation to secure these rights and freedoms to individuals outside its jurisdiction and within the jurisdiction of the other signatory states. If no obligation was due, what remedy could be sought? Individuals living in Northern Ireland acquired no right of redress under the Convention against the Irish Government. The most that could be done was that the United Kingdom Government might initiate a complaint against Ireland, but that could only relate to Ireland's failure to secure the rights and freedom to individuals within Ireland, and not within the United Kingdom. Equally, Lawless could not have pursued any remedy against the United Kingdom Government. Whatever obligations may have been due under customary international law was not at issue, and certainly the Commission was not the appropriate forum to settle that matter. The Convention relates to the very specific task of the protection of human rights, and the provision of some enforcement machinery, and these were not competent to determine wider issues of international law. If persons in Northern Ireland were in danger, or at risk, from IRA activity, even if it came from the Irish Republic, the obligation to provide "security of person"[49] rested, under the Convention, solely on the United Kingdom Government.

The next question was whether a breach of the Convention could be justified on the ground that the rights and freedoms enumerated therein were in jeopardy because of activity happening outside a state's jurisdiction and within the jurisdiction of another contracting state? The answer must be a definite no, because to accept such an interpretation would render the Convention ineffectual. As noted in the previous paragraph, the clear intention of the Convention was to place obligations on the signatory states for events within their jurisdictions, and conversely states bore no responsibility for events outside their own jurisdiction because they cannot prevent, control or otherwise manage those events. It must follow that a state cannot justify a breach of the Convention on the ground that the offending events took place within the jurisdiction of another state. To do so would result in some individuals within the contracting states of the Council of Europe being left without any relief under the Convention. In those circumstances such an individual cannot make a complaint against the state where the material events have occurred because that state owed him no obligation. When he makes a complaint against his own state he is met with the answer that the breach of the Convention was justified because of events taking place elsewhere. Such a construction could not have been intended by the signatories of the Convention and in the Lawless case should not have been entertained by the Commission. The proper course would have been for Ireland to initiate an inter-state application against the United Kingdom.

Even if these arguments relating to the competence of the Commission are unmeritorious then a more substantial issue remained. That was the rather slap-dash way the Commission performed its investigatory powers, a point discussed in the previous chapter. The consequence of this omission is clearly exhibited in the Commission report. Without any evidence, and merely on the strength of remarks, made in a sentence or two, the majority concluded that there was a threat to the friendly relations between the United Kingdom and Ireland. While not explicitly using the expression "war" other expressions were used, such as serious reactions, serious repercussions, which could be regarded as euphemisms for war. To have permitted this assertion to have gone unchallenged must, at least, have given the impression to Lawless's legal advisers, that the issue was not of major consequence. Subsequently to have relied on it, in such a material and substantial way, is somewhat shocking and must call into question the validity of this segment of the report, and by implication the whole report. Apart from that fundamental criticism, there was not one shred of evidence to support the probability, or even possibility, of such a war. True, the United Kingdom Government wished the Irish Government to continue to operate detention without trial in tandem with its own detention policy, but Taoiseach de Valera had, in Dail Eireann, expressly disclaimed that any threat of war had been made. While the United Kingdom Government later expressed its disappointment when *de facto* detention ended in 1959, the problems facing the Government, particularly with the Lawless case pending before the European Commission was appreciated. Incidentally, the leading exponent of this threat of war theory, Waldock, was the United Kingdom representative, whose natural inclination would have been to support the policy of his own Government, and who is known to have discussed some issues with his Government, albeit not this particular issue.[50] A rejection by the Commission that detention without trial in Ireland breached human rights, because an emergency existed, based partly on the possibility of war with the United Kingdom, would, indirectly at least, have exonerated the use, by the United Kingdom, of detention without trial in Northern Ireland for precisely the same reason. Finally, was it reasonable and practical to have expected a private individual such as Lawless to have been privy to the diplomatic and political manoeuvrings between his own Government and a neighbour, and even if he was, to have been able to call cogent and sufficient rebuttal evidence?

Another matter that requires analysis is the majority opinion that the threat of communal strife in Northern Ireland was potential and real. Objection can be mounted to this conclusion on a number of grounds. Again the fundamental criticism can be made of the extraordinary absence of evidence, this time concerning actual conditions in Northern Ireland. Granted there were illegal activities, some with deadly consequence, committed by the IRA. Undoubtedly those who used the territory of the Republic as a haven committed some of these activities. But to then make a quantum leap from those established facts to the conclusion that these activities could only lead to widespread community strife in Northern Ireland was incredible. Not one incident of community strife was hinted at, let alone proven. This again reiterates the criticism that the sub-Commission's investigations were flawed. Since this clearly was an issue which weighed with the majority, the sub-Commission should have made a vigorous investigation with a fact-finding visit to Northern Ireland, or should, at least, have called for supporting information from the Irish and United Kingdom Governments. Finally, it seemed grossly unfair to have burdened a private individual, such as Lawless, with the task of producing contradictory evidence concerning probable events which it was alleged might occur. While it might have been possible to rebut such a probability with regard to one's own state: to do so with regard to another state has an air of unreality about it.

B. The Measures Taken were Strictly Required

Opinion The Commission was of opinion,[51] by a majority of eight members[52] to six,[53] that detention without trial was a measure strictly required by the exigencies of the situation within Article 15 (1) of the Convention. Thus, the case for Lawless was defeated by the slimmest of margins. Had just one other member voted against, the Commission would have been evenly divided and deadlocked.

Jurisprudential Issues

Derogation reviewable Citing the authority of *Greece v United Kingdom,*[54] Sorensen said[55] it was beyond doubt that the Commission was entitled to evaluate the facts. It was not bound to accept the evaluation made by the government concerned. Waldock, citing the same case, concluded[56] that the Commission had both the right and duty to examine whether a measure taken was strictly required by the exigencies of the particular situation. Eustathiades said[57] that it must, in the nature of things, be left to the government concerned to appreciate the strictly exceptional character of measures derogating from its obligations. This could not mean that its view should prevail over that of the Commission, which was entitled to draw its own conclusion by comparing the actual situation with the express stipulation as to what was strictly required. Susterhenn said[58] that where the total or partial suppression of rights was notified it was the duty of the Commission, as guardian, to watch over the maintenance of the guaranteed rights and freedoms. Then it must determine by stringent enquiry whether the derogation was necessary in principle and taken only to the extent strictly required by the exigencies of the situation.

Government possesses margin of appreciation Sorensen accepted[59] that a government was in the best position to decide what measures were necessary to cope with an emergency, that a margin of appreciation must be left to the government. The task of the Commission was to answer the question whether or not this margin of appreciation had been exceeded. Waldock said[60] that the express purpose of Article 15 was to give governments the necessary authority to take special measures to meet the threat to the life of the nation. This must be interpreted as leaving to the government a reasonable discretion in judging the needs of the situation, and accordingly a government must be allowed a certain margin of appreciation.

Principle of proportionality applied There was a general consensus amongst the members of the Commission that, in the circumstances, the principle of proportionality applied. Expressing that view, Sorensen said[61] that one of the most difficult and delicate tasks was to evaluate the facts with a view to concluding whether the measures taken remained within the limits of what was "strictly required by the exigencies of the situation". Account must be taken not only of the measures as they appeared from the legal texts but also of the manner in which these measures had been applied in practice, and regard must also be had to the character of any alternative measure available. Eustathiades said[62] that in assessing the proportion between the measures adopted and the extent of the emergency, account must be taken of the very explicit instructions that clearly confirmed the measures to be adopted to "the extent strictly required". This was a specific and precise application of the principle of proportionality that must be objectively determined when the Commission exercised supervision. Susterhenn said[63] that the appreciation of the necessity of the measures taken to meet the danger depended essentially on the seriousness of the threat. Very drastic measures were necessary and expedient when the threat was very grave, but not when it was less so. The severity of the counter-measure must be proportionate to the gravity of the threat though account must also be taken of the importance of the guaranteed rights that might be prejudiced by the derogation. Waldock took the view[64] that when a public emergency actually existed, it became a question of getting into proportion the evil of interference with rights and the threat to the people as a whole.

Onus of proof Waldock felt[65] that the burden lay on the government concerned to satisfy the Commission that a measure derogating from the Convention was strictly required when it was imposed. Susterhenn said[66] that a government must be absolutely convinced, and must show proof, beyond all possibility of doubt, that the measures were in fact indispensable to avert the emergency.

Factual Issues

The adequacy or otherwise of the ordinary courts Sorensen, speaking for himself and four other members, said[67] that a difficulty arose where the normal functions of the courts were rendered impossible and the maintenance of public order and safety thus endangered. It had been contended that in some cases the normal functioning of the courts had been rendered impossible. Because the IRA and related organisations enjoyed a certain latent or manifest sympathy in wide sections of the population, the authorities were in a particularly difficult position because the general public was reluctant to give information to the police about such activities. It was a general experience that whenever the population refused to collaborate in the struggle against crime, the task of the police was rendered extremely difficult, with the result that sufficient evidence for the conviction of law-breakers could not be procured. It was significant that in the few cases relating to IRA activities, the convictions had been assured only on the testimony given by the police. In assessing the facts, the Government had remained within its margin of appreciation in finding that the operation of normal judicial proceedings had been rendered ineffective in cases like that of Lawless. Waldock noted[68] that there was a particular need to be satisfied that the normal processes of law and order were not reasonably sufficient to deal with the situation. Although there had not been any major dislocation of the normal processes, the special character of the emergency seemed to have created psychological and political obstacles[69] to their effective use. Having said that, he was not confronted with clear proof of the inadequacy of the ordinary processes of law and order to meet the needs of the emergency. Nevertheless, he formed the view that, because of the risk of IRA attempts to obstruct the course of justice and other factors, there were elements in the situation on which the Government might properly arrive at an appreciation that the application of the criminal law through the ordinary courts was not an adequate instrument for dealing with the particular threat which IRA activities constituted. Eustathiades[70] and Ermacora[71] supported that conclusion. On the other hand, Susterhenn concluded,[72] supported by Dominedo and Janssen-Pevtschin, that the Government had not shown proof that the ordinary criminal courts were invariably or even frequently inadequate in political cases. The IRA generally did not subject judges to intimidation, nor had civilian witnesses refused, generally through fear of the IRA, to testify or tell the truth. Granted that, in specific cases, the Government was justified in its criticism of acquittals or unduly mild sentences, it nevertheless did not take the necessary steps to improve the administration of justice either by proceeding against judges for dereliction of duty[73] or by increasing the minimum penalties by law. Erim said[74] that while there were diametrically opposed arguments regarding the normal operation of the ordinary courts, the difficulties encountered should not have prevented the Government from bringing every person arrested before a judge, even if the procedures had to have been simplified.

Would special courts have been a more measured response? On this aspect of the case, which proved to be the pivotal issue, there were mixed opinions on whether the establishment of special courts was more in conformity with the Convention than detention without trial. Sorensen[75] thought that, since these courts were bound by the same rules of evidence as the ordinary courts, they could hardly be considered an adequate alternative. They would not have overcome the difficulty of assuring the conviction of persons who might reasonably be believed to have engaged in illegal activities but against whom sufficient evidence could not be produced. Such special courts, even if adequate, would not be an entirely unobjectionable alternative because they did not enjoy the usual judicial independence, and the trials in such courts could not be considered as offering the usual guarantees against a miscarriage of justice. Faber agreed[76] that special courts were not adequate to deal with the situation. Waldock was more ambivalent in his conclusion[77] that it had not been established that special courts could not have been effective instruments for dealing with persons suspected of IRA activities. This conclusion, he admitted, merely meant that the possibility of special courts being effective could not, on the evidence, be altogether excluded. Eustathiades was of the view[78] that certain actions could have been removed from the jurisdiction of the ordinary courts by legislation that empowered the establishment of special courts that would have effectively met the situation. Such a course was a lesser restriction on freedom than detention without trial. The machinery of special courts, had it been promptly and firmly applied, as it could have been done without difficulty, would have effectively suppressed IRA activities. The establishment of special courts would have enabled the Government to prosecute and have punished militant IRA members. The preservation of public peace and order could thus have been assured by an effective administration of justice. Susterhenn, who had concluded that the ordinary courts were adequate, said[79] that if the ordinary courts were really inadequate it would have been possible, by setting up special courts, to make more effective provision for the prosecution of political offences and, hence, for the safety of the State. This was a measure that was specifically authorised under law.

Would military courts have been a more measured response? There was universal condemnation by the Commission of the possible use of military courts. Sorensen said[80] that an efficient alternative would, undoubtedly, have been military courts that were not bound by the ordinary rules of evidence. This was a particularly objectionable measure because a trial which excluded the usual safeguards against the conviction of innocent persons, and which might result in the most severe punishment including the death penalty, endangered the most elementary and precious human right, the right to life. This should not be accepted as a permissible measure as long as any less oppressive measure was available. The Government had rightly refrained from resorting to military tribunals. Waldock was strongly of the opinion[81] that trial by military courts, sitting in secret and applying different rules of evidence, was not a procedure which was demonstrably to be preferred to the procedure of detention without trial subject to safeguards. Eustathiades expressed the view[82] that the trial of criminal cases by military courts was not suitable, a conclusion shared by Faber.[83]

Assessment of detention without trial and its safeguards Sorensen said[84] that in assessing detention without trial, account had to be taken of the procedures and administrative practice. While the Detention Commission was not a court and did not enjoy the usual judicial independence, and although far short of a judicial remedy, recourse to it must be considered a certain safeguard against the abuse of detention powers. There was also the practice of releasing a detained person upon his giving an undertaking to respect the Constitution and the law, and not to engage in unlawful activities. Detention, as practised, had very little resemblance to those oppressive violations of personal liberty, which were known elsewhere. Waldock concluded[85] that the right to apply to the Detention Commission did provide those who had not given the authorities substantial cause to suspect them of engaging in IRA activities, a reasonable possibility of a remedy. The undertaking had no legal basis and it gave no legal right to detained persons that entitled them to release upon giving the undertaking. Nevertheless, in a parliamentary democracy a government statement of this kind constituted a definite political commitment. When some of those detained professed to find the form of the undertaking objectionable, the Government was willing to compromise on the form of the undertaking without troubling whether the objections were reasonable or unreasonable. This only served to confirm the seriousness with which the Government regarded its commitment not to detain persons who gave an undertaking as to their future conduct. Faber emphasised[86] the manner in which detention without trial was applied. Attention was drawn to the extreme moderation employed, with detention without trial not arbitrarily ordered but only in the light of very grave suspicions arising from police investigation. Furthermore, the prisoner enjoyed the right of appeal against an administrative decision[87] to a Detention Commission, recourse to which was not so very "*far* short of a judicial remedy," and detention was subject to parliamentary control. Also, the Government accepted a mere declaration of loyalty by the person detained, upon which he was immediately released. The Government had acted with such moderation that it was a long way from detention without trial (schutzhaft) practised under dictatorships. Dissenting, Eustathiades noted[88] that a detained person had no appeal against his detention and that the Detention Commission was not a court. Despite the desire to avoid any abuse, this administrative body offered no judicial guarantees, since the person had no right to be informed of the documentary and other evidence submitted by the Government. The detained person was not released unless the Detention Commission found, in the nature of things an unlikely contingency, that there were no reasonable grounds for detention, which was by no means synonymous with reasonable grounds for conviction.

Conclusions Sorensen said[89] that the Government had not gone beyond its margin of appreciation in adopting the measures of detention without trial under the special circumstances that pertained at the time. Waldock concluded[90] that, although he had great hesitation about some aspects, he was in general agreement with the majority opinion. Faber decided[91] that the Government could not be reproached for having committed the exceedingly grave act of violating fundamental rights. There was no manifest abuse, culpable negligence or irresponsibility on its part. On the contrary, it availed of the right with a moderation worthy of the democratic state it was. Dissenting, Eustathiades concluded[92] that detention without trial did not seem, in view of its rigorous character, to be in line with the "extent strictly required" by the exigencies of the situation. Susterhenn, with whom Janssen-Pevtschin agreed,[93] concluded[94] that the enforcement of the detention law, both in its general application and in the particular case of Lawless, was not strictly required. Dominedo agreed[95] with Eustathiades and Susterhenn. Erim said[96] that "having examined the Government's responsibility very carefully, taking their good faith into account [he] could not say as much for their having gone beyond the 'strict extent required' in acting contrary to...the Convention". Ermacora held[97] that the Government had not endeavoured to find less drastic means of dealing with the situation.

Comment The Commission majority correctly noted that the implementation of detention powers was subject to safeguards though they did not take cognisance of the fact that, in the circumstances, these were more theoretical and illusory than real. While Dail Eireann, the elected body, could annul the executive proclamation, the Commission failed to appreciate that Dail Eireann had been adjourned the day before the proclamation was made and stood adjourned for a further three-and-a-half months. Taking political considerations into account, the simple fact that the majority of Dail Eireann supported the Government, any effort made to annul such a proclamation was doomed to failure. Indeed, a motion calling for the release of detained persons was overwhelmingly defeated and further efforts to pass motions on detention without trial in the light of the Convention proved so sensitive that the Government successfully prevented their discussion on the ground that the matter was by then *subjudice*.[98] Yet again, the Detention Commission, in a legal context at least, looked a substantial precaution against abuse, though there were obvious deficiencies. For example, there was no automatic review of each detention: a detainee had to make application, which seemed to reverse the presumption of innocence. Leaving such inadequacies aside, the Commission paid scant attention to the Government's very decided attitude to the way that the Detention Commission was to perform its statutory functions when Lawless made his application.[99] In real legal terms, that would have rendered such a process ineffectual as a safeguard, though in fairness the Commission never explored the actual procedures settled by the Detention Commission. Turning to the last supposed safeguard, the undertaking, it was noted that it had no statutory basis. What is also immediately obvious is how shrouded in confusion the whole affair with regard to Lawless was, despite the contrary impression given by the Government to the Commission.[100] What is incontrovertible is that Lawless was only given a definitive wording in writing of such undertaking one month after his detention. The Commission seemed to conclude that the failure by Lawless to sign the undertaking, whatever its wording, prevented his release, or in some way justified his continued detention, and ignored the fact that many other detained persons were subsequently released without being obliged to give any form of undertaking.

Notes

[1] Article 31 of the Convention, and Rules of Procedure, Rules 65 and 66.

[2] Lawless case. ECHR 1960-61, Series B., p.241, per Waldock.

[3] BPRO. FO.371/146292/1738.

[4] Lawless case. op.cit. Report is 174 pages and contains detailed facts, selected extracts from the pleadings and arguments, and reasoned conclusions. An uncorrected copy can be seen on DJ File S.9/58/18. (1993 Release). There are minor differences between the uncorrected and published copies. See footnote 87, infra.

5 Lawless case. op.cit. p.184.
6 Ibid. para.80, pp.72-74.
7 Ibid. para.64, pp.63-66.
8 Ibid. para.111, pp.144-145.
9 Ibid. para.106, p.124.
10 Ibid. para.110, p.134.
11 Ibid. para.68, p.67.
12 Ibid. para.141, p.180.
13 Ibid. para.89, p.81.
14 Ibid. Waldock (who wrote the opinion), Berg, Faber, Beaufort, Petren, Sorensen, Crosbie, Skarphedinsson and Erim.
15 Ibid. Eustathiades, Dominedo, Susterhenn, Janssen-Pevtschin and Ermacora.
16 YBECHR 1958-59, pp.174-176. The Commission considered it was "competent to pronounce on the existence of a public danger which, under Article 15, would grant to the Contracting Party concerned the right to derogate". See also Human Rights Journal. vol.18, No.9-12, p.385.
17 Lawless case. op.cit., para.90, p.82.
18 Ibid. para. 92, p.93.
19 Ibid. para. 96, p.101.
20 Ibid. para. 90, p.82.
21 YBECHR 1958-59, pp. 174-176. The Commission stated that "the Government concerned retains, within certain limits, its discretion in appreciating the threat to the life of the nation". See Human Rights Law Journal. vol.18, No.9-12, p.387.
22 Lawless case. op.cit., para.93, p.98.
23 Ibid. para.90, pp.81-83.
24 Ibid. para.92, pp.90-93.
25 Ibid. para.93, pp.94-95.
26 Ibid. para.94, pp.98-99.
27 Human Rights Law Journal. vol..18, No. 9-12, p.385.
28 Lawless case. op.cit. para.90, pp.83-84. Speaking for Berg, Faber, Crosbie, and Erim. Sorensen and Skarphedinsson were of the same opinion. While Beaufort and Petren are not expressly mentioned they must be counted in the nine members.
29 Ibid. para.93, p.97.
30 Ibid. para.94, p.100.
31 Ibid. para.90, pp.84-86.
32 Ibid. para.92, p.93.
33 Ibid. para.93, p.95.
34 Ibid. para.96, p.101.
35 Ibid. para.90, p.87.
36 Ibid. para.93, p.96.
37 Ibid. para.95, p.101.
38 Ibid. para.96, pp.101-102.

[39] Ibid. para.94, p.100.
[40] Ibid. para.90, pp.88-89.
[41] Ibid. para.93, p.97.
[42] Ibid. para.90, p.90.
[43] Ibid. para.92, p.94.
[44] Ibid. para.93, p.95 and p.98.
[45] Ibid. para.94, pp.98-99.
[46] Ibid. para.95, p.101.
[47] Ibid. para.96, p.101.
[48] Article 1 of the Convention.
[49] Article 5 of the Convention: see Appendix 1.
[50] See p. 85.
[51] Lawless case. op.cit. para.105, pp.113-114.
[52] Ibid. Waldock, Berg, Faber, Beaufort, Petren, Sorensen, Crosbie,and Skarphedinsson.
[53] Ibid. Eustathiades, Dominedo, Susterhenn, Janssen-Pevtschin, Erim (who had sided with the majority on the public emergency issue) and Ermacora.
[54] YBECHR 1958-59, pp.174-176. The Commission held it was "competent to decide whether measures taken by a Party under Article 15 had been taken to the 'extent strictly required by the exigencies of the situation' ". See Human Rights Law Journal. vol.18, No.9-12, p.390.
[55] Lawless case. op.cit. para.107, p.130.
[56] Ibid. para.106, p.114.
[57] Ibid. para.110, p.135.
[58] Ibid. para.111, p.145.
[59] Ibid. para.107, p.130.
[60] Ibid. para.106, p.114.
[61] Ibid. para.107, p.130.
[62] Ibid. para.110, p.142.
[63] Ibid. para.111, pp.142-143.
[64] Ibid. para.106, p.129.
[65] Ibid. para.106, p.114.
[66] Ibid. para.111, p.145.
[67] Ibid. para.107, pp.130-133. Berg, Petren, Crosbie and Skarphedinsson were of the same opinion. The other eight members gave individual opinions. Once again, Beaufort is not mentioned but must be counted as one of the majority.
[68] Ibid. para.106, p.117.
[69] This expression originated with Crosbie (see p. 86) and indicates Crosbie's influence on Waldock. The British authorities suggested that the way to sway Waldock was through Crosbie (see p. 68). It is not known whether, and, if so, how the British influenced Crosbie.
[70] Lawless case. op.cit. para.110, p.136.
[71] Ibid. para.115, p.155.
[72] Ibid. para.111, p.148.

[73] See p. 45, footnote 18 for the forced retirement of a judge. This was never mentioned by either the Government or Lawless's advisers to the Commission or the Court.
[74] Lawless case. op.cit. para.114, p.155.
[75] Ibid. para.107, pp.131-132.
[76] Ibid. para.109, p.134.
[77] Ibid. para.106, p.121.
[78] Ibid. para.110, pp.137-140.
[79] Ibid. para.111, pp.149-150. Janssen-Pevtschin agreed: para.113, p.154.
[80] Ibid. para.107, p.132.
[81] Ibid. para.106, p.118.
[82] Ibid. para.110, p.136.
[83] Ibid. para.109, p.134.
[84] Ibid. para.107, pp.132-133.
[85] Ibid. para.106, p.123.
[86] Ibid. para.109, p.133-134.
[87] In the uncorrected text this read: "administrative decision by a police court" and is clearly a misunderstanding of the relevant law: see footnote 4 supra.
[88] Lawless case. op.cit. para.110, p.133.
[89] Ibid. para.107, p.140. Berg, Petren, Crosbie and Skarphedinsson were of the same opinion.
[90] Ibid. para.106, p.130.
[91] Ibid. para.109, p.134.
[92] Ibid. para.110, p.140.
[93] Ibid. para.113, p.154.
[94] Ibid. para.111, p.154.
[95] Ibid. para.112, p.154.
[96] Ibid. para.114, p.155. Erim had agreed that a public emergency existed.
[97] Ibid. para.115, p.156.
[98] See pp. 40-44.
[99] See pp.49-52 and pp.54-57.
[100] See pp. 48, 116 –118.

8 Lawless Case Referred to the European Court of Human Rights: preliminary procedural objections

Introduction

The Lawless case had made legal history by being the first instance in which the European Commission of Human Rights had rendered a report on the merits of a complaint lodged by an individual applicant. It was the subsequent decision to refer the case to the Court that propelled it into the unique place it holds in the annals of international human rights jurisprudence. As the first such international forum for the vindication of human rights the first case, irrespective of the issues raised and the final outcome, was guaranteed a place in the history of an international system for the protection of human rights, which was then in an embryonic stage of development. The Irish Government, having defeated the claim before the Commission, understandably did not relish the risk of a reversal before the Court. But the raising of many preliminary procedural objections not only prolonged the proceedings but was viewed as obstructionist.

Jurisdiction of the European Court of Human Rights

The European Court of Human Rights may only deal with a case after the Commission had acknowledged that efforts to achieve a friendly settlement have failed[1] and within a period of three months from the date of the transmission of the report to the Committee of Ministers.[2] The following may bring a case before the Court, provided the state concerned was subject to the compulsory jurisdiction of the Court or, failing that, with the consent of the state concerned: (a) the Commission; (b) a state whose national was alleged to be a victim; (c) a state which referred the case to the Commission; and (d) a state against which the complaint had been lodged.[3]

In that event the decision whether a measure was in conflict with the Convention rested with the Court[4] whose jurisdiction extended to all cases concerning the interpretation and application of the Convention.[5] Failing a referral to the Court, the Committee of Ministers decides, by a majority of two-thirds, whether there has been a violation of the Convention.[6] The Convention did not, at that time, confer any right on an individual applicant to refer the case to the Court. As already noted, the Court was formally established on 20 April 1959,[7] and it had to wait a year for the Lawless case to be referred to it, and a further six months for its first public hearing.

Deliberations of the Commission on its Report

The Commission session at which the report in the Lawless case was adopted terminated on the eve of the Christmas vacation, towards the end of which the point was raised as to what action the Commission should take concerning referral of the case to the Court. Having regard to the time-limit, it was clear that the Commission had to arrange its meetings so as to give itself a proper opportunity to take a decision on this question before the three month period expired. Accordingly, on Waldock's proposal, it was agreed to put the matter on the agenda for the next meeting. Early in January 1960, the Commission returned to Strasbourg for the purpose of drawing up its report on another important case, that of *De Becker v Belgium.*[8] It also had to decide on the admissibility of a considerable number of individual petitions. When this session ended on 9 January, the *Lawless* and *De Becker* reports had to be completed, apart from other business. The Commission then had two cases on which, sooner or later, decisions would need to be taken about referring them to the Court. It was not possible to get these two reports ready for transmission to the Committee of Ministers before the end of January. Accordingly, the Commission took the view that, unless there were special reasons for urgency, which there were not, it would be better to postpone a decision on this question and to wait until the governments had time to study and react to the report. Accordingly, the Commission decided to hold a plenary session in March and to take up the question of referring these two cases to the Court during that session.[9]

Government Requests Issue of Communiqué Stating Result

As noted in the previous chapter, the Commission, on 21 December 1959, issued a public communiqué[10] to the effect that it had adopted its report in the Lawless case which would shortly be transmitted to the Committee of Ministers. This statement gave no indication of the outcome of the case. The print media in Ireland carried considerable speculation, some incorrect, as to the outcome of the case that made the Government understandably unhappy. As a response,[11] the Government prepared a proposal for the Committee of Ministers. This stated that since the Government was specifically estopped from publishing the Commission report,[12] there seemed no reason why the Committee of Ministers should not be at liberty to announce the conclusion of the Commission without publishing the report. The Commission had announced its decision on admissibility in this case, though it did not publish the actual text of the decision. The Government believed there were good reasons why this should be done. Lawless's case had aroused considerable publicity in Ireland and prolonged silence on the conclusion reached could have harmful effects on public opinion. The fact that the report had been transmitted to the Committee of Ministers already received wide publicity in Ireland. The Government found it difficult to continue to maintain a negative attitude to many inquiries from the press and public. It suggested that the Committee of Ministers might issue a short communiqué immediately stating that it had received the report and that the Commission was of opinion that there was no violation of the Convention by the Government of Ireland. Unless the matter was referred to Court in the meantime, the Committee of Ministers would consider the report at the expiration of three months.

The British Embassy in Dublin reported[13] to London that it had been informed by the Irish Government that the Commission had, by a majority, decided that there had been no breach of the Convention. The Commission had submitted its report to the Committee of Ministers, which might consider it at their next meeting on 16 February. The Convention required that there must not be any publication of the report and Lawless had not been sent a copy. The press had reported on the matter and the Government could not say anything, with the result that there was an inference from its silence that the Commission had come down against the Government, which was embarrassing. The Irish Government was most anxious to secure publication of the decision of the Commission and requested UK support for its proposal, outlined in the previous paragraph. "It was earnestly hoped that we can support the Irish Government in securing publication of Commission's decision. This will prove a considerable shock to illegal bodies." The Colonial Office had misgivings about the request. Once a precedent had been established, then, despite the silence of the Convention, the Committee of Ministers may publish a summary of the report of the Commission, if the parties consented. It would be difficult for parties to resist pressure to give consent in all cases. The Home Office noted that in view of the political importance of helping the Irish as far as possible in dealing with the IRA, it was felt that Britain should not vote against any communiqué if the Irish succeeded in persuading other members of the Committee of Ministers to support it, which was very unlikely. The Foreign Office, in a response to the Embassy, stated that publication of a communiqué presented difficulties. While the reasons for which the Irish Government were anxious to secure early publication were fully appreciated, and while Britain sympathised with the embarrassment caused to the Government in dealing with IRA detainees, Britain could not, at this stage, support a communiqué. The Embassy later telegrammed London that when the matter was discussed in Dublin, the Department of External Affairs, whilst disappointed at the reply, was not entirely surprised, and concluded that if Britain was not prepared to accept the Irish proposal it was unlikely that other governments would do so. Despite this setback, the Government pressed ahead and the Committee of Ministers, at its February session, as predicted, refused to accede to this request.[14]

Transmission of Commission Report to Committee of Ministers

The Government was informed that, on 1 February 1960, the Commission had transmitted its report to the Committee of Ministers. A copy of the report was enclosed, which was not to be published.[15] It was noted that it was not for the Commission to send the report to Lawless.[16] The Secretary General of the Council of Europe, on the instructions of the Chairman of the Committee of Ministers, communicated to the Government a copy of the report of the Commission.[17]

The Department of External Affairs files covering this period are missing,[18] and bearing in mind that the most likely response would come from within that department, there is unfortunately very scant recorded reaction to the report of the Commission. In a hand-written note on a small torn piece of paper,[19] the Assistant Secretary in the Department of Justice noted that the report took a solid four-and-a-half hours to read. It was "most interesting and showed that in relation to 'exigencies' the Government had a very narrow victory which might easily have been reversed. Waldock's observations are acute and it is surprising that he found for us." Once again recourse must be made to British records for an indication of the Irish Government's reaction. In a report[20] in early December 1959 before the Commission's decision was publicly known, which may in itself be very significant, the Embassy in Dublin reported that even if Taoiseach Lemass "could be convinced in confidence of danger of reprisals he could clearly not make public use of this information to justify sterner measures. In any event it is not clear what more Government here could do now. You will remember that Sir Richard Pim [British Ambassador] sent message of appreciation to the commissioner of the police. Only other alternatives are increasing sentences or reopening the internment camp. On first, it would be imprudent for Government to say anything to judiciary concerned, mainly District Justices, if only because apart from other considerations, it would leak out, with effect reverse of what was intended. On the second, even if the Government was prepared to invoke state of emergency required by Human Rights Convention, it risked a rebuff in the Human Rights Commission. MacBride and others would use all possible legal means to frustrate them and to have to face, as they did in the past, severe criticism of the practice of imprisonment without trial from highly respectable persons and organisations. They would only take such steps because of very greatly increased IRA activity. Representations from us would make such action more and not less difficult for them politically." After the contents of the Commission report became known, the Embassy in Dublin, reporting[21] on contact with the Department of External Affairs, noted that "the officials concerned were understandably not prepared to be drawn on whether the results of the Lawless appeal would mean that, if, in future, the Government wished to re-open the internment camp, it would not face any further difficulties with the Human Rights Commission.[22] They seemed to think that all the legal argument and circumstances were so tricky that the Lawless case could not necessarily be regarded a precedent".

Once the Commission report was transmitted to the Committee of Ministers, the Commission and the Government had three months thereafter to refer the case to the Court. Unfortunately, as already noted, the archival material for this period is missing and it is impossible to discover whether the Government considered referring the case to the Court. Having had a decision in its favour the inclination would have been to leave well enough alone and settle for what it had achieved. Though it would have been very understandable had the Government, on its own initiative, sought a decision which would hopefully exonerate it from allegations of breaching the Convention from the highest judicial authority established under the Convention.

Government Informed of Referral of the Case to the European Court

The Commission informed Ireland's Permanent Representative in Strasbourg, on 1 April 1960,[23] that it had, at its session held between the 28 March and 2 April 1960, decided to refer the Lawless case to the European Court of Human Rights whose jurisdiction the Republic of Ireland had accepted. The Commission's decision was to be announced on 4 April, and enclosed for information was the text of the communiqué that was to be released to the press on that date. There is no evidence from the available published and archival material that Lawless's legal advisers made any representations to the Commission to refer the case to the Court.[24] Having regard to the continued interest which MacBride took in the case, after Lawless was formally excluded, it would not be a surprise to discover that some such representation was in fact made as a kind of collateral against the possibility of an adverse finding by the Commission against Lawless. The sequence of events adopted by the Commission, that of referring the case to the Court before sending a copy of its report to Lawless, had the effect, intended or otherwise, of forestalling representations from Lawless's legal advisers.[25]

There is no indication in the published material or in the incomplete archival material, for instance information from Crosbie as the most likely source, whether the decision to refer the case to the Court was the unanimous decision of the Commission or merely that of a majority. What is clear is that members of the Commission who had decided there was no breach of the Convention must have voted for referral to the Court. And it is likely, having regard to his role and attitude as principal delegate of the Commission before the Court, that Waldock was one of those who favoured referral. The Department of External Affairs noted[26] that the Court would be meeting on 11 April but it was doubtful whether it would be seized of the case. The procedure to be followed was that the Commission would make a "request" setting out the facts and giving the legal points on which they think the Court should give an opinion and the Government can offer observations on this submission. This request would be lodged with the Court and a copy sent to the Government. Three members of the Commission would be in attendance during the proceedings. There would not be two "parties" before the Court, the Government would in effect be the only party. The Commission would not be regarded as, so to speak, the "plaintiff". Counsel speaking in Lawless's name would not put the case but the Court would, apparently, be free to call him to appear. Much of this was tentative, pending a fuller examination of the Court rules, because, since this was the first case, there was no body of practice on which to draw.

The brief communiqué issued by the Commission mentioned that the Commission, by a majority, expressed the opinion that Lawless's detention had not violated the Convention, having regard to the public emergency and the right of the Government to take derogating measures. Since Ireland had accepted the jurisdiction of the Court, and because of the fundamental importance of the legal issues involved, the Commission considered that it should refer the case to the Court. The Government later took issue with the propriety of issuing this communiqué. This seems most peculiar and contradictory having regard to its earlier request to the Committee of Ministers that the Commission should have pronounced, in its very first communiqué issued on 21 December 1959, that the Government had not breached the Convention. The Commission defended its action on the ground that serious embarrassment might be caused to the Government if no mention had been made of the favourable finding. The prevention of any misunderstanding and the protection of the Government, in the interval before the public proceedings opened in the Court, was the sole object in issuing the communiqué. The Commission was convinced that the publication of the main finding was essential for the satisfactory working of the Convention, was appropriate and within its competence.[27] The Court neither passed comment nor made any decision on the action of the Commission in this regard.

Commission Submits Request to the Court of Human Rights

The President of the Commission informed the Court,[28] on 12 April 1960, that the Commission, on 1 April 1960, decided to bring before the Court the case of Lawless and that accordingly the request was submitted to the Court. The report had been transmitted to the Committee of Ministers on 1 February 1959.[29] The Commission appointed Waldock as principal delegate,[30] Eustathiades and Petren as assistant delegates, to take part in the consideration of the case before the Court.[31] The Government was informed,[32] on 14 April 1960, that the Commission had filed a request referring the Lawless case to the Court. Copies of the request and report were attached and it was also stated that the Committee of Ministers had been so informed.[33] The Government was invited to reply within 30 days whether it wished to appear as a party.[34] By telegram,[35] on 13 May 1960, the Court was informed that the Government wished to appear as a party and that a letter was to follow.[36] The Government's initial response[37] was a complaint that it had been "severely handicapped in considering the matter by being unaware of the precise reasons for the Commission to bring the case before the Court". While the Government was required to state whether it wished to appear as a party, it had not been told what were the "legal issues of fundamental importance in the application of the Convention". It was essential that, at the meeting, which it was assumed would be convoked, the Attorney General should be present so that the matters at issue should be clarified and the procedure determined. The Government was informed[38] that after the Chamber of the Court had been constituted, its letter would be submitted to the President of the Chamber and that the Government and the delegates of the Commission would be consulted when fixing the most convenient date for a meeting.

Reasons for Referral of the Case to the Court

The Commission stated that it referred the case to the Court because legal issues were raised which were of fundamental importance in the application of the Convention. The Court was the appropriate tribunal rather than the Committee of Ministers to deal with such issues.[39] The sole task of the Commission remained that of ensuring the observance of the engagements of the contracting states undertaken in the Convention, which was also the task of the Court. For the Commission this meant the establishment, by an authoritative Court pronouncement, of whether or not a violation of the Convention was disclosed. The Commission referred the case with the general object of obtaining a ruling on several questions dealt with in its report, to allow the Court to adjudge whether the facts disclosed any breach of the Convention and because an opinion by the Commission was not conclusive. The Commission's opinion was unanimous on all the issues, except two questions under Article 15 on which there was a substantial minority vote on each. The proper interpretation of the limits of the authority given to governments to suspend, in time of war and other public emergency, the enjoyment of rights was a matter of fundamental importance, an interpretation that was not merely of theoretical importance. The Commission had previously applied Article 15 in *Greece v United Kingdom*,[40] and since the Convention came into force, notices of derogation in respect of twelve different territories had been made.[41] The Commission emphasised that its decision to refer did not qualify its opinion. On the contrary, the Court was being asked to confirm the report and to find that no breach of the Convention had been established.[42] While these stated reasons are laudable, and clearly weighted heavily with the Commission, the more fundamental and implicit reason for referring the case to the Court was, so to speak, to put the last piece of the Strasbourg jigsaw into place. The Government later took serious issue with the Commission in this regard. The Government appreciated the desire to seek confirmation, at the highest level, for principles that may be a guide to future actions. It wished that the Convention should enjoy full effectiveness. Nevertheless, such a lofty aim did not permit any departure from the rules and principles clearly laid down by the Convention. It was not the function of the Court to lay down, without necessary application to the Lawless case, general principles of interpretation. While general principles of international law may eventually evolve from decisions of international tribunals, they did so as a result of the application of existing or new law to the facts under dispute in the particular case and not in abstract.[43]

Committee of Ministers *functus officio*

The Secretary General of the Council of Europe, on 25 April 1960, informed the Government[44] that the Court had notified him, on 13 April, that the Commission had lodged with it a request referring the Lawless case to the Court. Consequently, the Committee of Ministers would not be required to perform any function in this regard.

Composition of the Court Chamber

The Government was informed,[45] on 13 May 1960, that the President of the Court would proceed to constitute a seven-judge Chamber of the Court for the consideration of the case.[46] Richard McGonigal, having the nationality of the Irish Republic, would sit as an *ex officio* member of this chamber.[47] Lord McNair proceeded, on 17 May 1960 in London, to choose by lot the six remaining judges. In a case that raised a serious question affecting the interpretation of the Convention, the Chamber of the Court may, at any time, relinquish jurisdiction in favour of the plenary Court.[48] Despite the fact that serious questions arose in the case, such as the right of states to derogate in time of emergency, a point on which the Commission members were fairly evenly divided, it is somewhat surprising that the Chamber of the Court so appointed did not relinquish jurisdiction in favour of the plenary Court.

Settling Procedural Issues

The President of the Chamber, Rene Cassin, on 1 June 1960, met with the Attorney General and the Commission delegates to ascertain views on the procedure to be followed.[49] Cassin emphasised the fact that there was only one party, the Government, in the strict sense, appearing before the Court and that the Commission appeared in an advisory capacity. The Attorney General said there was some speculation that the Commission, when appearing before the Court, would assume the role of public prosecutor. Waldock intervened to say that there was no question whatever of that. The Commission regarded its function as being that of protecting the public interest.[50] The Attorney General mentioned misleading references to the case in the press[51] and suggested there should be no publicity about the proceedings before the Court. The Registrar of the Court said that he had, subject to the obligations of secrecy attaching to his official duties, to reply to all inquiries concerning the work of the Court, including inquiries from the press.[52] Cassin stated that the obligation of secrecy in relation to pleadings, etc., must obviously be observed but that it was for the Registrar, within his discretion, to give any necessary publicity to the purely functional side of the Court's work.[53] The Commission was to file its memorial by 30 June and the Government was to file its counter-memorial, containing any preliminary objections, by 20 August 1960.[54]

Preparation of Government Counter-Memorial

The task facing the Government, in preparing for the case, was momentous. It was the first time that Ireland, as a State, was to appear before an international tribunal. It was monumental in that the task ahead, without precedent as it was, was bound to impact in a major way on the unfolding jurisprudence, not alone of the European Convention of Human Rights, but on international human rights in general. Mindful of the task ahead, the Government decided to enlist the assistance of Prof. Paul Reuter of the Law Faculty, Paris. This was done, through the Irish Embassy in Paris,[55] sometime after the meeting with the President of the Chamber in June 1960. From the limited archival material available, it appears that Reuter was concerned mainly with the procedural issues raised in the Government's counter-memorial of 12 August 1960. He was engaged to assist in the furtherance of these views, as part of the Government's team at the Court hearing in October 1960. Unfortunately, no written material exists of the exact input made by Reuter at this juncture. From the scant archival material available, it seems that the drafting of the Government's counter-memorial was undertaken by the Department of External Affairs and the Attorney General, with, of course, some input by Reuter.

Overview of the Proceedings

Since this was the first case before the Court it was understandable that, in the absence of an established jurisprudence, particularly with regard to procedural matters, issues of such a nature would be raised. But the sheer volume of such objections, raised exclusively by the Government, resulted in ponderous proceedings, "heavy with objections".[56] The Government did not appear to appreciate that international tribunals tended to be more impervious to procedural rectitude than domestic courts. Thus, there were two sets of pleadings, two hearings, three judgments[57] and the case, referred in April 1960, was not concluded until July 1961. The first Court hearing, preceded by written submissions, dealt exclusively with matters of procedure, such as the role of the Commission vis-à-vis the Court, the propriety of the communication by the Commission of its report to Lawless, and the preliminary objection made by the Government to the exercise of the Court's jurisdiction. A judgment on these issues was rendered on 14 November 1960 and is covered in this chapter. An issue that straddled both hearings, and consumed considerable time and intellectual effort, was the status to be afforded to Lawless, and to his views on the Commission's report, before the Court. Because of the importance of this issue it is dealt with separately in the next chapter. The second Court hearing, again preceded by written submissions, dealt mainly with the merits of the case, detailed in Chapter 10, although a further point of procedure awaited argument and decision.

First Historic Hearing of the European Court of Human Rights

The first historic hearing of the Court, at which preliminary objections were argued, took place in public on 3 and 4 October 1960,[58] in the Conference Room of the Council of Europe building in Strasbourg. The judges wore formal black gowns, with blue shoulder blades lined with ermine. On the shoulder blade was an insignia bearing twelve stars representing the twelve Council of Europe states that had ratified the Convention of Human Rights. Most of those who attended, apart from the media, were legal professionals and university professors interested in the workings of Europe's first Court of Human Rights case. The Chamber of the Court[59] was composed of Judges Cassin, as President, Maridakis, Rodenburg, McGonigal, Balladore Pallieri, Arnalds, and Arik, as substitute for Holmback.[60] Waldock, as principal delegate,[61] represented the Commission, and the Attorney General, Aindrias O Caoimh, represented the Government. Cassin noted how this was a memorable moment in the history of the movement for the international protection of human beings and human values. Waldock said that the establishment of the Court had completed the system of guarantees envisaged by the Convention. He congratulated the Court on beginning the exercise of its high jurisdiction, expressing the conviction that its judgments would win the confidence and sustain the hopes of the governments and peoples of the Council of Europe.[62] The Attorney General recorded that he had the great honour to be the first advocate to address the Court. While the Convention was a very notable attainment, the introduction for the first time of the individual's right to have limited access to an international tribunal was its most noteworthy achievement. The Court would play a great part in securing for the peoples of Europe, and by its example for the peoples of the free world, the proper observance of the fundamental rights that the Convention assured to the peoples of the Council of Europe states.[63]

At the hearing, Waldock presented the case for the Commission with meticulous and minute care. He scrupulously submitted, on each of the contentious issue, the views of the Commission, together with the views of the Government, despite the Government having separate representation. This was a method which, incidentally, tortuously prolonged the hearings but is readily explained by the view which the Commission took of its role before the Court. The Court delivered its judgment a little over a month later,[64] in public, in French and in English, the French text being authentic, on the preliminary objections and questions of procedure, on the afternoon of 14 November 1960. The Attorney General[65] and the delegates of the Commission were present.[66] It is interesting to note that the Irish member of the Court sided with the majority and decided all the procedural issues against the Government. The Government was informed in advance and notified that the President of the Chamber would discuss, immediately after the Court's public session, with the parties the procedure to be followed for the consideration of the merits of the case. At that meeting it was agreed that the public hearing would begin on 7 April 1961.[67]

Role of the Commission vis-à-vis the Court

The Commission contended[68] that it acted on behalf of the governments and peoples of the Council of Europe. Its duty was to submit, with complete objectivity and impartiality, all relevant matters of fact and of law, that it did not wish to be argumentative, and did not regard this task as litigious. The Commission would be stultified if it did not present its own conclusions as the correct conclusions to be drawn, which it asked the Court to confirm, though it would have compromised its objectivity if it had not drawn attention to dissenting opinions. The proposition that the opinion of the Commission majority be treated as *res judicata* before the Court, and that opinion alone submitted, was incorrect. The Commission report was not a judgment. It was a report of an enquiry conducted by a committee of experts which was intended to provide the material for a binding decision either by the Committee of Ministers or by the Court, and the Convention expressly provided that the opinion of all the members may be stated.

The Government argued[69] that while the functions of the Commission in some respects were clearly defined, the Convention was silent as to the precise status of the Commission before the Court. It was never intended that the Commission should refer a case, such as the Lawless case, where its opinion was favourable to a state. The Commission could not criticise the validity of its opinion, but must support it, because any other contention would bring both the Convention and the Commission into ridicule. It was impossible to imagine that "taking part in the consideration"[70] envisaged the Commission adopting an attitude of indifference, or worse, that it would impugn the cogency of its conclusions. The Commission was obliged to endorse the work it had already accomplished, a considerable juridical achievement, as much in clarifying points of facts as in resolving points of law, and to endeavour to convince the Court in that sense. It was no mere committee of experts. It was one of the two bodies set up to ensure the observance of the engagements undertaken by the signatory states. It was an important judicial organ to which was entrusted the primary duty of establishing the facts and of forming an opinion as to whether or not the facts disclosed breaches of the Convention, even though its opinion need not bind the Committee of Ministers or the Court. This judicial organ must not only be impartial but it must be obvious to all that it was impartial and it must not be open to the criticism, whether well founded or not, that it had leant more to one party than to another. Decisions of the Commission were taken by majority[71] and there could be no question of differing or contradictory decisions as to the facts which must be established by a majority decision, and when so established became the decision of the Commission. The Court would, in most cases, be content to accept the facts as found, although the Court would not wish to lay down a firm principle that in no case would it conduct its own examination of the facts. The decision to refer a case to the Court was an important judicial decision involving serious consequences for the state concerned and also for the Commission. The judicial role of the Commission required that its attitude of impartiality must be maintained throughout the whole course of its activities. When it came to assist the Court, it must present the facts so found, and the opinion so formed, as being the objectively found facts and objectively formed opinion, unaffected by any influence, either from the individual or from the state, after its judicial decision was arrived at.

Court Decision

The Court acknowledged, *passim* and without expansion, that the role of the Commission before the Court was cast as "the defender of the public interest".[72]

The Propriety of the Commission Communicating Report to Lawless

The Commission, on 5 April 1960, four days *after* the decision to refer the case to the Court, when adopting additional rules of procedure to cover relations with the Court, included a rule[73] that permitted the Commission to communicate its report to the applicant. Accordingly, the Commission, on 13 April 1960, sent its report to Lawless, advised him that the document was secret and must not be communicated to persons unconnected with the case, and invited him to submit his written observations before 4 June, which he did on 23 May 1960. The Government was notified of these events.[74]

The Attorney General for the Government argued[75] that the only provision of the Convention on the publication of the Commission's report provided that it "shall be transmitted to the Committee of Ministers. It shall also be transmitted to the state concerned, who shall not be at liberty to publish it."[76] This express provision was not by implication an indication that there was no restriction on the Commission, but an indication that, except for the purposes clearly required, that was to be the only publication: no power in express terms was given to communicate it to any other person or body. A power to do something could not be implied merely because the doing of that thing was not prohibited. Secrecy was an important feature of the Commission's proceedings and a continuation of that secrecy must be implied, except in the special cases indicated in the Convention. The Commission, when transmitting its report to the Committee of Ministers, indicated in the clearest terms that this was its view and to later transmit its report to an individual not bound to secrecy was a strange action to take. The Commission's power to draw up rules of procedure[77] must be confined to when it was acting as a judicial tribunal carrying out its functions of investigating a petition assigned to it, and not of drawing up rules for its relations with the public. It was abundantly clear that the Commission's work was completed the moment the Court's jurisdiction was invoked, and, save in so far as its delegates may be called to assist the Court in the further examination of the case, the Commission was *functus officio*. If further information was required, it was for the Court to indicate how it should be obtained, and not for the Commission. The Commission had suggested that once a decision was taken to refer the case to the Court, the Commission may publish the report, since the Court hearing would be public. While the hearing would probably be public, the Court reserved an express power to hear a case in private and the Commission had anticipated a decision that in no case would the hearing be in private. Furthermore, if reference of the case to the Court relieved the Commission of its secrecy obligation, did it also relieve the state of this obligation? Once a case was referred to the Court, all the documents were, in accordance with established practice, under its control and could not be published without its consent. The Commission had, after the court was seized of the case, abrogated one of the Court's functions, namely the control over the publication of documents. There was no sanction that could be attached to the individual if he disclosed this report. The Government had entered into a formal Convention under which it was obliged to maintain the secrecy of the report. Would the Commission refuse to forward an applicant's comments on the report to the Court, not because the case was a bad one, not because the comments were unwarranted, not because the comments might not be of assistance to the Court, but as a form of punishment? The Court should know, before giving a decision, what steps the Commission would propose to take in such a case. The absence of a prohibition on publication by the individual was attributable solely to the fact that it was never contemplated that the Commission would take such an action. The Government formally asked[78] that a correct interpretation of the Convention did not permit an action contemplated by the new rule.

In defending its actions[79] the Commission argued that it represented all the contracting states and served only the purposes of the Convention. It was natural that in entrusting special responsibilities and functions to it, the signatory states intended it to possess all the powers necessary for the effective discharge of those responsibilities and functions. That must include the power, as it thought fit, to communicate its report to any person. The Convention was not as explicit on this point as it might have been and there were two notable omissions. The Convention was silent concerning (a) the communication of the report to an applicant, and, (b) the publication of the report. When the Convention spoke of publication it undoubtedly meant giving the report to the public because that might frustrate a last-minute effort at conciliation. This desire not to impede efforts at conciliation only had relevance during the proceedings before the Commission, whose express function was to conciliate, and before the Committee of Ministers, a political organ inherently invested with a conciliation function. No doubt a case may be settled in proceedings before a judicial tribunal, but confidential conciliation to secure a settlement was not a normal function of a judicial tribunal, except in special spheres like matrimonial cases. In contrast, there was nothing whatever relating to the Court about either publication of the report or secrecy of the proceedings. The Commission had felt some uncertainty as to its proper course of action when the report was before the Committee of Ministers. The express prohibition placed on any publication by the state did appear to indicate an intention to keep the report secret whilst it was being dealt with by that body. If it had been intended to place the Commission under the same absolute prohibition, it would have been very easy and natural for the Convention to say so. Moreover, it was quite possible that occasions might make some statement as to the findings necessary, for example if false rumours or distorted accounts appeared in the press. The Commission considered that normally it should not make any announcement in regard to its findings while the case remained with the Committee of Ministers. Obvious consideration of equity militated in favour of a party being informed of the Commission's conclusions concerning his own case. Having regard to the conciliation functions of the Committee of Ministers who were seized of the case, at least provisionally, the Committee were informed that the Commission did not make any communication to Lawless except it informed him that it would be for the Committee of Ministers to decide whether he should receive knowledge of the report. This was a procedure of ordinary caution. When the case was brought before the Court, the proceedings entered an entirely new phase with its removal from the jurisdiction of a political body to a judicial organ and the position of secrecy was very different. If the contracting states intended the report to be kept secret in these proceedings, unless otherwise ordered by the Court, it was astonishing that neither the Convention nor the *travaux preparatoires* contained a single word upon the point. Yet the Commission's report was obviously the centre-piece, the main subject matter, of the proceeding before the Court and it was impossible to suppose that the contracting states were unaware that the general rule in judicial proceedings was that the hearings were public. After all, that very rule had been written into the Convention,[80] which guaranteed the right to a fair and public hearing, and only allowed the public to be excluded in exceptional cases. While the Convention expressly provided that the Commission met *in camera*, no such rule was made for the Court. The Commission found it impossible to accept that the signatory states intended the report to remain secret, and not subject to any publication in connection with the Court's proceedings, unless specially authorised. This thesis was not accepted by the court when it laid down the rule[81] that hearings shall be public except in exceptional circumstances and the rule[82] that the report was to be considered in the proceedings. The Commission concluded that, subject to the possibility of an exception, it was free if it thought fit to publish or communicate to any person its report in connection with the proceedings before the Court. At the same time it recognised that this discretion ought only to be exercised responsibly in the due discharge of its functions. For the Commission to properly discharge its functions before the Court, it was desirable to know Lawless's comments. Rule 76 was carefully drafted so as to be limited to obtaining the applicant's comments and it absolutely made clear that the Commission reserved a complete discretion as to the use, if any, which it would make of any such comments. The Commission, in a formal submission,[83] requested the Court to decide that the new rule, and the Commission's communication of its report to Lawless, fell within the competence conferred upon the Commission by the Convention.

Court Decision

The Court, by six votes to one, was of opinion[84] that, since it could not interpret the Convention in an abstract manner, but only in relation to specific cases, it was not competent to delete a rule from the Commission's Rules of Procedure. That would amount to rulings on matters of procedure or rendering advisory opinions. Accordingly, the Court had no power to consider a point raised in a general manner. It had the duty to ensure that the Convention was respected and, if need be, to point to any irregularities and to refuse to apply any provisions or regulations that were contrary to the Convention. The Court was of opinion,[85] as regards the communication of the Commission's report to Lawless, that the procedure in a case before it differed from that applicable before either the Commission or the Committee of Ministers. The proceedings assumed a judicial character and in any democratic society proceedings before the judiciary should be conducted in the presence of the parties and in public, a fundamental principle which, with regard to domestic civil and criminal law, was upheld. The provisions of the Convention governing the Court contained no stipulation that it should meet *in camera*. In fact, hearings of the Court shall be public unless the Court in exceptional circumstances decided otherwise[86] and the Court's judgment shall be read at a public hearing,[87] and it followed that proceedings before the Court were public. Although Lawless was not entitled to bring the case, nor to appear before the Court, nor even to make submissions through a representative appointed by him,[88] he was nevertheless directly concerned since he had instituted the proceedings. If the Court found that his complaint was justified, he would be directly affected by any decision.[89] The Court was authorised[90] to hear any person whose position seemed useful in the fulfilment of its task, as was admitted both by the Government and by the Commission. The Court was of the opinion that the Commission was enabled under the Convention to communicate the report to Lawless, with the proviso that it must not be published, and in communicating its report to Lawless the Commission did not exceed its powers.

Dissenting, Judge Maridakis said[91] that it was apparent from the Convention that the jurisdiction of the Commission ceased as soon as the report had been transmitted to the Committee of Ministers. Since the Commission no longer had any powers, then *a fortiori* it had no further powers after the case had been referred to the Court. But, if neither the Committee of Ministers nor the state to whom the report had been transmitted were at liberty to publish it, then *a fortiori* the Commission had no right to do so: to communicate the report to Lawless was to publish it. What action could the Commission take in respect of Lawless's comments since the report could not be amended once it had been transmitted to the Committee of Ministers? Since the case had been in the hands of the Court, the Commission was not entitled to present them simply as having come from Lawless because the Commission was placed above the parties.[92] From the moment the Commission referred the case, the Court had sole jurisdiction and if it considered that points needed clarification and that

Lawless was the only person capable of doing so, the Court may, as sole judge call and hear him. Judge Maridakis also concluded that the new rule was contrary to the Convention. While the Court was not empowered to declare null and void any procedural rule of the Commission, it had the duty to refuse to apply any rule that it regarded as contrary to the Convention.

Objection to Court's Jurisdiction

The Government noted[93] that there was an unexplained delay of 42 days from the date the Commission adopted its report to the date on which it was transmitted to the Committee of Ministers and to the Government. An interval of six days (viz. from 26 September 1958, when it was adopted, to 2 October 1958, when it was transmitted) was adequate for the much more elaborate report in the Cyprus case. The Government submitted that jurisdiction should be declined unless (a) the Court was satisfied that between the two dates the reference of the case to the Court was not discussed in any way, and (b) even if the Court was so satisfied, it ought to refuse to entertain the case while the delay had not been satisfactorily explained.

In explaining and defending this delay, Waldock said[94] that the Commission felt disappointment that the Court should be confronted with an objection to the exercise of its jurisdiction which was out of harmony with the Irish Government's progressive attitude towards the acceptance of the compulsory jurisdiction of the Court. If the contracting states had intended that the Commission transmit its report to the Committee of Ministers forthwith upon its adoption, they could, and no doubt would, have so provided. Having created an international tribunal of wholly independent individuals, the contracting states were content to assume that the Commission would carry out its duties in good faith and would send forward its report when it considered it ready. The Commission in transmitting the report may make such proposals as it thought fit. This clearly contemplated that, after drawing up its report and before transmitting it, the Commission might proceed to further discussion as to whether it wished to make any specific proposals to the Committee of Ministers. This procedure was inconsistent with the thesis that the signatory states intended that, on adopting its report, the Commission was under an obligation forthwith to transmit it to the Committee of Ministers. The Commission did recognise that it must act with reasonable expedition. But the Court was being asked to rule that after the Commission had voted upon adopting the report, the report must forthwith, that was, within a few days, be transmitted. Since the report in the Cyprus case had been transmitted within six days, this implied that the Commission was guilty of an improper delay in the Lawless case, a contention which completely disregarded the exigencies of the Commission's work. The Commission felt strongly that the demand that it should explain to the Court precisely why six weeks elapsed between the vote of adoption and the transmission was totally without justification under the Convention. In the hope and belief that the Government would withdraw its objection, the Commission noted that it was composed of part-time members who came from the four corners of Europe. Nearly all had heavy responsibilities in their own countries, whether as judges, university professors, or in other spheres. Consequently, it was difficult to meet whenever it wished, or for long periods of time, a difficulty that the Court appreciated, since it was composed in the same way, and this necessitated a certain measure of flexibility in the procedure adopted for handling a case. The preparation of a report by a body working in two languages was a substantial piece of work and, in addition, some members might wish to include individual opinions on various points, and that was very much so with the Lawless case. Exactly how soon after the vote of adoption had been taken a report would be ready for transmission depended, therefore, on a number of factors. These included the extent to which alterations might have to be made in the drafts, the course of the meetings leading up to the vote, the extent to which individuals members wished to revise or to check their separate opinions, the requirements of translation, the Commission's other work, and the demands on secretarial and technical services. Accordingly, the fact that in the Cyprus case it proved possible to transmit the report within six days did not mean that the same thing could and should have been done in the Lawless case. The Commission had no intention of giving the Government, a party to the proceedings before the Commission, a detailed account of the private and secret deliberations and internal working of the Commission.[95] This confidentiality was founded upon the highest considerations designed to ensure the independence, integrity and impartiality of the Commission's work. The Commission was the master of its own procedure.[96] The drawing up of a report was an internal and purely private procedure. The Commission felt bound to put on record for the future that it was for the Commission alone to determine the procedure of drawing up a report and transmitting it to the Committee of Ministers. The argument made that jurisdiction should be declined was based on the contention that it was a fundamental principle of the Convention that there should be equality of opportunity as between the Commission and the state in arriving at a decision whether to refer a case to the Court. That was asking the Court to take rather strong liberties with the Convention. The three months period was not introduced primarily for the purpose of defining the extent of the right of the state or of the Commission to refer a case to the Court. The role played by this period was unmistakably of a constitutional provision marking the boundary between the respective competencies of the Committee of Ministers and of the Court to give final decision on whether or not the Convention had been violated. The Court was being asked to set aside these constitutional provisions and to hold that, although the Commission had referred the case to the Court within the three months period, the jurisdiction to give a final decision belonged to the Committee of Ministers and not to the Court. The primary object[97] was to fix a time limit, after which it would no longer be valid to institute proceedings before the Court. The three months period clearly related, not to the opportunity to consider whether to seize the Court, but to the actual institution of proceedings before the Court and it was with regard to the actual institution of proceedings that the Commission and the state were placed in the same position. No proceedings may be instituted before the Court until the Commission had transmitted its report to the Council of Ministers, because until then the case was exclusively within the jurisdiction of the Commission. Nor could any proceedings be instituted when three months had elapsed after the transmission, because then the case falls exclusively within the jurisdiction of the Committee of Ministers. But during the three months period the Commission and the state may alike refer the case and certainly each were in a position of equality in regard to the legal power to refer a case to the Court. The Commission's report must be transmitted to the state so as to enable the state to consider whether it wished to exercise the right to refer the case to the Court, a right which accrued only after the transmission of the report to the Committee of Ministers. But this provision, the only one in the Convention which could in any way touch upon the question of opportunity to consider whether to refer a case to the Court, did not establish equality of opportunity as between the Commission and the state. On the contrary, there was nothing to prevent the Commission from referring the case immediately after the transmission of its report, and thus before the state concerned had even had the time to open the parcels containing the report. Had it been intended to lay down as a fundamental rule the principle of equality of opportunity for considering whether to refer the case to the Court, the Convention would certainly have deferred the right of the Commission to seize the Court to a date some considerable time after the transmission of the report. While the Commission's jurisdiction derived entirely from the consent given by signature and ratification of the Convention as did that of the Court, that did not mean that there was any intention to put individual states in a position of inferiority vis-à-vis the Commission or the Court. To ensure the observance of their engagements undertaken in the Convention, the signatory states conferred on both the Commission and the Court large powers of jurisdiction vis-à-vis individual states and were established to serve the common public purpose of all the Council of Europe states. The signatory states entrusted to the Commission the power to investigate a complaint against one of themselves, to ascertain the facts, to attempt to conciliate, to state an opinion as to whether the state had violated the Convention, and to bring the case before the Court. These powers were entrusted to the Commission as one of their chosen instruments for ensuring the observance of the human rights guaranteed in the Convention. This being so, it was difficult to see how the Commission, which derived its jurisdiction from the consent of the contracting states, could come to the conclusion that the states must have intended that before the transmission of its report, the Commission should be totally debarred from any consideration of what ought to be its decision after that date, in regard to referring the case to the Court or leaving the case with the Committee of Ministers for final decision. The Commission was created as a wholly independent body and its members did not represent their governments. The Commission did not pursue any interest of its own but the public interest of all the Council of Europe states in the maintenance of human rights. The Commission was in no sense an antagonist of the state against which complaint was made. The Commission was intended to, and did, act in all matters with complete impartiality, favouring neither the state nor the individual against the state. When the Commission decided to refer a case to the Court it did not do so as to obtain an advantage over the state. It did so because it believed that the Convention would be best served by reference of the case to the Court for final adjudication, and for no other reason. When doing so it discharged a responsibility rather than exercised a right. The Commission expressed the hope that, in the light of this statement as to how the Commission in fact acted, the Government may not wish to press its objection to the Court's jurisdiction. Public opinion everywhere in the Council of Europe states would regard it as a splendid augury for the future work of the Court if the Government withdrew its objection. In a formal written submission the Commission requested the Court to reject the preliminary objections to the Court's jurisdiction.

In reply the Attorney General said[98] that the Government had not renounced the Court's jurisdiction but asked for a ruling on a preliminary point as to whether the Commission had by its conduct ousted the jurisdiction of the Court. That point was not of great importance in the Lawless case, but was fundamental in the application of the Convention and one which the Government felt obliged to raise. If it was not clearly established that the Commission did not in any way discuss the question of reference to the Court before the transmission of the report to the Committee of Ministers, the equality of opportunity which the state, in virtue of its sovereign status was entitled to expect, would have been denied. Such a circumstance would demand that the Court decline jurisdiction unless the report was referred to it within three months of the date of its adoption. The Commission claimed that it was not under any duty to send its report to the Committee of Ministers within any time, specified or unspecified, that it could take as long as it liked. The state had the right to be given a copy of it at the same time as the Committee of Ministers. The reason for that view was that the Convention did not say that the two things had to be done at the same time. The Commission was unwilling to read into the Convention even the most reasonable provisions. It was fundamental that, when the Commission adopted a report, it must send it promptly to the Committee of Ministers and, at the same time, send it to the state concerned. It was essential for the proper working of the Convention that delay on the part of the Commission in transmitting its report, once the report was adopted, must be discountenanced. The objection raised as to jurisdiction on the ground of delay was designedly framed so as to enable the Commission to explain the delay and the Court to entertain the case, if the Court thought fit. The Government was prepared, in the light of the explanation, not to press the preliminary objection, but in doing so, the Government reserved the right to maintain that the duty imposed on the Commission was as outlined. In a formal written submission, the Government made no mention that the preliminary objection was withdrawn.

Court Decision

The Court took notice of the Government's withdrawal of the preliminary objection to jurisdiction and accordingly did not rule on the issue.

Notes

[1] Article 47 of the Convention.

[2] Ibid. Article 32.

[3] Ibid. Article 48. The Committee of Ministers could not refer a case to the Court.
[4] Ibid. Article 50.
[5] Ibid. Article 45.
[6] Ibid. Article 32 (1).
[7] See p. 10.
[8] See p.89, footnote 18. The Commission adopted its report in this case on 8 January 1960, which held there had been breaches of Article 10 (freedom of expression), transmitted it to the Committee of Ministers on 1 February 1960 (the same day as the Lawless report) and referred the case to the Court on 29 April 1960. Following changes in Belgian law, the Court struck out the case on 27 March 1962.
[9] Lawless Case. ECHR 1960-61. Series B. pp.240-41.
[10] BPRO. FO. 371/146292/1738.
[11] BPRO.FO. 371/154531/1732/6.
[12] Article 31 (2) of the Convention.
[13] BPRO. FO. 371/154531/1732/6. The UK Government received a copy of the report on 15 February 1960 from the Council of Europe, as presumably did all the member states.
[14] Lawless case. op.cit. p. 282.
[15] Article 31 (2) of the Convention.
[16] Lawless Case. op.cit. pp. 281-282.
[17] DJ File S.9/58/3.
[18] Letter from DFA to author: 25 December 1996.
[19] DJ File S.9/58/3.
[20] BPRO. FO. 371/146292/1738.
[21] FO.371/154531/1732/6.
[22] There were two other applications from detainees (Brady and Cunningham) before the Commission: see pp. 221-222.
[23] DFA File 417/39/19/4/2. Part 6.
[24] The place to find such correspondence is in the Council of Europe archives but these are closed to public inspection. Letter to author from Registrar of the European Court of Human Rights, dated 21 October 1996.
[25] According to Gormley, this "indirect right of petition" is available to an individual who has been unsuccessful before the Commission and who may try to persuade that body to transfer his case to the Court in order to secure an additional hearing and perhaps a favourable result though he notes that no example of the "indirect petition" exists. *The Procedural Status of the Individual before International and Supranational Tribunals.* (1966) p.107.
[26] DJ File S.9/58/3.
[27] Lawless Case. op.cit. p.252.
[28] Ibid. p.6.
[29] Ibid. pp.6-8.
[30] FO 371/154531/1732/11 contains a record, dated February 1960, made by the Legal Adviser to the Foreign Office, that "the conduct of the case before the Court raises a number

of problems, some of which Waldock discussed privately with me a few days ago...the case of Lawless is certainly of interest to us...".

[31] Rules of Court, Rule 29 (1), as it was then.

[32] Lawless Case. op.cit. p.185.

[33] Rules of Court, Rule 32 (1), as it was then.

[34] Rules of Court, Rule 21 (2), as it was then.

[35] Lawless Case. op.cit. p.186.

[36] Ibid. p.189.

[37] Ibid. p.189.

[38] DJ File S.9/58/3.

[39] Lawless case. op.cit. Request to Court, pp.6-7; Commission memorial, par.49-54, pp.205-207; Waldock's address, pp.234-236.

[40] YBECHR.1955-56-57. pp.128-130.

[41] United Kingdom in respect of Malaya and Singapore, Kenya, British Guinea, and Uganda (1954); Cyprus (twice in 1957 and 1959); Northern Ireland (1957); Northern Rhodesia (1957);Nyasaland (1959), and Aden (1960).

[42] Lawless Case. op.cit. Commission memorial, para.54, p.206.

[43] Ibid. Government counter-memorial, para.7, p.220. The Government was not beyond using the same argument when it suited: see later in this chapter at p. 175.

[44] DJ File S.9/58/3.

[45] Lawless case. op.cit. p.187.

[46] Rules of Court, Rule 21 (3), as it was then.

[47] Ibid. Rule 21 (1), as it was then.

[48] Rules of Court, Rule 48 (1), as it was then.

[49] AG File SR 54/38 contains a summary of what took place.

[50] Ibid. AG referred to proposed role of Lawless which is covered in Chapter 9.

[51] Irish Independent, on 24 February 1960, reported that "sources close to the Commission said its transmission to the Irish Government was an indication that the opinion favoured Lawless". Irish Times, on the same day, said that a Reuters report from Strasbourg that the transmission of the report to the Irish Government would suggest that "the report favoured Lawless but if this were the only reason for the suggestion, it would appear to be wrong, as the...Convention provides that the report must be sent to the state concerned".

[52] Rules of Court, Rule 14 (3), as it was then.

[53] A very detailed statement on the issue a few days before the proceedings opened noted that the Commission should not be regarded as "against" the Irish Government.

[54] Lawless case. op.cit. p.192.

[55] DFA File 417/39/19/4/2B. Sanction was given to pay Reuter 5,000 new French francs (approx.£380). Paris Embassy noted (1 November 1960) that this sum was "paid in cash" to Reuter. Travelling and subsistence expenses were also paid in cash for his visit to Strasbourg. A further fee of 1,000 new French francs (approx.£75), in cash, was paid for the court attendance.

[56] Lawless case. op.cit. p.364.

[57] Lawless case. ECHR. 1960-61. Series A. Judgments and decisions. Contains 67 pages.

[58] The Commission's submission took most of the first day, and the Government's submission began on late afternoon of the first day and concluded on late afternoon of the second day when a short reply for the Commission was made.

[59] See Appendix 2 for biographical notes on members of the Court.

[60] Of the seven members of the Chamber, four were from states which did not recognise the jurisdiction of the Court. Thus Cassin (France), Maridakis (Greece), Balladore Palleri (Italy) and Arik (Turkey) sat in judgement on states which had recognised the jurisdiction of the Court. This deficiency was commented on by H.Golsong, (during the Lawless case he was Deputy Registrar of the Court): "One may recall the critical attitude in Belgian public opinion when the Court in 1968 decided the Belgian Linguistics case and a French judge presided (Cassin) although France had not yet ratified the Convention." *On the Reform of the Supervisory System of the European Convention of Human Rights.* vol. 13 Human Rights Journal. (1992). pp.265-269.

[61] Eustathiades and Petren assistants, and McNulty, Secretary of the Commission.

[62] Lawless Case. Series B. op.cit. p.233.

[63] Ibid. p.270.

[64] Lawless case. Series A. pp.4-20.

[65] DJ File S.9/58/3 contains a noted from Secretary of the DEA: "As expected the Court has found against us...on the preliminary objections...however, their decision on one important point is as follows: 'The Court sees no reason at this stage to authorise the Commission to transmit to it (the Court) the applicant's written observations on the Commission's report.' This is a very big point for us...gives us satisfaction on the substance of the issues...the view taken by the Court is not irreversible".

[66] Lawless case. Series A, pp.4-20. The record does not note attendances.

[67] Lawless case. op.cit. Government formally notified on 16 January 1961.

[68] Ibid. Commission memorial, paras.55-58, page 207; Waldock's address, pp.234, 266-268 and 305.

[69] Ibid. Government counter-memorial, para.7, pp.219-221; AG's.address, pp.278-280 and 287-294.

[70] Rules of Court, Rule 29 (1), as it was then.

[71] Article 34 of the Convention.

[72] Lawless case. ECHR. 1960-61. Series A. p.16.

[73] Rule 76 provided: "When a case brought before the Commission in pursuance of Article 25 of the Convention is subsequently referred to the Court, the Secretary of the Commission shall immediately notify the applicant. Unless the Commission shall otherwise decide, the Secretary shall also in due course communicate to him the Commission's report, informing him that he may, within a time limit fixed by the President, submit to the Commission his written observations on the said report. The Commission shall decide what action, if any, shall be taken in respect of those observations."

[74] DJ File S.9/58/3. By letter dated 28 April 1960 which refers to a Government letter written to the Commission on 15 March 1960 (before the Commission referred the case to the Court). The Commission, from 28 March to 2 April 1960, examined "the written observations of the Government which related to relevant extracts from the written pleadings...". No copy of the March 1960 letter exists.

[75] Lawless Case. op.cit. pp. 214-216 and pp.280-287.

[76] Article 31 (2) of the Convention.
[77] Ibid. Article 36.
[78] Lawless Case. op.cit. p.320.
[79] Ibid. Waldock's address. pp. 247-253 and 311-314.
[80] Article 6 of the Convention.
[81] Rules of Court, Rule 18, as it was then.
[82] Ibid. Rule 29 (2), as it was then.
[83] Lawless case. op.cit. pp. 316-317.
[84] Lawless case. Series A, pp.11-12.
[85] Ibid. pp.12-14.
[86] Rules of Court, Rule 18, as it was then.
[87] Ibid. Rule 51, as it was then.
[88] Lawless's role before the Court is considered in Chapter 9.
[89] Article 50 of the Convention.
[90] Rules of Court, Rule 38 (1) provided that "the Chamber may, at the request of a party or of the delegates of the Commission or *proprio moto*, decide to hear a witness or expert or in any other capacity any person whose evidence...seems likely to assist it in the carrying out of its task".
[91] Lawless case. Series A. pp.17-20.
[92] Article 19 of the Convention.
[93] Lawless case. op.cit. pp.212-214.
[94] Ibid. pp.236-247.
[95] Which the Government were privy to already: see p. 86.
[96] Article 36 of the Convention.
[97] Ibid. Articles 32 and 47.
[98] Lawless case. op.cit. pp.270-272.

9 Status of Lawless before the European Court of Human Rights

Introduction

Despite the impressive charter of human rights enumerated and declared in the European Convention of Human Rights, and the inclusion of an enforcement mechanism which could be activated by individual petition, the Convention did not afford any explicit status to the individual before the European Court of Human Rights. This lacuna produced the anomalous situation that while the individual initiated the claim, and had carriage of it before the European Commission, the individual was prevented from litigating his claim to final judgment in the Strasbourg system. With the Court now seized of its first case, the Commission was aware of this patent anomaly. An effort by the Commission to afford Lawless some partial role in the proceedings was successful though it fell short of recognising his standing as of right. This achievement was to open the way to further expansion in this regard in subsequent cases. This chapter covers the tussle between the Commission and the Irish Government on this vital issue.

Settling Procedural Matters

The President of the Chamber, following the pronouncement by the Court of its decision on 14 November 1960, invited the representatives of the Government[1] and the Commission to his office to consider the arrangements for the exchange of memorials so that the Court might give a decision on the merits.[2] Having ascertained the views of the Government and the Commission, the President ordered the Commission to file its memorial by 16 December 1960 and the Government to file a counter-memorial by 5 February 1961, which was done on 31 January 1961.[3]

Another Major Issue of Conflict Identified

Despite the Court ruling on matter of procedures, these further pleadings identified a remaining fundamental difference of opinion on the general question as to the status to be accorded to Lawless. The particular question was how far it was proper for the Commission, of its own accord, to put before the Court the views of Lawless on the Commission's report. Much of the written pleadings and an entire day, 7 April 1961, were consumed with this issue, which had already been addressed at some length in the previous proceedings and Court judgment. Since this issue straddled both hearings, it is dealt with in this chapter for convenience and had three distinct facets, each of which is discussed presently.

Commission's Contact with Lawless after Referring the Case to Court

As noted in the previous chapter, the Commission sent a copy of its report to Lawless, on 13 April 1960, and invited him to submit his written observations thereon, which he did on 23 May 1960. No complete copy of these observations is to be found in the archival material. This is understandable because it is probable that the Commission did not forward a copy to the Government. It is equally probable that, having regard to the stance taken by the Government, which is discussed later, the Government did not request, nor would have accepted a copy of these observations. The Commission included Lawless's views, in its statement to the Court on the merits, though these were deleted from the published material in accordance with the judgment of the Court of 7 April 1961,[4] which is discussed presently. However, an edited version of these observations was included in the statement of the Commission that was forwarded to the Government and is available in the archives.[5] Waldock made an accurate assessment of these observations: "any comments...will be decidedly critical of the Commission's findings, which are, of course, adverse to him."[6]

On 7 January 1961, Lawless's solicitor wrote to the Court that Lawless considered that the adequate presentation of his case before the Court required the presence of his legal advisers in some capacity. He inquired whether the President of the Commission would propose to the Court that Lawless should be separately represented if the Commission did not have the intention to call on Lawless's legal advisers for assistance.[7] The Commission, on 23 February 1961, wrote to Lawless enclosing a copy of the counter-memorial of the Government and requested him to submit to the Commission, before 25 March 1961, if he so desired, a statement of his views on matters that arose therein. The Commission noted that neither the Rules of Court nor the previous judgment empowered the Commission to request the Court to establish the separate representation of Lawless before the Court. Notwithstanding this conclusion, Lawless was asked whether he wished to be present at the public session of the Court, beginning on 7 April. He was also asked whether he wished to nominate a person to be present at that session who may be available to give such assistance to the Commission delegates as they may think fit to request.[8] It is interesting to note that this suggestion that Lawless's legal advisers may be of assistance to the Commission first came from Lawless and not from the Commission. In response,[9] Lawless's solicitor supplied views on the Government's counter-memorial. This document is not available even in the archives and is only referred to in passing.[10] In the same letter, Lawless said that he did not wish to be present at the Court hearing and that he nominated Sean MacBride to attend the session to give such assistance to the delegates as they might desire. There is no record of Lawless, or his legal representatives, making direct contact with the Court, nor did the Court make direct contact with Lawless.

The Government expressed concern that "rumours are circulating in Dublin" that Lawless or his legal advisers had been invited by the Court to attend the public hearing of the case, which the Government felt sure was not so as it had received no notice to that effect. The Government asked the Court to confirm that it had not been in communication with Lawless or his legal advisers. There is no record of a reply of this request.

Communication of Lawless's Views to the Court: Discussion at the First Court Hearing

In documentation to the Court prior to the first hearing the Commission noted[11] that, without wishing to prejudge this procedural question, it had not appended Lawless's comments to its memorial. Instead, it requested leave to file these comments and to receive directions as to the right to communicate these comments to the Court. At the hearing Waldock said[12] that while the Convention made clear that the individual was not to have any direct relations with the Court as a party to the proceedings, it was silent as to his relations with the Commission during these proceedings. It was also silent as to the right of the Commission to obtain and communicate to the Court the individual's comments on any point. It also said nothing as to the right of the Court to call him before it, or to request his comments in writing upon any material point of fact or of law. These omissions make it difficult to suggest what exactly was intended to be the individual's role before the Court. The Commission found it difficult to attribute to the Convention an intention to place an impenetrable curtain between the individual and an organ specifically set up as a judicial tribunal to make a judicial determination on his case. There was nothing in the Convention to prevent the Government from introducing new facts or arguments or to prevent the Court from taking new points missed in the Commission proceedings. Yet the Commission was not, apparently, to have any right to ascertain the individual's view on new matters of fact or of law and still less to communicate them to the Court. Similarly, while the Government was free to criticise and comment upon the Commission's report, neither the Commission nor the Court was to be allowed to know whether the individual contested the report's findings. The Commission doubted whether the Convention created such a marked degree of inequality in the presentation of a case to a judicial tribunal.

In the *Judgments of the Administrative Tribunal of the International Labour Organisation* case,[13] individuals obtained decisions against UNESCO. Under the Statute of the International Court of Justice, only states and international organisations had direct access in advisory opinions, and on the question of equality of opportunity the Court pronounced that "the judicial character of the Court requires that both sides directly affected...should be in a position to submit their views and their argument to the Court....The principle of the equality of the parties follows from the requirements of good administration of justice".[14] The expedient was then adopted whereby UNESCO undertook to transmit to the Court the observations of the individuals in writing, without exercising any control over their contents, and not to exercise its own right to present oral observations, since the individuals were precluded from doing so. Only on this basis did the Court feel justified in entertaining the request for an advisory opinion. In the *Danzig Legislative Decrees* case,[15] a referral to the Permanent Court of Justice for an advisory opinion, the Court informed the petitioners that it would be prepared to receive an explanatory note supplementing the statements in their petitions. But at the oral hearings, while the representatives of the Free City were heard, the petitioners, owing to the provisions of the statute, were not invited to present oral observations. In that case, therefore, there was not complete equality in securing a hearing, and this drew grave criticism from Judge Anzilotti, in a dissenting opinion. In the *Former Officials of the Governing Commission of the Saar Territory* case,[16] the Council of the League of Nations foresaw the difficulty of equality between the parties. Accordingly, it approved a procedure whereby written pleadings with fixed time limits were exchanged beforehand, and these were then appended to the request for an advisory opinion. And at the same time, the League, by a formal resolution, renounced its right to present oral observations, because it did not wish to have any greater opportunities of furnishing information than the complainants. Owing to the outbreak of war, the Court never pronounced upon that procedure. These cases underlined the importance of giving, even in advisory proceedings, a fair opportunity to both sides of the dispute. There was another case, the *United Nations Administrative Tribunal* case,[17] which, on a superficial view, may seem to point the other way. After UN officials had obtained final judgments from the Administrative Tribunal in their favour for wrongful dismissal, the General Assembly referred the matter to the Court for an advisory opinion, but in a general form, asking whether the organisation might be entitled to refuse to execute these awards. The Court refused to allow the individuals to present written statements and refused to disclose to the individuals the written observations presented by states and by the organisation when it was suggested that the individuals might ask one of the member states to present observations to the Court on their behalf. The procedural decision did not run counter to the principle of equality, because the case submitted to the Court was not the case of the individual officials but was a request, couched in general terms, for an advisory opinion as to the general powers of the General Assembly.

The situation that confronted the European Court differed from that which was confronted in these cases. In the present case, the Commission, although not a party to the case, participated in the proceedings and stood in an intermediate position between the Government and the individual. Moreover, if the Commission considered the rights of the individual had been violated, it was the Commission's duty to state that in its report, and to present that opinion to the Court. It could be urged that both sides had been presented to the Court through the medium of the Commission, and certainly, before the Commission, the Government and the individual were in a position of complete equality. But the report represented new elements in the case. Before the Court the Government had the right to comment upon these new elements and to introduce new points. Yet it denied the individual any right to do the same, or to reply to the Government's comments, or to the Government's new points. The Commission thought it unacceptable to act as the mouthpiece of Lawless without reference to him. It would be one thing to transmit to the Court his views, and quite another to formulate Lawless's views to the Court without any consultation with him, which the Commission was not prepared to do. This request was criticised as an attempt by a subterfuge to bestow on the individual the quality of a party before the Court. The Commission believed that it had the duty to place before the Court with all impartiality and objectivity, the elements relevant for the Court's consideration. It recognised that whether the comments of Lawless were relevant was a question for the Court, and that was why, having obtained Lawless's comments, the Commission did not file them with its memorial. The delicacy of this question was fully recognised. The Commission would be ready, if the Court so required, to obtain and place before it, either orally or in writing, the comments of Lawless upon the questions that would be under examination at these hearings. It would also comply with any other procedure ordered for placing Lawless's comments before the Court. But the Commission would feel unable to identify with Lawless before the Court and plead his case for him, for that would compromise the impartiality and objectivity of the Commission's work, and be wholly contrary to its conception of its own duties. The Commission did not seek any right or privilege for Lawless which the Convention withheld. The Commission sought the Court's guidance as to the manner in which, under the Convention, the individual's side of the case was to be handled before the Court and placed itself under the direction of the Court on this question. The Commission rejected the idea that Lawless should have the opportunity to re-open the whole case and present his arguments to the Court *de novo*. The Commission's concern was that the individual should, by some procedure or other, be able to submit his views to the Court on any new element in the case, such as the Commission's report, or any criticism by the Government of the Commission's findings, and any new point of law or fact that might arise in the proceedings. The Commission was not thinking of Lawless alone, but of all individuals whose cases would hereafter come before the Court for final decision. Therefore, the Commission[18] requested the Court: (a) to give leave to the Commission to transmit Lawless's written comments upon the Commission's report, and (b) to give such direction as to the Commission's right to communicate Lawless's comments in regard to matters arising in the proceedings, and (c) to reject the submission formulated by the Government.

The Government, in its counter-memorial,[19] contended that individuals had no capacity before the Court. It was first proposed at The Hague Congress in 1948 that individuals should have an immediate and direct access to the Court. The Consultative Assembly instead proposed that an individual should have a right to appeal to the Court only with the authorisation of the Commission. These proposals were unacceptable to the governments. The final proposal was that individuals should have the right to petition the Commission but should never have the right to petition the Court. While the Commission recognised this position it attempted by a subterfuge to bestow on Lawless the quality of a party before the Court by enabling him to make submissions in a document which the Commission wished to append to its memorial. If permitted, this would enable Lawless to play an active part before the Court in the same way as if he were a party. The Government asked that any comments of Lawless should not be received by the Court because: (a) no argument in favour of their admission had been submitted; and (b) the admission of such comments would amount to an oblique method of amending the Convention; and (c) such comments had come into existence only through a breach by the Commission of its obligation of secrecy, and (d) such comments were not material.

The Attorney General said[20] that in no circumstances should the Commission tender to the Court the comments of an individual received after the conclusion of its primary function, that was the adoption of a report. The cited cases demonstrated that the receipt by an international court of written submission from individuals had been exceptional and only agreed when all the parties who had the right to appear had either expressly or by implication consented to that course. The Commission adopted this approach because of the element of inequality. While that was true, the inequality was more fanciful than real, because the individual had already presented his case fully to the Commission, and that case could and ought to be put by the Commission in supporting its own report. This inequality was deliberate, not in the sense of states placing individuals at a disadvantage, but because in agreeing to the Court's limited jurisdiction created by the Convention, states had gone as far as they could in recognising for individuals a status of any kind in international law. This settled practice of international courts must have been well known. It was regrettable that, when the opposition of the Government was known, the Commission adhered to its intention and endeavoured to force a decision from the Court. If implemented, this may create a doubt as to the impartiality of the Commission and as to its suitability to deal with any further petition against the Government. It was not suggested that the Commission was partial or biased. The Government must be sensitive to public opinion and must ensure, so far as it could, that the impartiality of any tribunal before which it appeared was obvious to all. The Government asked the Court to rule that Lawless's comments on the report should not be received and that no further comments of his should be received by the Court.[21]

Court Decision

The Court noted[22] in its judgment that it was not called upon to examine in detail the precedents invoked by the Commission, and though recognising their force noted that none of the cited cases was that of an individual appealing against the action of his own government. These proceedings were instituted by Lawless against the state of which he was a national. The solution must be sought in the special nature of the procedure laid down in the Convention. The contracting states and the Commission were alone empowered to bring a case, or to appear before the Court. Nevertheless, the Court had the duty to safeguard the interests of the individual who may not be a party to any court proceedings, and the proceedings in the instant case related to issues which concerned Lawless. Accordingly, it was in the interests of the proper administration of justice that the Court should have knowledge of, and take into consideration, if need be, Lawless's point of view. Towards this end, the Court had at its disposal (a) the Commission's report, which set out Lawless's allegation with regard to the facts and his legal arguments, even if the Commission did not endorse them, and (b) the Commission's written and oral observations. The Commission, as the defender of the public interest, was entitled, even if it did not share them, to make known Lawless's view to the Court as a means of throwing light on the points at issue. The Court was also entitled to hear Lawless[23] and, as part of the inquiry, was entitled to invite the Commission, *ex officio*, or authorise the Commission at its request, to submit Lawless's comments on the report or on any specific point which arose in the course of the debates. While formal note must be taken of the request for authorisation to submit Lawless's comments, the Court said that since it had been unable to examine the merits of the case, it was not in a position to reach a decision on this request and reserved its right to do so when it deemed fit. The Court declared, by six votes to one, that at this stage there was no reason to authorise the Commission to transmit to it Lawless's written observations on the Commission's report.

Communication of Lawless's Views: Discussion of the Issue at the Second Court Hearing

In the preparation for the second hearing the Government gave consideration to the possibility of requesting the Court for an interpretation of the Court's previous judgment. There is a copy of such a draft request in the archival material, together with the Government's draft observations on the statement of the Commission.[24] In the draft request the Government complained that following a full argument of the issue and despite the Court's refusal to authorise the Commission at that stage to transmit to it Lawless's written observations on the Commission report, the Commission had included the whole or part of these observations in its statement. The Government did not believe that the Court's decision was intended to mean that where the Court refused its authorisation, the Commission could transmit the observations without such authorisation. The Government's attitude was supported by the discussion on procedure between the President of the Chamber, the President of the Commission and the Attorney General following the delivery of the November judgment. This made it clear that the President of the Chamber did not envisage a decision on the question of the inclusion of Lawless's comments until the court had seen the pleadings on the merits from both sides. The Government felt sure that the interpretation of the judgment would bear out the Government's view and did not anticipate that the Court would require a re-argument of the case before giving its decision. If the Court could be convened a few days in advance of the date to be fixed for the public hearing, it would not be necessary to postpone the hearing of the case. The Government in its observations did not include any plea as to the views of Lawless on the report of the Commission. It was more appropriate that it should be left to the Court to take such action as it considered warranted in the circumstances. The Government formally requested an interpretation of the point as to "whether the decision of the Court declaring 'that at this stage there is no reason to authorise the Commission to transmit to it the applicant's written observations on the Commission's report' meant...that the Commission might, subsequent to such decision, and without any request or authorisation from the Court, submit to it the applicant's written observations on the report of the Commission".[25]

Waldock noted[26] that the Commission had included Lawless's written comments because it was believed that this was in conformity with the Court's judgment and was necessary for the effective application of the Commission's responsibilities under the Convention. The importance of the propriety of presenting Lawless's comments on its report was emphasised, because until this was known, the Commission could not determine what was a proper course of action to pursue. The Commission was anxious not to exceed its functions, but equally it was anxious not to fail to do its full duty. The Court was requested to rule that the Commission was entitled to consider, as part of the proceedings, Lawless's comments on the Commission's report, as indicated in the Court's previous judgment.[27]

The Attorney General said[28] that, in the previous judgment, it was expressly recorded that the Court had Lawless's allegations with regard to the facts and the law in the Commission's report. The Government did not agree that the Court, in its judgment, intended the Commission to act in the manner in which it had done and placed on record the Government's disappointment at the departure from the course that the Court desired to see adopted. The Government had not sought any deletion from the Commission's submission. It did not ask the Court to take any action. It was entirely a matter for the Court to do what it thought proper to ensure that the case was conducted in the manner that the Court itself desired.

Court Decision

In pronouncing its decision the Court noted[29] that, in its previous judgment, it had declared that there was no reason at that stage to authorise the Commission to transmit Lawless's comments on the Commission's report. The Court had recognised the Commission's right to take into account ('de faire etat de'), on its own authority, those views as a proper way of enlightening the Court. The Commission was entirely free to decide by what means it wished to establish contact with Lawless and give him an opportunity to make known his views to the Commission. The Court decided unanimously[30] that Lawless's comments, as reproduced in the Commission's statement, were not to be considered part of the proceedings. Though the Commission had all latitude, in the course of debates and in so far as it believed that they might be useful to enlighten the Court, to take into account those views.

Communication of Government's Pleadings to Lawless

The Government took the strongest exception[31] to the Commission communicating its pleadings to Lawless, because, as a Court document, the Commission had no authority to transmit them to anyone and to request a statement on matters which arose therein. No justification could be found in the Court's judgment and this constituted a further attempt to circumvent the Convention.

The Commission argued[32] that sending the pleadings to Lawless had been endorsed in the Court's judgment and was part of its internal procedure by which it might be apprised of Lawless's views on matters which had arisen in the pleadings. The Commission had not asked to introduce this document, nor was there any intention of doing so, nor was there any question of new facts being introduced. The Commission felt that it ought to be informed of Lawless's views. The Commission requested a ruling that it was entitled to make known Lawless's point of view on points arising in the course of the Court's debates, as indicated in the Court's judgment.

Court Decision

The Court decided[33] unanimously that the Commission had all latitude, in the course of debates and in so far as it believed they were useful to enlighten the Court, to take into account Lawless's views concerning any other specific point which might have arisen since the lodging of the report.

Status before the Court of a Person Nominated by Lawless

Waldock said[34] that, having regard to the strong expression in the Court's previous judgment as to the interest of Lawless in these proceedings, the Commission had invited him to nominate a person to be present at the session to give such assistance which the delegates might think fit to request. That invitation was carefully worded: it was not an invitation to appoint a person to form part of the Commission's delegation. The Commission was entitled, if it so desired, to have the assistance of any person of its choice.[35] It was emphasised to the Court at the previous hearing that the Commission did not identify with Lawless, and that applied *a fortiori* where the Commission's finding was in favour of the Government. The Commission was ready, and regarded it as its function, to objectively expose to the Court the elements in the case, including so far as it might think proper, the views of Lawless and that would be done, if it was done at all, impartially and objectively. If the Commission had no contact with Lawless there could be no question of the Commission's representing to the Court his views and it would be irresponsible to represent Lawless's point of view, except so far as it was found explicitly in the pleadings. It was as a precautionary measure that Lawless had been invited to nominate, if he wished, a person who would have his authority in the proceedings. If the Commission had unwittingly gone beyond its duty it was sorry to be the cause of objection, but it did not think that it had exceeded its duty. The Court in its judgment had stressed the interest of Lawless during the progress of these judicial proceedings, and expressly recognised the Commission's rights to communicate documents to him and to make known to the Court his views. It was prepared to take what responsibilities may be put upon it and since this was the first case it had no guidance other than the rules of procedure, the Convention, and the Court's judgment. Guidance was requested because, when it came to the merits, the Commission must be in a position to know whether it was proper to take further account of Lawless's views. The Commission requested a ruling that it was entitled to consider that the person nominated by Lawless was available to give such assistance to the delegates as they may think fit. This was in order to make known Lawless's views on any specific points arising in the course of the debates to the Court.[36]

The Government, in a letter of 28 March 1961, noted that the Commission, by inviting Lawless to nominate counsel to be present at the hearing, "departed from that impartiality which should characterise the work of the Commission...".[37] The Attorney General said[38] that this was a public court and if Lawless chose to come, the Government could not raise any objection. If the Court felt that Lawless's attendance was necessary, that was for the Court to decide. It was not for the Commission to both invite Lawless to the hearing and to nominate a person who was accepted by the Commission to assist them in their deliberations before the Court. The Government made no request to the Court but took public exception to the Commission's conduct, so that the public may know how unfavourably that action had been viewed.

Court Decision

The Court noted that it had declared in its previous judgment that the Commission was entirely free to decide by what means it wished to establish contact with Lawless and to give him an opportunity to make known his views. In particular, it was free to ask Lawless to nominate a person to be available to the Commission's delegates though it did not follow that person had any *locus standi in judicio*. Accordingly, the Court decided unanimously that it was for the Commission, when it considered it desirable to do so, to invite Lawless to place some person at its disposal.[39]

Notes

---

[1] No record of this meeting exists. The Government successfully prevented the publication of the record of this meeting: see pp. 222-225.

[2] Lawless case. ECHR 1960-61. Series B. p.322.
[3] Ibid. p.323.
[4] Lawless case. op.cit. p.336.
[5] DJ File S.9/58/23. (1993 Release).
[6] Lawless case. op.cit. p.263.
[7] Ibid. p.348.
[8] Ibid. p.348.
[9] Ibid. p.347.
[10] Ibid. pp. 347 and 364. There is no record of this document in the Government archives.
[11] Ibid. Commission memorial, para.56-59, pp.207-208.
[12] Ibid. pp.253-266.
[13] 1956 ICJR 77.
[14] Ibid p. 86.
[15] 1935 No.A/B, No.65 pp. 43-44.
[16] No reference was given and despite an extensive search, none has been found.
[17] 1954 ICJR 47.
[18] Lawless case. op.cit. p.319.
[19] Ibid. para.6, pp.216-218.
[20] Ibid. pp. 287- 293.
[21] Ibid. p.320.
[22] Lawless Case. ECHR. 1960-61. Series A. pp.15-16.
[23] Rules of Court, Rule 38 (1), as it was then.
[24] DJ File S.9/58/3.
[25] This request, rather unusually, is not published in the Series B material and there must be doubt whether it was actually sent.
[26] Lawless case. op.cit. pp.358-367.
[27] Ibid. p.373.
[28] Ibid. pp.368-370.
[29] Ibid. p.373, and Series A, pp.29-30.
[30] Ibid. p.374.
[31] Ibid. pp.352-354.
[32] Ibid. pp.363-367.
[33] Ibid. p.374.
[34] Ibid. p.365.
[35] For Rule 29 (1) see p.258, footnote 82.
[36] Lawless case. op.cit. p.373.
[37] Ibid. p.354.
[38] Ibid. pp.369-370.
[39] Ibid. p.374.

10 Judgment of the European Court of Human Rights on the Merits

Introduction

Finally, after a process spread across four years, the European Court of Human Rights was ready to deliver, in a historical moment, its first judgment under the European Convention of Human Rights. Had the Government of Ireland, in the particular circumstances, "secured to everyone within its jurisdiction the rights and freedoms defined in...the Convention".[1] The Court concluded that, while detention without trial contravened the Convention, there had been no breach of the Convention because the Government had properly derogated from its obligations under the Convention. Primary and seminal issues touching the interpretation of the European Convention were elucidated in the judgment. These pronouncements subsequently impacted on the new and challenging international protection of human rights that was beginning to unfold. Unfortunately, the judgment is flawed for the same reasons that the Commission's report was flawed. The Court ignored an obvious issue of interpretation. This was whether a government's obligations under the Convention had mere territorial effect within that government's state or whether the Convention had a wider European application which obligated all governments to give extra-territorial effect to the Convention. This issue has been totally ignored in the very extensive literature on the Convention published over the years.

Government Preparation for the Court Hearing

As noted in the previous chapter, the Commission and the Government were required to lodge written pleadings. The statement of the Commission was sent to the Government.[2] Within days, a copy of the covering letter, which had been sent with the statement from the President of the Commission to the Court, was forwarded to the Government. It stated that the Commission reiterated that the interpretation of Article 15 of the Convention in the present case raised issues of fundamental importance. The Government was notified in January 1961 that the public hearing on the merits would begin on Friday, 7 April. The archival material suggests that the observations of the Government were prepared within the Department of External Affairs. Prof. Reuter offered advice in a number of letters. In the first, having seen the statement of the Commission and the Government's draft observations, he believed that the comments regarding the Cyprus case would embarrass the Court. While he was of opinion that the Court would have desired that the Commission had not raised them, the Court would not blame them for having done so. He offered assistance on Article 17. In the second letter, he advised that the reply should be very short because the Commission had not submitted many new arguments. The Government should not reply to the views of Lawless and should state that it refused to do so. As a result of telephone conversations between the Department of External Affairs and the Irish Embassy in Paris in which Reuter was a participant, he wrote a third letter expanding on the two issues that were obviously causing the Government continuing concern. The first was the inclusion of the Cyprus material. He stated that the Court would regret that the Commission had taken an attitude that was "aggressive, cutting and clumsy".[3] While not in agreement as regards the method, it would be in agreement on the final objective to be attained. This was to safeguard the individual and to make the procedure flexible. The second issue was the inclusion of Lawless's views. Reuter said that the November judgment was very subtle in that it authorised the Commission to make known, under its own responsibility, Lawless's views, but at the same time hoped that the Commission would not avail of this right. He did not favour raising a request for a preliminary interpretation on this issue. The Department of Justice supplied an outline of Lawless's history, compiled from the various documents and the oral testimony at the sub-Commission hearing[4] and events leading up to the making of the Government proclamation in July 1957. The Attorney General prepared in writing his oral address to the Court. The Commission informed the Government of a list of documents that were to be filed with the Court.

Inclusion of Material from the Cyprus Case

In the statement of the Commission, filed on 16 December 1960, extracts were quoted from the *Greece v United Kingdom* case, with regard to the emergency in Cyprus. The Government, in its observances,[5] noted with concern this reference to *in camera* proceedings and that no authority had been given for the publication of the report in that case, which had been transmitted to the Committee of Ministers on 3 October 1958. The Government envisaged that the two relevant Governments might take exception to the quotation of part of the proceedings. Apart from that objection, the Government was placed at a disadvantage, for without seeing the transcript and the pleadings, it could not know whether the statement attributed to the United Kingdom Government, taken out of context as it was, correctly and fully represented the submissions put forward. Even if possessed of the documentation the Government was not free to use them without the consent of all other contracting states. Unless all reference to these proceedings were deleted, the Government would be unable to proceed with its argument until it had obtained (a) a complete transcript and copies of the pleadings in that case, and (b) the consent of all other contracting states to use these documents in the course of the present case.

Waldock wrote, on 14 March 1961,[6] that the quotation from the Cyprus case was used exclusively with regard to the interpretation of certain provisions of the Convention which fell to be applied also in the Lawless case. According to a well-recognised rule of interpretation, the subsequent conduct of the signatory states with respect to the application of a treaty was, in case of doubt, a relevant element which may be taken into account in determining the meaning of the treaty.[7] The Commission did not attribute to the signatory states an intention to place the Court in a different position from both the Commission and the Committee of Ministers in regard to the availability of legal material that had a bearing on the interpretation of the Convention. Legal views expressed as to the meaning of the Convention when recorded in the reports of the Commission were automatically available to the Commission and to the Committee of Ministers. It would be strange if they were not to be accessible to the Court, the third organ of the Council of Europe. This would result in the Commission being unable, in interpreting the Convention in its report in one case, to refer to the meaning of the same provisions in another case. Such a system would clearly be inimical to the development of a coherent interpretation of the Convention. The Commission could not perceive what objection there could be to referring to the legal contentions of a government recorded in the Commission's report to the Committee of Ministers as to the meaning to be attributed to the Convention. It was natural to assume that governments, when they placed before the Commission their view as to the legal interpretation of the Convention, did so with a full sense of responsibility. They recognised that the interpretation of the Convention was a matter that concerned all the other signatory states and all the peoples within their jurisdictions. Under another well-recognised rule of interpretation, the *travaux preparatoires* of a treaty were, in case of doubt, legal elements that might be taken into account in the interpretation of the treaty. The Government had relied on the *travaux preparatoires* to support its own interpretation of the very provisions of the Convention in regard to which the Commission had referred to the views of the two governments in the Cyprus case. No authority had yet been given for the publication of the *travaux preparatoires* of the Convention, which were still classified as confidential in the archives of the Council of Europe. The Commission did not object to the Government's having recourse to the *travaux preparatoires* though it did not think that the Government's recourse to these was appropriate or legitimate, because the text of the Convention was clear. But this point apart, the Commission was at one with the Government in thinking that, despite their confidential status, recourse may be had to the *travaux preparatoires* for this purpose. The documents in the Cyprus case formed part of the archives of the Commission, an independent organ. The Commission could see no objection to the Government, or the Court, having access to the records in the Cyprus case for the purpose of verifying the contentions of the governments on legal points in that case which also arose in the Lawless case before the Court.

Taking note of the remarks of the Government, and having regard to the desire of the Court to have the proceedings completed at its next session, the Commission was prepared not to rely on the quotation from the Cyprus case. While not deleting the legal material which it considered it was entitled to include, the Commission said that the interpretation contended for was fully supported by the Convention text and the Commission's reasoning in its report in the Lawless case.[8]

Government Fears Audience will be Accorded to Lawless's Counsel

In a letter to Reuter,[9] the Department of External Affairs, having noted that the Commission did not propose to rely on the extracts from the Cyprus case, claimed that this was virtually an admission that such extracts should not have been included. What the Government found particularly irritating was the invitation to, and acceptance by Lawless's counsel "to act as adviser to the delegates at the hearing". The Government could envisage a situation in which it would be endeavoured to secure that Lawless's counsel should be entitled to speak.[10] It was "believed that the Commission had already dropped any pretence of impartiality in this matter and any attempt to secure an audience for Lawless's counsel would be strongly opposed".

European Court of Human Rights Hearing on the Merits

The President of the Court, Lord McNair, held a reception in the Assembly Hall of the Council of Europe on the Wednesday evening at which the Irish representatives attended. The hearing on the merits finally opened on Friday the 7 April[11] and concluded on Tuesday the 11 April 1961. The Chamber of the Court was composed of Judges Cassin (President), Maridakis, Rodenburg, McGonigal, Balladore Pallieri, Arnalds, and Arik, with Rolin as the substitute judge. Lawless did not attend the hearing though Sean MacBride SC was present as the person nominated by him. MacBride sat behind the Commission delegates who consulted him from time to time though he took no actual role in the proceedings.[12] Sir Humphrey Waldock, as principal delegate, made submissions on behalf of the Commission. These were confined to matters of legal interpretation, including Lawless's views of such matters. Waldock did not comment on the appreciation of the facts because, as he explained, the opinions of the members of the Commission were a matter of record and he took this course "on a directive from the Commission itself".[13] This course of action, so publicly stated, may have been a signal to MacBride that the factual findings in the Commission report were not open to review. The Attorney General, Andrias O Caoimh SC,[14] made submissions on behalf of the Government. The first day was taken up with submissions on the remaining procedural question,[15] with the Court pronouncing a decision in the early evening. Saturday morning was occupied with Commission submissions that were carried over to Monday morning when the views of Lawless on legal issues were presented to the Court.[16] Government submissions[17] occupied the Monday afternoon and evening sessions, which included a long and detailed statement on Irish history,[18] submissions on the legal issues,[19] a summary of Lawless's activities, not always an accurate one, and detailed reasons for the introduction of the powers of detention. Pointedly, the claim that the activities of the IRA might have lead to war between the UK and Ireland, an element which weighed decisively with the majority of the Commission,[20] was not pursued before the Court, probably because the hearing was in public. The replies were taken on Tuesday morning.[21]

Having regard to the fundamental issues of substance and of procedure that arose during the exercise of its jurisdiction for the first time, it is extremely difficult to understand why the Chamber did not relinquish jurisdiction in favour of the plenary Court. While it is invidious to compare one case with another when the subject matter of later cases which warranted the attention of the plenary Court are considered, they do pale into insignificance by comparison.[22] It is highly likely that had a plenary Court sat and considered the case it is possible that the final outcome might have been different to the one that resulted. Or, even if the result was the same, at least some divergence of opinion on the various issues might have emerged.[23] Severe criticism has already been levelled at the Commission because of the lack of a proper investigation of the conditions that prevailed in Ireland at the material time. More serious still was the failure to expound some opinion on the interesting and very obvious separate legal issue which was thus raised, whether one government could justify breaches of the Convention because of events taking place in another jurisdiction, a point argued in a previous chapter. By accepting the factual situation it seems that the Court implicitly accepted the principle that signatory states not only owed obligations under the Convention to persons within their own jurisdictions but also owed obligations to all persons residing within the signatory states of the Council of Europe.

The Court based its decision on the Commission's report[24] and did not carry out any independent investigation.[25] The consequences of these serious inadequacies of the Commission are further highlighted and emphasised, and must, in a major way, impugn the judgment of the Court. Instead of subjecting the events to careful analysis, the Court merely depended on the written pleadings and oral submissions. This omission is compounded by the fact that the submissions of the Government on the reasons for the introduction of detention powers went unchallenged. Waldock expressly refused to comment on any factual matter and simply allowed the opinions of the Commission members to stand in this regard, which of course, as detailed in Chapter 7, were fairly evenly divided. It was at this point that the injustice of shutting Lawless out from the Court hearing became particularly acute. The judges did not interrupt the submissions with queries, or if they did, the verbatim record of the proceedings does not register these. The Court seemed content to leave the matter in the hands of the advocates, each of which had a different agenda. Waldock was acting in the greater public interest, and the Attorney General was defending the actions of the Irish Government.

The Court, in reaching the decision it did, performed a very fine balancing act. On the one hand, the Court had to establish itself, in the minds of the general populous of Europe, and indeed far beyond that regional boundary, as a place where the human rights of individuals would be respected and protected. On the other hand, the Court, because its continued existence depended on the goodwill of the governments of Europe, had to be sensitive to the perceived needs of States. There clearly were political considerations at play. The major political powers in Europe had not at that time wholeheartedly embraced the Convention,[26] though conversely representatives from those powerful states had enormous influence on the developing jurisprudence of the Convention. The Court, particularly Cassin, must have been mindful that France had not ratified the Convention[27] and that the United Kingdom had not accepted the Court's jurisdiction.[28] It would have been a most inauspicious beginning, in this first decision, to condemn the action of a government taken when that government perceived, possibly wrongly, that its national security was in danger. Undoubtedly, that was a particular issue that would at all times be an extremely sensitive one for governments. To have held otherwise would probably have stunted the development of the Court and might even have spelled the death-knell for the Convention. To sacrifice individual justice, in its first case, in order to protect the integrity of the institution was a tariff that the Court was prepared to suffer. Consequently, in pandering to governments, the Court guaranteed its continued existence and insured a stronger and respected role for itself in the future. It also gained a certain level of flexibility in its interpretation of the Convention, particularly as regards the status to be accorded to the individual, a development later supported by governments.

Lawless's Influence on the Proceedings

As noted in the previous chapter, Lawless was not accorded any formal status before the Court. Despite this exclusion Lawless continued to exert some influence on the proceedings. The first way this was achieved was by Lawless submitting his observations on the report of the Commission which he considered material for the further consideration of the case by the Court. In turn, an edited version of these observations formed part of the statement of the Commission. By the Court's judgment of 7 April 1960, these observations were not to be considered part of the proceedings and were deleted from the published records of the case[29] though they are available in the unpublished archival records.[30] Despite this ruling, these observations must have been read by the judges prior to their decision to suppress these comments. These observations were substantial, and while issue was taken with a number of factual errors in the Commission's report, the major challenge was to the findings in relation to Article 15, and criticism was made of the finding that a margin of appreciation was available to governments in such situations. Criticism of the application of the law to the facts was made under two broad headings: "majority finding which was unsupported by the evidence" and "majority findings that were contradictory". The second way that Lawless influenced the proceedings was through the submission of his views on the Government's observations. This document is neither available in the published or unpublished records of the case. The third way was through MacBride, who, as already noted, attended the Court hearing to assist the delegates of the Commission. Waldock encapsulated Lawless's views on the legal issues from these various sources and presented them briefly and as accurately as possible to the Court on the last day of the hearing.[31] Waldock said that Lawless, not unnaturally, was afraid that the delegates might experience a certain conflict of interest in explaining his position to the Court, this being a case in which the Commission had found in favour of the Government. This suggestion was not accepted since the sole interest and function of the delegates was to assist the Court in the search for truth.

Comments on the Judgment

Each of the questions the Court sought to answer was examined as to facts, the law and a full debate on the terms of the Convention to be applied. This lead to a rather turgid judgment both in style and content. While the judgment contains a statement of facts, both as regards the background to events in Ireland at the time and in relation to Lawless's activities, it is questionable whether a potted history of the IRA was necessary. There is a recital of provisions of Irish law though some provisions quoted are clearly superfluous.[32] The written and oral pleadings are repeated together with considerable paraphrasing of the Commission's. Whilst the judgment contains some judicial reasoning, on which the conclusions of the Court are based, some of the voluminous repetition could have been sacrificed in return for the inclusion of a greater elucidation of judicial reasoning. This would not in any way have affected the impact of the decision. The shortage and lack of breath of such reasoning is disappointing to the common law jurist. The probable blame for which rests with the influence which the continental jurists, particularly Cassin as President of the Chamber,[33] had on the composition of the judgment.

The single most disappointing feature of the judgement is its unanimity. It is difficult to envisage such uniform agreement among such a diverse group of jurists, bearing in mind that the Commission members from similar diverse backgrounds were so evenly divided. The fact that it was a mere Chamber of the Court which rendered a decision rather than the plenary Court has already been noted. There may be two reasons to blame for such an outcome. The first is that courts of similar status in continental countries, or courts such the European Court of Justice, may be obliged to render a single unitary judgment. This practice may have been invoked in this tribunal despite the express provision that each judge was entitled to deliver a separate opinion.[34] The reasoning behind such a rule is the perceived need for certainty, authority and credibility. The second reason may have been the adoption of caution and wariness since this, the first judgment of the Court, would be eagerly awaited and would have a great influence on the emerging jurisprudence, and accordingly, division and disagreement was to be avoided if that was possible.

Various Canons of Construction used in the Judgment

The Court in its judgment resorted to a number of canons of interpretation. The first of these, the literal interpretation, demanded that a treaty be interpreted in good faith according to the ordinary meaning attributable to its terms: the text illustrates the common intention of the parties. The Court, when looking at Article 15, spoke of the "natural and customary meaning of the words" and when examining Article 5 declared that "the plain and natural meaning...follow[ed] from the precise words used...". This literal rule was used in conjunction with the systematic approach which demanded that the words should be understood "from the impression created by their context...".[35] The Court confirmed this literal interpretation by referring to the *travaux preparatoires*. It noted that "the preparatory work...leaves no room for doubt about the intention of the authors of the Convention...".[36] The teleological interpretation looked to the purpose and objective of a treaty. The Court resorted to this canon of construction when looking at Article 5, when it stated that "whereas the meaning thus arrived at by the grammatical analysis is fully in harmony with the purpose of the Convention...".[37] The Court also looked to "the purpose" of Article 17.[38] In addition, the Court referred to the French text of the Convention[39] to confirm its interpretation of Article 5 in the English text.

Judgment of the European Court of Human Rights

The Chamber of the Court unanimously decided,[40] on 1 July 1961, that the facts as found did not disclose a breach by the Government of its obligations under the European Convention for the Protection of Human

Rights and Fundamental Freedoms. The judgment of the Court, read by the President of the Chamber, Judge Rene Cassin, was done in French and in English, the French text alone being authentic.[41] The Attorney General was present, as were the Commission delegates. The published material notes that the Chamber examining the Lawless case met twice to deliberate, the first time in Paris from 26 to 30 May, and the second time in Strasbourg from 26 to 27 June 1961.[42]

Article 17 of the Convention

Waldock said[43] that the Commission had not made an express finding that Lawless was personally engaged in IRA activities. It was unanimously of the opinion that, even if that were true, Article 17[44] did not preclude him from claiming the protections, nor did it relieve the Government from observing Articles 5 and 6. Article 17 was one of those negative clauses found in international agreements that made a reservation. It provided that nothing was to justify the implication from the language of the Convention of any right to engage in certain activities. It could not be used to authorise a government to treat any person who engaged in such activities as outside the law. A contrary view would involve the proposition that once established as a fact that the person fell within the scope of Article 17, he was, so far as the Convention was concerned, outside the law. Could he then be tortured and shot without trial? Admittedly, that was a *reductio ad absurdum.* Persons were easily accused of activities against the state and it was easily said that such activities were against human rights and it was easy for persons to be put in prison for long periods on the supposition that they engaged in such activities. If that was done under the law of the state, under exceptional powers, under a special law, then it was not *reductio ad absurdum*. The Commission did not conceive that the signatory states, with laws based on the rule of law, could have intended to lay down so drastic and extraordinary a principle. The Court could not legitimately derive such a principle from Article 17 which was cautious in language and made clear that it was not its purpose to give authority to states to set aside all the guarantees in the Convention. Article 17 contained an express principle that a person could not derive from the Convention a right to engage in activities aimed at the destruction of rights. It was expressly aimed at the attempt to derive, from such rights as freedom of association and freedom of expression, a right to engage in such objectionable activities. That was the point raised in the *German Communist Party* case, where the domestic courts had established, as a matter of proof, that the aims of that party assumed the form of an activity which fell within Article 17. The recital in the Commission's decision on admissibility was widely stated. It was that the party could not "rest upon any provision of the Convention, least of all on Article 9, 10 and 11".[45] While the Commission conceded that statement was widely framed, when looked at very closely, its impact was essentially intended in the fields of expression and association. The Commission recommended that the Court should take this view of Article 17.

The Attorney General argued[46] that Article 17 was not very explicit in its terms. Its intention was that those who engaged in activities aimed at the destruction of the Convention rights were deprived, not of their rights under the Convention, but of their right to invoke the Convention for the purpose of securing those rights. A state, group or person engaged in the activities indicated in Article 17 was precluded from relying on any provision of the Convention, and that contention was supported by the express decision in the *German Communist Party* case. The Commission, in explaining the difference between that case and the Lawless case, said that this was "not a case of the same type" without any elaboration. It also said that if the view of the Government was accepted, it would be permissible to shoot without trial, to torture persons, or to imprison indefinitely persons so engaged and to do that even when there was no war or other public emergency. The Government contended that this lurid picture of the total collapse of the rule of law was without foundation and sensing that these suggestions were out of place the Commission then said that this was a *reductio ad absurdum*. Where Article 17 applied, there was no question of the abandonment by a government of the rule of law and a government was not relieved from the obligations to ensure that its code of conduct was in accordance with the Convention. Article 17 placed outside the protection of the Convention those engaged in certain activities. It was clear that the Commission and the Government differed radically on the meaning of Article 17. The Attorney General outlined Lawless's activities in great detail[47] though not with complete accuracy.[48] He then asked could it be doubted that the detention of such a person was reasonably necessary to prevent him committing offences? Nor could it be doubted that he was one of those persons, who, by their activities, had deprived themselves under Article 17 of the right of recourse to any provision of the Convention? The Commission had omitted to arrive at a finding on this most crucial point, and while not critical, it was a little strange that the body charged with the duty of ascertaining the facts should have failed to make a determination on this essential fact. The Government contended it was a material fact which should be ascertained and that the answer was clear and that the Court ought to have no doubt in arriving at a decision on it.

Court Decision

The Court was of opinion[49] that the purpose of Article 17 was to make it impossible to derive from the Convention a right to perform any act aimed at destroying the rights in the Convention. Consequently, no person could take advantage of the Convention to perform acts aimed at destroying these various rights. This negative provision could not be construed *a contrario* as depriving a person of the fundamental rights guaranteed by Articles 5 and 6. Lawless had not relied on the Convention to justify or perform acts contrary to these rights but complained of being deprived of the guarantees in Articles 5 and 6. The plea advanced by the Government on Article 17 of the Convention was dismissed.[50]

Article 5 of the Convention

Waldock said[51] that Article 5 (1) (c) was in the clearest and most unequivocal terms and only authorised lawful arrest or detention for the purpose of bringing the person before a competent legal authority. This was entirely and inescapably confirmed by Article 5 (3) that expressly referred back to sub-paragraph (1) (c). When both were read together they were unambiguous and there was no vestige of doubt left as to what the text authorised. Detention without trial was not for the purpose of bringing a person before a competent judicial authority. Accordingly, the Commission found that this measure was not authorised under Article 5 (1).

The Government argued[52] that Article 5 (1) (c) was limited to cases where the arrest or detention was reasonably necessary to prevent the commission of an offence. Article 5 (3) did not apply to this kind of case because such an arrest could not be followed by a trial for a criminal offence. Article 5 (1) (c) related to cases where the evidence was not such as would enable the person to be charged. In that limited class of case it was possible to detain him for the purpose of preventing the commission of an offence and the provision about bringing a person before a judicial authority did not apply.

Court Decision

The Court noted[53] that the question referred to it was whether or not, in Article 5 (1) (c), the expression "effected for the purpose of bringing him before the competent judicial authority" qualified only the words "on reasonable suspicion of having committed an offence" or also the words "when it is reasonably considered necessary to prevent his committing an offence". The wording was sufficiently clear and it was evident that the expression "effected for the purpose of bringing him before the competent legal authority" qualified every category of arrest or detention. The clause permitted deprivation of liberty for the purpose of bringing the person arrested or detained before the competent judicial authority. That was irrespective of whether such person was reasonably suspected of having committed an offence, or it was reasonably considered necessary to restrain him from committing an offence, or was reasonably considered necessary to restrain him from absconding after having committed an offence. Article 5 (1) (c) could be construed only in conjunction with Article 5 (3), with which it formed a whole, and which stipulated categorically that "everyone arrested or detained in accordance with Article 5 (1) (c) shall be promptly brought before a judge..." and "shall be entitled to trial within a reasonable time". This plainly entailed the obligation to bring everyone arrested or detained in any of the circumstances contemplated by Article 5 (1) (c) before a judge for the purpose of examining the question of deprivation of liberty or for the purpose of deciding on the merits. This was the plain and natural meaning of Article 5 (1) (c) and (3), a grammatical analysis fully in harmony with the purpose of the Convention, which was to protect the freedom and security of the individual against arbitrary detention or arrest. If this construction was not correct then anyone suspected of harbouring an intention to commit an offence could be arrested and detained for an unlimited period on the strength merely of an executive decision without its being possible to regard this arrest or detention as a breach of the Convention. Such an assumption, with all its implications of arbitrary power, would lead to conclusions repugnant to the fundamental principles of the Convention. The detention of Lawless was not "effected for the purpose of bringing him before the competent legal authority" and during his detention he was not brought before a judge for trial "within a reasonable time". It followed that his detention without trial was contrary to Article 5 (1) (c).[54]

Article 7 of the Convention

The common case was made that Article 7 was inapplicable. Waldock said[55] that the Commission had unanimously concluded that Article 7 had no application because Lawless was not detained as a result of a conviction on a criminal charge. His detention without trial could not be regarded as a heavier penalty within the meaning of Article 7, because it had not the character of a penalty. The Commission felt that detention without trial was, in substance as well as in form, a preventative measure which could not legitimately be brought within the scope of the mischief that Article 7 was intended to forbid. The Attorney General agreed[56] with the report of the Commission that Article 7 was of no relevance.

Court Decision

The Court noted[57] that Lawless was detained for the sole purpose of restraining him from engaging in activities prejudicial to the preservation of public peace and order or the security of the State. That being a preventative measure it could not be deemed to be due to his having been held guilty of a criminal offence. It followed that Article 7 had no bearing on the case.[58]

Article 15 (1) of the Convention

The Commission said in its statement to the Court that it had been unanimous[59] in holding that it always had the competence to examine into and to express its own appreciation of a government's determination as to the existence of a public emergency and as to whether the measures taken were strictly required by the exigencies of the situation. That stand had been taken previously in *Greece v United Kingdom.* The United Kingdom Government stated that it was:

> …never suggested [that] it is beyond the competence of this Commission to form a view on the existence of an emergency and similarly...that this Commission is not competent to form a view on the necessity of the measures required to meet the emergency. But...the Government of the territory is in the best position to judge whether an emergency threatening the life of the nation has arisen. That is a question on which governments always tend to reserve their own discretion, and...it would be very, very risky if the Commission were not at least to lean very favourably towards the opinion of the Government, because the Government has in its possession all the relevant information, much of which must, in the nature of things, be subject to security classifications, and the same considerations apply to the measures which have to be taken to meet the emergency...the Commission should not examine too critically what a Government has considered necessary to meet an emergency…[60]

At the hearing Waldock said[61] that many Commission members recognised, though perhaps to a varying degree, that some discretion and some margin of appreciation had to be allowed to a government in determining these questions. All the members agreed that objective criteria must be applied, meaning that it was only after certain minimum objective conditions had been established that the principle of the margin of appreciation came into play. The Government challenged the doctrine of the margin of appreciation as being too unfavourable to it while, before the Commission, Lawless contented for a restrictive interpretation that would leave either no room for any margin of appreciation or only the smallest conceivable margin. This was one of the questions that led the Commission especially to bring this matter before the Court.

The Commission majority recognised that the good faith of a government was an important element but it was definite in its opinion that Article 15 laid down objective criteria and established minimum conditions that must be satisfied before the exceptional power to derogate may be invoked. An acceptance of this view did not mean that the opinion of the Court or the Commission was substituted for that of the government. But it did mean that the opinion of either of these bodies were superimposed on the determination by a government as a check upon any misuse of its exceptional power to put in abeyance fundamental rights. The Convention left the determination of these issues solely within the discretion of the government concerned and therefore within its own unaided judgement as to whether the conditions that existed required it to have recourse to Article 15. The Commission said that if a such a determination was subsequently challenged, the Commission and the Court were empowered to make their own appreciation as to whether the government had kept within the limits of discretion conferred on it by Article 15. This might mean the Commission or the Court concluding that the government had not legally, under international law, been justified in resorting to Article 15. There was nothing that compelled the Court to read into Article 15 a limitation of the functions of the Commission or of the Court to that of appreciating a government's good faith. Wherever a treaty or customary rules of international law left a matter within the discretionary powers of a government, it remained a normal task of an international tribunal to appreciate whether in exercising its discretionary powers a government had kept within the limits delineated and defined in the treaty or in the customary rule of international law. The Commission did not feel that sufficient grounds had been advanced by the Government for asking the Court to imply this doctrine of good faith and thus to limit the examination by the Commission or the Court to this question of good faith.

Recourse to Article 15 involved temporarily putting into abeyance the most fundamental guarantees of the rule of law and the maintenance of democracy. It was often in times of disturbance and danger, which may have their source in political tensions, that these guarantees assumed their greatest importance. Recourse to arbitrary powers may often appear to be, and actually be, the simplest and speediest way for a government to put down a disturbance. But the Commission, as defender of the public interest, felt that to recognise a government's power too easily to adopt this simpler course of resort to special powers would undermine to too great a degree the guarantees of human rights enshrined in the Convention. The intention of Article 15 was to trace definite limits, definite objective conditions, by reference to which any resource to exceptional powers had to be justified. The Commission recognised that whether or not exceptional powers were employed involved problems of appreciation and timing for a government that may be most difficult in a democracy, where governments were always susceptible to the impact of public opinion. It recognised that the government had to balance the ills involved in a temporary restrictions of fundamental rights against the risks of a situation deteriorating with even worse consequences for the people and perhaps larger diminution of fundamental rights, if it was to put the situation right again.

Waldock noted[62] that Lawless said that there was nothing expressed in the Convention of this doctrine of the margin of appreciation and thus this was ruled out by the express terminology of Article 15, a view reflected in the opinions of the minority of the Commission. Lawless reinforced this by saying that if the more liberal view were really intended the Council of Europe states would have said so.

The Attorney General noted[63] that the Government approved the decision of the Commission that a public emergency existed in Ireland in 1957 and that the measures taken were permitted under the Convention. But it criticised the method adopted in arriving at its decision that recognised that some discretion and some margin of appreciation must be allowed to governments though the nature of the discretion went undefined and the measure of appreciation unmeasured. Article 15 was vital for governments when there was an emergency and the conditions under which it can be availed of must be such that, if some unusual steps were not taken, most likely to be arrived at with speed, serious consequences might follow. An examination of the Convention showed the idea of legitimate defence of the State. How was Article 15 to be construed as to be an effective provision available to governments, without being a weapon that could be abused by governments? When a government realised that there was an emergency, a delay in such circumstances might mean submission to destructive elements and might lead to the obliteration of the rights that the Convention sought to safeguard. When ultimately that action came under review, the Commission seemed to suggest that if, by a majority of a single vote, the Commission held that there was no emergency or that the measures taken were inappropriate, a government must be penalised and subjected to international odium. A government in that event might refrain from taking measures. If as a result a non-democratic group seized power, and the rights of citizens were suppressed, would not those who were essentially interested in human rights be the first to condemn the government for the failure to take adequate steps to protect rights? It must have been intended that governments in those circumstances should not be afraid to act in the manner which prudence dictated though they must not disregard their duty to safeguard the fundamental human rights guaranteed by the Convention.[64]

The Government had not adopted the view that once a government made a determination, the Court could not question that, though there were eminent jurists who supported the proposition that it was for the government alone to decide when an emergency existed and the measures taken to deal with it. It was open to the Court, as it was open to the Commission, to determine in every case whether a government had acted in good faith and this provided an important control over governments. If the Court, having reviewed the matter, came to the conclusion that a government had acted in bad faith in determining that an emergency existed, or that the measures taken were unnecessary, the Court should hold that reliance on Article 15 would not be permitted. This gave an important control over the decision of governments as to when and how derogation may be used, and it was an adequate control to prevent abuse. A government, having acted in good faith, might arrive at a determination that was wholly unreasonable. This was an argument that would be frequently heard from an individual though not from responsible bodies such as the Commission that had not put forward the argument that a government might act in a manner which was wholly unreasonable. But if it was thought that such eventuality was possible there was a formula that was a reasonable way to deal with the situation and would provide a reasonable guard against the actions of a foolish or reckless government. If the Court would not accept the view that the determination of a government shown to be acting in good faith should be left unquestioned, then an alternative test might be as follows. If, upon a consideration of all the relevant facts and circumstances it was shown that a *prima facie* case existed to support the judgement of the government and if that judgement was shown to have been arrived at in good faith then the judgement of the government should not be open to question. This gave control over the decision of a government that an emergency existed, or what measures were taken to deal with it. A government, when its decision was questioned, should satisfy the Court that (i) a *prima facie* case warranted its decision existed, and (ii) it had acted in good faith. Beyond this the Court ought not to go in declaring what was the burden to be imposed on governments. This was not very far removed from the position of the Commission. In putting forwards these arguments, the Government was trying to avoid a declaration of the law that would be too restrictive of the actions of governments. The Government was conscious that on the facts, which would be disclosed to the Court, and judged by the most severe standard, the Government's decision in this case ought to be upheld.

Court Decision

Derogation reviewable The Court noted[65] that it followed from Article 15 that, without being released from all undertakings assumed in the Convention, a government had the right, in case of war or public emergency threatening the life of the nation, to take derogating measures, provided that such measures were strictly limited to what was required by the exigencies of the situation, and also that they did not conflict with other obligations under international law. It is for the Court to determine whether the conditions laid down in Article 15 for the exercise of the exceptional right of derogation had been fulfilled.

Definition of "public emergency threatening the life of the nation" It is necessary to quote from both the English and French texts, the latter being the authentic text, because the wording of each is different. According to the English text, the natural and customary meaning of these words was sufficiently clear. They referred to "an exceptional situation of crisis or emergency which affected the whole population and constituted a threat to the organised life of the community of which the State was composed". The French text reads: "une situation de crise ou de danger exceptionel *et imminent* (missing from the English translation) qui affecte l'ensemble de la population et constitue une menace pour la vie organisee de la communaute composant l'Etat."[66] Thus, the Court adopted, using slightly more refined language, the definition supported by the majority of the Commission.

Public emergency existed The Court found that the existence of a public emergency was reasonably deduced by the Government from a combination of several factors, such as (a) the existence in the territory of a secret army engaged in unconstitutional activities and using violence to attain its purposes, and (b) the fact that by operating outside the territory this army seriously jeopardised the relations of the Irish State with its neighbour, and (c) the steady and alarming increase in terrorist activities from the end of 1956 and throughout the first half of 1957. Despite the gravity of the situation, the Government had succeeded, by using ordinary legislation, in keeping public institutions functioning more or less normally. But the homicidal ambush on 4 July in Northern Ireland near the border, just before 12 July, a date, which, for historical reasons was particularly critical for the preservation of public peace and order, highlighted the imminent danger to the nation caused by the continuance of unlawful activities in Northern Ireland by the IRA and various associated groups, operating from the territory of the Irish State.

Measures taken were strictly required The Court concluded that the Government was justified in declaring that there was a public emergency threatening the life of the nation and entitled, applying Article 15 (1), to take measures derogating from its obligations under the Convention. The application of the ordinary law in 1957 had, in the judgment of the Court, proved unable to check the growing danger that threatened the Irish State. The ordinary criminal courts, or even special courts or military courts, could not have sufficed to restore peace and order. The amassing of necessary evidence to convict persons involved in IRA activities and its splinter groups was meeting with great difficulties caused by the military, secret and terrorist character of those groups and the fear they created among the population. The fact that these groups operated mainly in Northern Ireland, their activities in the State being virtually limited to the preparation of armed raids across the border, was an additional impediment to the gathering of sufficient evidence. The sealing of the border would have had extremely serious repercussions on the population as a whole, beyond the extent required by the exigencies of the emergency. None of these means would have made it possible to deal with the situation. Therefore, the administrative detention of individuals suspected of intending to take part in terrorist activities appeared, despite its gravity, to be a measure required by the circumstances, a measure which was subject to a number of safeguards designed to prevent abuses in its operation. The application of the statute was subject to constant parliamentary supervision, which not only received precise details of its enforcement at regular intervals but could also at any time, by a resolution, annul the executive proclamation that brought the statute into force. A Detention Commission must be established to which a detained person could refer his case and whose opinion, if favourable, was binding on the Government, and this body could be compelled by the ordinary courts to carry out its functions. Immediately after the introduction of detention, the Government publicly announced that it would release any detained person who gave an undertaking to respect the Constitution and the law and not to engage in any illegal activity. The wording of this undertaking was later altered to one that merely required the individual to refrain from activities contrary to certain laws. The detained persons were informed immediately after their arrest that they would be released following the undertaking in question. In a democratic country such as Ireland the existence of this guarantee of release given publicly by the Government constituted a legal obligation to release all persons who gave the undertaking.[67] With regard to Lawless there was nothing to show the Court that the powers of detention were employed against him, either for a purpose other than that for which they were granted, or by virtue of a measure going beyond what was strictly required by the situation at the time.

Lawless's position The Commission had observed that the general conduct of Lawless, his association with persons known to be active IRA members, his conviction for carrying incriminating documents and other circumstances, were such as to draw on himself the gravest suspicion that, whether or not he was any longer a member, he was still concerned with IRA activities at the time of his arrest. The Government had informed Lawless at the beginning of his detention that he would be released if he gave a written undertaking to respect the Constitution and the laws and not to be a member of or assist any organisation that was an unlawful organisation. This offer was renewed in a different form and was accepted by Lawless when he gave a verbal undertaking not to take part in any activities that were illegal under certain statutes. He was immediately released.

Conclusion The Court stated that Lawless's detention was founded on the right of derogation duly exercised by the Government under Article 15.[68]

Article 15 (3) of the Convention

The Commission[69] hesitated to say that the right of a state to justify its actions may never be affected by its failure to keep the Secretary General of the Council of Europe informed. The aim of the signatory states was to establish a system of collective enforcement of a collective guarantee of human rights. Article 15 (3) was a vital link in the effectiveness of this system. The Commission had made its reservation simply out of a cautious reluctance to pronounce in advance of the concrete case calling for a pronouncement on this issue. The Government had accepted this conclusion and only raised the point whether, in some circumstances, a failure to comply with Article 15 (3) might attract the sanction of nullity, or some other sanction. It took the position that such a failure could not, in any circumstances, affect the validity of a government's measures even if these constituted a violation of the obligation in Article 15 (3). This was an interesting question but was not one that justifiably called for an urgent anticipatory answer.

Waldock said that Lawless had challenged the right of the Government to rely on the letter of 20 July 1957 as a notice of derogation on a number of grounds. The first was that it had not been forwarded with the intention of filing a genuine notice of derogation but only of doing so if the Government afterwards found such a notice to be necessary. It had not been pleaded in the domestic courts and it had not been notified to Dail Eireann until 23 October 1957.[70] The Commission considered this contention to be misconceived. The second contention was that the notice of derogation was defective. This was so because it did not give, as a reason for the introduction of detention without trial, that a time of war or other public emergency existed. Also the nature of the measure was not correctly stated in that it said that detention was necessary to prevent the commission of offences while the statute empowered detention where a person was engaged in certain activities. The Commission considered that this complaint was groundless in that the text of the statute had been annexed to the letter. The Commission thought that the notice was open to criticism because it did not indicate with sufficient clearness the reasons that had led the Government to derogate from the Convention. The Commission held that the measures taken could not be regarded as invalidated merely by the reason of this criticism. Lawless made a new point[71] which was that the Commission ought to have held that the Government's act of derogation was ineffective and not binding until 23 October 1957, the first date it was published and came to the knowledge of persons in Ireland. Lawless was of the view that unless the Secretary General was notified of acts of derogation with reasonable promptitude and with reasonable detail, the other signatory states could not appreciate their position. Also that if a contracting state took a measure which was in apparent conflict with the Convention, the citizens of such a state were likewise unable to appreciate their position under the law if there had not been a promulgation of the notice of derogation.[72] The Commission was doubtful how far this new legal point deserved the Court's consideration. The Commission was of opinion that this point had no basis in Article 15 (3). That article only spoke of keeping the Secretary General fully informed to ensure the effectiveness of the system of collective guarantee on the international level. It could not offer a ground for implying that they intended also to impose on signatory states an obligation to promulgate a notice of derogation within their respective domestic jurisdictions. If the signatory states had so intended they would have said so.

The Attorney General said[73] that while the Commission had unanimously decided that the Government had complied with its obligations under Article 15 (3) it added a reservation that was a little unfortunately worded. It conveyed the impression that the Commission questioned in a serious way what the position of a government would be in the event of a notice being inadequate. Since it now appeared that the Commission did not intend to do so and merely wished to have the question left open, the Government did not wish to force a decision on a matter which the Commission considered undesirable to have decided. The contention of Lawless that until the Government announced in Dail Eireann that it had notified the Secretary General the Government should not be entitled to avail of the measures of derogation taken under Article 15 (1) had been adequately demonstrated by the Commission to be completely without foundation. He endorsed what had been said in respect of that point.

Court Decision

The Court stated[74] that it was called upon to examine whether, in pursuance of Article 15 (3), the Secretary General of the Council of Europe was duly informed both of the measures taken and of the reasons therefor. A copy of the 1940 Act and the proclamation were attached to the letter in which it had been explained that the measures were taken in order to prevent the commission of offences against public peace and order and to prevent the maintaining of military or armed forced other than those authorised by the Constitution. The Government thereby gave sufficient information of the measures taken and the reasons therefor and this information was forwarded only twelve days after the entry into force of the measures taken and that accordingly notification was made without delay. The Convention did not contain any special provision to the effect that the State concerned must promulgate in its territory the notice of derogation. The Court accordingly found that the Government fulfilled its obligation under Article

15 (3) and that the letter of 20 July 1957 constituted sufficient notification within the meaning of Article 15 (3).[75]

Notes

[1] Article 1 of the Convention.

[2] AG File SR 54/38.

[3] "Une agressive, tranchante et maladroite."

[4] Attorney General File SR 54/38.

[5] Lawless Case. ECHR 1960-61. Series B. pp.338-329.

[6] Ibid. pp.344-347.

[7] Competence of the International Labour Organisation, Series B, No.2, p.40; International Status of South-West Africa, 1950 ICJR 135.

[8] As a result of these, and later, objections (see pp.222-225) when Lawless case, Series B. came to be published, p.324 notes that "By decision of the President, the passage in this statement where the Commission referred to the position taken by the two Governments concerned in the (non-public) proceedings before the Commission concerning Application No.176/56 (Greece v United Kingdom) has been deleted [cf. Observations of the Government of Ireland (31 January1961) and the letter form the President of the Commission (14 March 1961)]".

[9] DFA File 417/39/19/4/2. Part 6.

[10] Rules of Court, Rule 37 provided that "the President of the Chamber shall direct the hearing. He shall prescribe the order in which the agent, the advocates or advisers of the parties and delegates of the Commission, as well as any other person appointed by them in accordance with Rule 29 (1) shall be called upon to speak".

[11] The President of the Chamber met the AG and Commission delegates on Thursday evening to discuss the arrangements for the hearing.

[12] The published material of the hearing does not acknowledge the presence of MacBride or Ciaran McAnally, solicitor for Lawless.

[13] Lawless case. Series B. p.398.

[14] Reuter was not part of the legal team at this hearing.

[15] Lawless Case. op.cit. pp. 357-374.

[16] Ibid. pp.405-414.

[17] Ibid. pp.414-476.

[18] Ibid. pp.418-426.

[19] Ibid. pp.427-467.

[20] See p.136.

[21] Lawless case. op.cit. pp.468-475 and pp. 483-492.

[22] When considering its third case, the Belgian Linguistic case, the Chamber relinquished jurisdiction to the plenary Court. Series A. (5) 1967 p.4.

[23] Ibid. The Court declared that the Convention had been breached but only by 8 votes to 7.

[24] Lawless case. op.cit. para.27, p.56 and para.34, p.57.

[25] Rules of Courts, Rule 38 (2) provided that "the Court may, at any time during the proceedings, depute one or more of its members to conduct an inquiry, to carry out an investigation on the spot or to obtain information in any manner".

[26] France and United Kingdom were permanent members of the UN Security Council.

[27] France only ratified the Convention and accepted the jurisdiction of the Court in April 1974. Whether France (and the UK) should have had a judge on the Court when those countries had not accepted the Court's jurisdiction is debatable.

[28] Did so only in 1966. Italy, Greece and Turkey were in similar situations.

[29] Lawless case. op.cit. p.336.

[30] DJ File S/9/58/23. (1993 Release).

[31] Lawless Case. op.cit. pp.405-414.

[32] e.g. section 30 of the Offences Against the State Act 1939, pp.32-33.

[33] Eustathiades was of the opinion that Cassin wrote the judgment: see YBECHR. The Greek Case. 1969, para.182, p.82.

[34] Article 51 (2) of the Convention. The Irish Supreme Court is bound to implement such a practice in certain circumstances: Articles 26.2.2° and 34.4.5° of the Constitution.

[35] Lawless case. Series A. p.52.

[36] Ibid. p.50.

[37] Ibid. p.52.

[38] Ibid. p.44.

[39] Ibid. pp.47 and 51.

[40] Lawless case. Series A. para.48, p.62. Judge Maridakis, while concurring with the operative part of the judgment, annexed an individual opinion, pp.64-67.

[41] Lawless case. Series A. para.48, p.63.

[42] YBECHR (4) 1961. p.96.

[43] Lawless Case. Series B, pp.398-404 and 481-482. Commission's memorial, paras.44-46, pp.204-205; Commission's statement, paras.13-18, pp.329-332.

[44] See Appendix 1 for articles of the Convention.

[45] YBECHR 1955-56-57, pp.222-225. The decision was given only in French: "Considerant qu'il resulte de tout ce qui precede que la requete du Parti Communiste ne peut s'appuyer sur une disposition de la Convention et notamment sur les Articles 9, 10 et 11 de celle-ci."

[46] Lawless Case. Series B. pp.433-438. Government's counter-memorial, para.13, pp.228-229; Government's observations, para.5, pp.339-340.

[47] Ibid. pp. 468-475.

[48] Ibid. For example, the AG told the Court that Lawless "joined the lawful forces of the Armed Forces of the State" (p.468), which gave the impression that he was a full-time soldier, subject to rigorous military discipline. In fact, Lawless had enlisted in the Army reserve (see p. 29 of this book), which was part-time and where attendance tended to be rather casual. The AG said Lawless was discharged in 1956 (p.468). While technically correct, Lawless had in fact ceased attending parades in late 1955. The AG repeated the police information that Lawless was implicated in an armed raid on an explosive store (p.470) but failed to mention that Lawless had accounted for this movements for that time and was never charged (p.32 of this book), that he denied involvement in his affidavit read to the Detention Commission (see p. 57 of this book) and that the AG himself, when he had

the opportunity to cross-examine Lawless on this issue before the sub-Commission, did not deliberately it seems, do so. (see pp.113-117 of this book).

49 Lawless Case. Series A. pp. 44-46.

50 Ibid. p.62.

51 Lawless Case. Series B. pp.375-381. Commission's memorial, paras.28-29, p.201; Commission's statement, paras.5-12, pp.325-329.

52 Ibid. pp.427-432. Government's counter-memorial, paras.9-10,pp.222-224; Government's observations, para.4, p.339.

53 Lawless Case. Series A. pp. 46-51.

54 Ibid. p.62.

55 Lawless Case. Series B. pp.381-383. Commission's memorial, paras.30-31, p.201.

56 Ibid. p.433. Government's counter-memorial, para.10, p.224; Government's observations, para.3, p.339.

57 Lawless Case. Series A. pp.53-54.

58 Ibid. p.62.

59 Lawless case. Series B. Commission's memorial, paras.23-26, pp.199-200; Commission's statement, paras.19-25, pp.332-334.

60 This is the material quoted by the Commission and objected to by the Government. It was only published as late as 1997. See Human Rights Law Journal. vol.18, No.9.12, p.382.

61 Lawless case. Series B. pp.392-396.

62 Ibid. pp.396-397.

63 Ibid. pp.439-445. Government's counter-memorial, para.11, pp.224-227; Government's observations, para.6, pp.340-341.

64 While the AG must here have been speaking generally, there may have been the veiled suggestion that the IRA, in the circumstances that pertained in Ireland during that period, posed a threat to democratic order. If this was so, then it is yet another wild and exaggerated example of how the Government portrayed events in Ireland at that time.

65 Lawless Case. Series A. pp.54-60.

66 For a discussion on this point, see p. 245.

67 Whether these were adequate safeguards, see p.147.

68 Lawless case. Series A. p.62.

69 Lawless Case. Series B. pp.384-391. Commission's memorial, paras.33-34, p.202; Commission's statement, paras.26-29, pp.334-336.

70 See p.39.

71 Lawless Case. Series B. pp.390-391.

72 BPRO. FO.371/154531/1732/15. Lawless's solicitor wrote, on 8 September 1960, to the Commonwealth Relations Office in London, to ascertain what procedure had been adopted in the various colonial territories when derogation was made under the Convention. A reply was made that, apart from informing the Council of Europe, it was "...not the practice for the Colonial Governments concerned to publish such notifications...".

73 Lawless case. Series B. pp. 438-439. Government's counter-memorial, para.12, pp.227-228; Government's observations, para.7, pp.341-342.

74 Lawless Case. Series A. pp.60-62.

75 Ibid. pp.62-63.

11 Postscript

Introduction

The pronouncement by the European Court of Human Rights of its judgment in the Lawless case brought the judicial aspects of these events to a close. However, there remained some outstanding matters that are considered in this chapter.

Reactivation of Special Courts to Quell Political Violence

The IRA border campaign faltered somewhat in 1960. Despite this lull, the following year opened with the killing of a police officer in Northern Ireland, and while there was a lapse during the summer months, there was the killing of another police officer on 12 November 1961.[1] Protests from London, Belfast and Dublin followed. The Government[2] considered the situation and decided that as the campaign of violence was continuing, and as trial by jury was not feasible for "political" offences, and the punishments inflicted by the District Court were not adequate, it was necessary to take new measures. Accordingly, the Government[3] took steps, on 22 November 1961, to enable the Special Criminal Court[4] to once again function by the appointment of additional members drawn from the Defence Forces. Speaking in Dail Eireann, on 23 November 1961, the Taoiseach, Sean Lemass, said:

> …the Government was determined to do everything in their power to bring these acts of violence to an end. As existing measures have not yet succeeded in the purpose we have decided that it is now necessary to strengthen them...the only cases which will be brought before the Special Criminal Court will be those arising from the armed conspiracy of violence. I hope that these special measures...will be effective in dealing with the situation but if they do not prove to be so, the Government will not hesitate to take still further steps…[5]

While detention without trial was not expressly referred to, it was hinted at, though how serious an option it was, is considered in the next chapter. Already, the first lesson learned from the Lawless case was implemented.

That was that detention powers could only be used as a last resort. Between 27 November 1961 and 25 January 1962, the Special Criminal Court, sitting in a military barracks, convicted and sentenced 30 persons to terms of imprisonment ranging from four months to eight years.[6] When the Government was satisfied, on 2 October 1962, that the ordinary courts were once again adequate to secure the effective administration of justice and the preservation of the public peace, the Special Criminal Court ceased to function.[7] This episode tends to prove that special courts were an adequate response to political violence and, consequently, these should have been used during the period under review in this work, before detention powers were invoked. That being so, the argument which the Government used against the establishment of special courts, in the Lawless case, was seriously undermined. Thus, the European Court and the Commission majority made an incorrect appreciation of the situation and granted too wide a margin of appreciation to the Government. Accordingly, Lawless's argument, together with the opinions of the Commission minority, with hindsight, stood vindicated.

Termination of IRA Campaign

When the IRA perceived that the Government was intent on taking drastic measures to scotch the continuing campaign, the IRA Army Council, on 26 February 1962, issued a statement calling off the border campaign that had begun on 12 December 1956.[8]

De Jure Ending of Detention without Trial

The Minister for Justice, in a memorandum to Government,[9] in March 1962, set out the background to the bringing into effect of Part II of the Offences Against the State (Amendment) Act 1940, and the powers of detention without trial it conferred. He noted that while the:

> ...exercise of the powers of detention had been challenged before the Commission of Human Rights and the International Court of Justice [sic]. Although, it was held firmly that the Government had not acted improperly in all the circumstances, nevertheless a feeling prevailed both at home and abroad that the powers of detention should not again be exercised except as a last resort and only where any other effective means of a less repugnant kind were not available.

It was noted that the reactivation of the Special Criminal Court had "proved adequate and that the situation had been brought under control" and that the IRA had called off its campaign. It appeared that the time was opportune for the Government to consider whether the powers of detention should be formally prorogued. The Minister was of opinion that the cesser:

> ...would have a good effect on public opinion both at home, where concern has been expressed from time to time at the imprisonment of persons without trial, and abroad, particularly before the Council of Europe where questions of this kind come alive in connection with proceedings before the Commission of Human Rights and the International Court of Justice [sic] pursuant to the European Convention of Human Rights. Accordingly, it was recommended to Government the making and publication of a proclamation declaring that Part II of the 1940 Act shall forthwith cease to be in force.

Accordingly, the Government,[10] on 6 March 1962, declared that Part II of the Offences Against the State (Amendment) Act 1940 ceased to be in force. The Department of External Affairs, on 3 April 1962, informed the Secretary General of the Council of Europe.[11] The Clerk of the Consultative Assembly circulated to members a copy of this letter, in accordance with Article 15 (3) of the Convention and stated that "the provisions of the Convention are again fully executed in that country".[12]

Other Applications to the European Commission of Human Rights

There were two other applications to the Commission arising out of the same events chronicled in the Lawless case. The first of these, that of Rory Brady, who had been elected to Dail Eireann in the general election of March 1957, was lodged with the Commission on 30 March 1957[13] following his conviction and sentence by the District Court. He was interned from 14 July 1957 until he escaped. In January 1959, he was further sentenced to six months imprisonment for failure to account for his movements. In his application, he asked the Commission to investigate the Offences Against the State Acts 1939 and 1940 on the ground that these statutes "were unconstitutional and the negation of democracy and of all human rights". Following an invitation by the Commission, the Government submitted observations on 27 January 1958.[14] The Commission adjourned this application until it finished its examination of the Lawless case. While it seemed that Brady did not pursue his application with any great vigour,[15] the Commission ruled, on 29 March 1960, the application inadmissible on two grounds.[16] The first reason was that the Commission was not competent to examine *in abstracto* the question of the conformity of domestic legislation with the Convention and therefore the applicant was not the victim of a violation of the Convention. The second reason was that, since the applicant had not availed himself of his right to appeal to a higher court against his convictions, he had not exhausted the domestic remedies at his disposal.

The second application, that of Joseph Cunningham, a solicitor, was lodged on 3 April 1959 and arose out of his internment from February 1958 to the time when he escaped in December 1958. After remaining in hiding for some time he showed himself openly and was not rearrested. Cunningham claimed that he was not an IRA member and that he was detained because he was a Sinn Fein organiser and that the Government saw him as a political opponent. When requested, the Government submitted its observations on 15 March 1960. The Commission decided to adjourn the application until after the Court gave its decision on the merits in the Lawless case. Following the judgment in that case, the Commission ruled the application inadmissible on 27 July 1961. It held that, in the light of the Court's findings in the Lawless case, the applicant's contention that the conditions which obtained in the Ireland in February 1958 did not justify the Government in invoking the powers of detention, was manifestly ill-founded. Furthermore, an application to the Detention Commission was a legal remedy that offered an effective means of establishing promptly the absence of any reasonable grounds for his detention and of securing his early release from detention.[17] The Commission had pointed out in *Nielsen v Denmark*[18] that the rules of international law governing the exhaustion of domestic remedies, as were generally recognised, in principle required that recourse should be had to all remedies available under local law which were capable of providing an effective and sufficient means of redressing the wrong which was the subject of the claim submitted to an international tribunal.

Publication of the Lawless Case by the Council of Europe

The judgments of the Court in the Lawless case were, it seemed, published speedily and without controversy. It was foreseen that problems might arise in relation to the publication of the other materials. As early as the plenary session of the Court, held on 5-6 April 1961, which coincided with the hearing of submissions in the Lawless case, the Court decided to set up a working party,[19] composed of Judges McNair, Cassin, Holmback, Rolin and

Ross to discuss the questions raised by the application of Rule 52 of the Rules of Court.[20] It met on 20 October 1961 and obviously drafted a new rule because the plenary Court adopted a new Rule 52 on 24 October 1961.[21] The Deputy Registrar of the Court, Herbert Golsong, wrote on 13 July 1962, to Ireland's Permanent Representative at the Council of Europe. He noted that in pursuance of the Rules of Court certain decisions and documents would shortly be published and that certain other documents would be made accessible to the public. The Government requested an extension of time to consider the matter, though it immediately proposed the deletion from the Commission's memorial of 27 June 1960 of matters relating to efforts at reaching a friendly settlement. A later reply stated that it appeared that the rule on which the proposal to publish was based was adopted long after the proceedings in the Lawless case were completed. The relevant rule was the one that stood before amendment. That being so, much of what was proposed to publish or make accessible should remain confidential. These views should be conveyed to the Court and, in the meantime, it was assumed that publication would not take place.

The Vice-President of the Court, Rene Cassin, wrote from Paris, on 17 October 1962. He said that the Chamber which examined the Lawless case, having regard to the importance of the precedent it established, referred to the plenary Court the question of the publication of documents other than the judgment and the verbatim reports of the hearings. The plenary Court was of the unanimous opinion that the publication of all the documents in the Lawless case would involve considerable expense. It was specifically for this reason that the rule was modified in order to confine the volume of documents for printing solely to memorials, reports and verbatim reports of proceedings, all other documents being simply made available to the public. When the Court modified the rule, it was clearly understood that the publication of the documents in the Lawless case was governed by the new rule. He again requested the Government to state any objections to particular documents. Having regard to the fact that this was the first application of the rule, and as a gesture to the Irish government, he proposed to inform his colleagues, on the occasion of the next plenary session of the Court, of the exchange of letters on the subject, there being no question, however, of going back on that decision. The Department of External Affairs noted that the Court was anxious for a friendly settlement to the dispute and having regard to Cassin's letter there seemed no point in continuing to fight the issue of which rule applied, though the Attorney General may have another reaction. While the Court was incorrect in altering the rules and applying them retrospectively, there was no possible way of persuading the Court they were wrong. So it seemed that the

Government must indicate any objections that they entertained in respect of the documents. Despite this advice, the Government replied that the view was still held that publication was governed by the rule as it stood prior to amendment. In support it referred to the judgment of 14 November 1960 which stated: "it is true that the debates and the judgment alone are public and that other documents in the case can only be published...if the Court expressly authorises such publication."[22] The Government had not been informed of any Court decision expressly authorising such publication.

Next, the Attorney General took the matter up directly with Richard McGonigal, Ireland's judge on the Court, though the attitude was softening with specific objections outlined. The Attorney General wrote, on 11 May 1963, pointing out that he, McGonigal, had, no doubt, received copies of the correspondence that passed between the Government and the Court concerning the publication of documents. The President of the Chamber that heard the Lawless case, who incidentally would not appear to be the appropriate person to deal with this matter on behalf of the Court, had inferred that the Court was obliged to publish all the documents. It was strongly felt that the transcripts of the oral proceedings heard *in camera* by the Commission should not be made available to the public. Apart from the obvious objections on grounds of principle, he, the Attorney General, was personally reluctant to having them made available, as he was required to address the Commission *ex tempore* and without a prepared text. He would not have been willing to do so had he realised that what he said would later be made available to the public in a permanent form. This objection on grounds of principle also applied to the part of the Commission's memorial to the Court filed on 16 December 1960. In that document there was noted what purported to be a record of a statement made by the United Kingdom Government at a secret session of the Commission in the Cyprus case. The Court had been asked to delete the offending passage but made no ruling on this matter. McGonigal then wrote to the Registrar of the Court, on 23 May 1961. McGonigal on his return from Strasbourg told the Attorney General that he had quite a struggle but that eventually it was agreed that there might be some grounds for objecting to the publication of the transcript of the proceedings before the sub-Commission and also the extract from the Cyprus proceedings. The members of the Court felt that they should not take cognisance of the objection that the Attorney General had conveyed to McGonigal and that some formal objection on behalf of the Government would be necessary. It was apparently thought that it might be said that publication of the record would cause difficulties for the Government vis-à-vis Northern Ireland. It might be said that the Government objected to publication of the transcript on the ground that it was *ex tempore* and not a prepared speech. As regard the Cyprus quotation, it seemed that some objection would be required from the Government before the Court would take action. Cassin wrote, on 10 June, that the Court confirmed that the publication of documents was governed exclusively by the modified rule. Accordingly, the Government was requested to make its observations before 30 July 1963. The Government responded that it remained of the view that the position should be governed by the rule as it stood prior to amendment. Nevertheless, in compliance with the request, the following documents should not be published for the reasons stated: (1) the transcript of the proceedings before the Vice-President of the Court on 1 June and 14 November 1960;[23] and, (2) memorial of the Commission which contained an extract from *in camera* proceedings in another case, details of which had never been made public; and, (3) verbatim records of the oral hearings before the Commission in June 1958 and in April 1959 before the sub-Commission, because the persons addressing the tribunals spoke *ex tempore* and without knowledge that the matters would subsequently be made public.[24] It is not known whether the Court corresponded with Lawless's advisers on this matter.

This episode came to an end in March 1964, nearly three years after the Court gave final judgment. The Registrar of the Court forwarded to the Government, a copy of the printed publication, the Series B volume and a copy of the order made by the President of the Chamber.

The lobbying by the Government was successful in that only a heavily truncated version of the verbatim hearings before the Commission and the sub-Commission was published and the material from the Cyprus case was deleted. Thus the allegations made by the Attorney General in his carefully prepared address to the sub-Commission of Human Rights[25] of the likelihood of war between Ireland and the United Kingdom was suppressed and has remained so until published in this work for the first time. While this matter is referred to in the Commission report by some of the members it looks from the published material that that was a conclusion they reached on the appreciation of the facts.[26] There is little or nothing to suggest that they were directed to the issue by remarks made by the Attorney General. This view is supported by the fact that the Attorney General did not repeat this contention in public hearings before the Court.

Subsequent Careers of the Major Participants

Gerard Lawless later emigrated to England, where he dabbled in journalism and participated in local government politics in London, where he currently lives. Sean MacBride continued to practise at the Bar, appearing in many leading constitutional cases. He became Chairman of Amnesty International (1961), Secretary General of the International Commission of Jurists (1963), President of the International Peace Bureau (1974) and Assistant-Secretary General of the United Nations and UN Commissioner for Namibia (1973). He was awarded both the Nobel Peace Prize (1974) and the Lenin Peace Prize (1977). Tommy Connolly continued a successful practise at the Bar, appearing in many leading constitutional cases. Seamus Sorahan is a leading criminal advocate. P.C.Moore was elected President of the Law Society. The Attorney General, Aindrias O Caoimh, became a judge of the Supreme Court (1965), President of the High Court (1967-1974) and a judge of the European Court of Justice (1984-1985). Brian Walsh was appointed to the High Court (1959) and later to the Supreme Court (1961) where he had a seminal influence in judgments he delivered in constitutional and other important legal cases. He was appointed President of the Law Reform Commission and was elected a judge of the European Court of Human Rights (1980-1998). Anthony Hederman became a Supreme Court judge in 1981 and was at one time President of the Law Reform Commission. Peter Berry became Secretary of the Department of Justice, and Philip O'Donoghue, who had been Legal Advisor in the office of the Attorney General, became judge of the European Court of Human Rights in succession to Richard MacGonigal.

Subsequent Resurgence of Political Violence in Northern Ireland

The suppression of political violence, without addressing its underlying causes, may only garnish a temporary respite. As events were later to prove, this is precisely what happened with regard to Northern Ireland. The Irish, United Kingdom and Northern Ireland Governments must have greeted the suppression of the 1957-1962 border campaign with relief. But within the very short space of eight years political violence was to flare again and this time with a fury, duration and intensity that dwarfed the border campaign. Since 1969 there has been over thirty years of death, destruction and untold misery. Unlike the border campaign, which was essentially aimed at the ending of the political partition of the island, the later "troubles" were sparked by a repressive governmental response, coupled with a violent Loyalist paramilitary reaction, to a Nationalist campaign for what was then loosely called "civil rights". Because of the intensity of these responses, the IRA regrouped, initially as the defender of the Nationalist community, though subsequently targeting the continued

British political and military presence in Ireland. Accordingly, this "armed struggle" brought further governmental repression, some of which were clear breaches of human rights, and further Loyalist violence directed at the Nationalist community. A by-product of this terribly tragic sequence of events in Irish life was the conclusion of the first successful inter-state application, that of Ireland v United Kingdom, by the European Court of Human Rights under the European Convention. As this work draws to a close there are hopeful signs that some political solution in the nature of a compromise is in sight and can be achieved. But equally it must be recognised that these efforts and hopes may end in failure. Whatever the outcome, hopefully the Strasbourg organs will never again be called upon to adjudicate on governmental measures taken in response to political violence in any part of the island of Ireland.

Notes

[1] See Bowyer Bell. op.cit. pp.391-393.

[2] Following the General Election of October 1961, the Sinn Fein vote collapsed and the four Dail Eireann seats won in 1957 were lost.

[3] Government minute. Item 1. 22 November 1961.

[4] Part V of the Offences Against the State Act 1939, which permitted the establishment of such courts, had been activated by Government order on 24 August 1939 and while it functioned until 1946 that order had never been annulled.

[5] 192 DD 838-842.

[6] 193 DD 378-379 (15 February 1962) prints convictions and punishments.

[7] Government minute. Item 1. 2 October 1962.

[8] See Coogan. op.cit. p.418.

[9] DT File S.13710.

[10] Government minute. Item 1. 6 March 1962.

[11] DFA File 417/39/19 Part IV.

[12] YBECHR. 1962. (5). p.6.

[13] Some seven months before Lawless lodged his claim.

[14] Incorporated in the first set of observations in Lawless. Thereafter, the two applications were treated separately.

[15] Brady's application by made by his election agent and the remarks of Waldock (p. 62) are very apt here.

[16] YBECHR. 1960. (3). pp.214-222. While the applicant's name is not printed, his identity is known from the DFA files on the Lawless case.

[17] The Court in the Lawless case saw the Detention Commission as a safeguard and not a remedy: see p.212.

[18] YBECHR. 1961. (4). pp.302-322.

[19] YBECHR (4) 1961. p.96.

[20] "The Registrar shall be responsible for the publication of judgments and of such other decisions and documents whose publication may have been authorised by the Court."

[21] "1. The Registrar shall be responsible for the publication of: judgments and other decision of the Court; documents relating to the proceeding including the report of the Commission but excluding any particulars relating to the attempt to reach a friendly settlement; reports of public hearings; any document the publication of which is considered as useful by the President of the Court. Publication shall take place in the two official languages in the case of judgment and other decision, applications or introductory request for proceedings and the Commission's reports; the other documents shall be published in the official language in which they occur in the proceedings.

2. Documents deposited with the Registrar and not published shall be accessible to the public unless otherwise decided by the President of the Court, either on his own initiative, or at the request of a party , of the Commission or of any other person concerned."

[22] Lawless case. Series A. p.13.

[23] See p. 163 for a record of June meeting, no record exists of the November meeting.

[24] It is obvious that the addresses of the AG were carefully prepared in advance. The only *ex tempore* submissions would have been the replies which were rather innocuous.

[25] See p.123.

[26] See pp. 138-139.

12 Lawless Case in Retrospect

Introduction

Consequent upon the pronouncement by the European Court of Human Rights of its judgment, the Lawless proceedings finally came to an end, though the case then began a new and potentially perpetual lease of life as an important precedent in the field of international human rights. The international protection of human rights has been a major preoccupation of many in the second half of the twentieth century. This cause was first espoused with the United Nations Universal Declaration of Human Rights in 1948 and culminated in the International Covenant on Civil and Political Rights in 1966. Charters with geographical effect followed, such as the European Convention of Human Rights in 1950, the American Convention on Human Rights in 1969 and the African Charter on Human and Peoples' Rights in 1981. Charters that focused on specialised issues became commonplace, such as the Convention on the Status of Refugees in 1951 and the Convention on the Rights of the Child in 1989. The Lawless case, decided against this unfolding backdrop, was undoubtedly a major influencing factor in this context. In this chapter, an analysis is made of the impact that the case has had in a number of broad areas.

The Lawless Case and an Irish Human Rights Jurisprudence

Assists the Discovery of Human Rights in Irish Law

While an impressive charter of human rights has been expressly enshrined in Irish law, dating from the enactment of the Constitution of the Irish Free State in 1922, and carried over into the Constitution of Ireland in 1937, it was not until many years later that constitutional and human rights in their generality came to be explored, declared, protected and enforced by way of litigation generally.[1] This trend began as late as 1960. As this process gradually unfolded, and later accelerated in pace, volume, variety and complexity, the relationship between the individual and the State, and the individual within the State, was to undergo fundamental metamorphosis. While there had been some notable cases with implications for constitutional rights prior to 1960, these were rather sporadic and isolated.[2] The question must then be posed: why was there such a sudden and extraordinary explosion in constitutional rights litigation at that precise moment in time?[3] Some reasons have been offered why this should have occurred at that time. It has been suggested that the improvement in legal education in Ireland and events abroad, such as the civil rights movement in the USA, were influential.[4] While there were changes in legal education at that time, the results were not to be seen for a further decade or so. The campaign for racial equality in America only reached its zenith in the latter part of the 1960s.[5] Another more accurate though rather general suggestion was the awareness of the sacredness of the citizen's human rights brought about by the Council of Europe's Convention of Human Rights. Therefore, what event raised the general consciousness, and focused the collective legal and judicial mind, on constitutional and human rights? It is this writer's opinion that the catalyst for the sudden and massive interest in human rights in Ireland at that time is directly attributable to the impact that the Lawless case made on the national consciousness. This influence has never, until now, been alerted to, let alone been adequately and properly acknowledged. While a European dimension as an influencing factor in the development of Irish human rights at that time was credited it did not expressly identify the Lawless case as the source. By dating this awareness of rights to the year 1960 it appears that the Lawless case is being expressly excluded.[6] On a more careful scrutiny, that is not a correct conclusion because, while the Lawless case was litigated in the domestic courts in 1957 it did not appear in the Irish law reports until 1960. Thus the Lawless case fits neatly into the tranche of cases which are correctly seen as the foundation stone of constitutional rights in Ireland. There are three broad inextricably inter-connected reasons why the Lawless case played such a crucial role in this early exploration period.

The first explanation why the Lawless case exerted such an influence, as it meandered its way, first through the domestic courts, and then on into the Strasbourg system, for a four year period, from September 1957 to July 1961, was the considerable media attention accorded to the case on each step of the way. The Convention had received scant coverage in the printed media, both at the original signature and thereafter, and this writer can find no discussion on the implications of the Convention for Irish law in the legal literature in the decade following its signature. When the printed media commented on Strasbourg affairs, it tended to concentrate on the reporting of debates in the Consultative Assembly and on isolated events, such as the establishment of the European Court of Human Rights. Because there had been nothing of any substance dealt with prior to the Lawless case, there had been little or no media coverage in Ireland on the work of the European Commission, though this could justifiably be explained by the relative inertia of that body. Indeed, the only notable case in the Strasbourg system prior to the arrival of the Lawless application, that of *Greece v United Kingdom*, ran in parallel with the Lawless case for much of the time. Since the bulk of the media reportage of European affairs, in the context of human rights, concentrated on the Lawless case, one is driven very firmly to the conclusion that if there was a European dimension to the development of constitutional rights in Ireland at that time then the Lawless case must have been the singular influencing factor. Of course, it would be trite to suggest, and it is not suggested, that it was the sole influencing feature in this regard. However, the proposition is advanced that the Lawless case has not been credited, until now, as the major influencing force that it undoubtedly was.

The second major outcome of the Lawless case was the influence it exerted in awakening within the legal fraternity of an awareness that constitutional rights offered the individual a shield of protection, particularly from an ever-increasing intrusive State, even if the intention of the measures adopted were well-meaning and benevolent. The Lawless case as it moved though the Strasbourg system proved how a judicial mechanism could be effectively used both to protect human rights and highlight related issues, even if victory was not always assured to the individual in a particular case. Could such a mechanism that protected human rights in a European context be replicated in a domestic forum? Courage, creativity and ingenuity would be required to mould an efficient and sufficient jurisprudence in this regard. That task fell primarily and squarely on the shoulders of the legal profession. It is highly significant that the legal personnel involved in the Lawless case were professionally involved in most of the constitutional cases from this formative period,[7] all of which postdate the bulk of the Lawless proceedings.[8] This tranche of cases only commenced after the Lawless case was nearing completion. Given the media publicity that the case attracted, and given the additional fact that the senior branch of the legal profession, the Bar, was small in number and worked in a single setting which was intimate, if not claustrophobic,[9] it is reasonable to conclude that this case provided, in part at least, the impetus to the advocacy side of the legal profession to become decidedly more proactive in the protection of human rights within the domestic setting.

This evolution of the acknowledgement and protection of constitutional rights would have been still-born without a receptive judiciary. To coincide with the other changes that were occurring in this formative period, there were fundamental changes in judicial personnel.[10] The older generation of judges may have been too cautious and slow either to invalidate what the legislature had done or to take it on themselves to supply what it had left undone.[11] It may also been that their legal education and formation was done at the time when written constitutions were unknown in this part of the world and the common law principle that parliament was supreme was the ruling dogma. Though in fairness that conclusion may be somewhat inaccurate.[12] Be that as it may, under our code of law the judiciary can neither of their own volition initiate change nor implement change: they are in a sense the captives of the litigants and their advocates. It is futile to speculate on how the judges of the superior courts, prior to 1960, would have responded to the avalanche of constitutional litigation that was to follow in later years. The factual situation was that there were changes in the judiciary at this crucial moment. This, combined with the other factors discussed already, led to an upsurge in constitutional litigation that in turn resulted in decisions and pronouncements that, as a consequence, formed the nucleus of a developing constitutional human rights jurisprudence. Once again, the influence of the Lawless case lurks in the background. One jurist who has exercised an influence of colossal magnitude on the development and protection of human rights, the late Brian Walsh,[13] was a member of the Government's legal team in the early stages of the Lawless case. This experience must have influenced not alone his perception of human rights, but the realisation of the trend towards the internationalisation of the protection of human rights. If Ireland were not to be isolated from this international trend, then the judiciary would have to take a leading role domestically in this process. Otherwise, there was a real risk of a flood of cases invoking the Strasbourg system and this drift would have reflected badly on the judiciary, which in democratic states at least, is seen as the bastion which offers protection to the individual from an over-jealous legislature and executive. It has transpired that it is the judiciary that is the organ of government most attuned to the obligations contained in the European Convention and, without necessarily expressly referring to its provisions, has incorporated the various rights stated therein into a series of judgments.

In a sense, in Irish law, the Lawless case looks two ways simultaneously. On the one hand, it marked the end of a rather sterile period in Irish legal history, and, on the other hand, it heralded the beginning of the development of a human rights law in Ireland. Henceforth, the legal landscape was to witness the co-operation of willing litigants, adventuresome advocates, thought-provoking academics and receptive judges working in combination. This was to result in an accelerating and expanding process that has resulted in a vibrant code of human rights law of which Ireland can be justifiably proud.

Jolted a Complacent Executive

Having caused ripples in the legal profession and in the judiciary, the Lawless case had a corresponding effect on the executive arm of government. In an adversarial context, great credit must be given to the Government for achieving victory in the Lawless case. From an international human right perspective, the behaviour of the Government, in the circumstances, was judged to have been responsible and measured, and the Government's conduct of the case before the Strasbourg organs was positive, if not always fair, and even if sometimes too formalistic. Having made those obvious acknowledgements, it must with equal force be noted that Ireland's appearance, as a first defendant before the bar of an international human rights tribunal on complaint from one of its citizens, must have proved both a chastening and uncomfortable experience. This was particularly so for a small jurisdiction with relatively limited experience and standing in international affairs and diplomacy. It must surely have come as a surprise to the administration to find itself in that predicament, at least in the initial stages until it settled comfortably into the process. Nevertheless, the most obvious consequence was that the case provided a severe knock to the complacent attitude that the State had displayed towards the European Convention from the outset and towards human rights in general. This is particularly so when it is remembered that the Lawless case was initiated and partly heard before the explosion in human rights litigation in the Irish courts chronicled earlier in this chapter. The attitude within the administrative organ of government to the advent of the European Convention was summed very aptly up with the comment that "the likelihood of this country being brought before the [Strasbourg organs was] very remote as all the 'rights' set out in the Convention are already conceded here".[14] This typified a smugness, which, with hindsight, was extraordinarily foolish, though similar views were expressed by other signatories to the European Convention, such as the Netherlands[15] and Iceland.[16] Though these sentiments were ultimately vindicated in the Lawless case, it came at a cost of scrutiny in a very public way in an international forum. Nevertheless, the entire process must have been a severe shock to the executive arm of government,[17] though as already noted, victory went a long way towards mitigating the trauma.

Ireland and the European Convention after the Lawless Case

It is not the purpose of this work to examine in any detail the relationship between Ireland and the European Convention over the years since the Lawless case was decided. Nevertheless, it is pertinent to ask in passing whether, as a consequence of the acquaintance with the Strasbourg organs which that case forced upon Ireland, the consciousness of legislators and administrators was raised to the implications of the Convention when considering the content of legislative measures and contemplating administrative action. The number of cases decided by the European Court, in the almost forty years of its existence, in which Ireland has been a party is modest - only eight cases, including Ireland's complaint against the United Kingdom. But when judged on a ratio of cases to population, Ireland appears to fare no worse than the other signatories to the Convention.[18] In this respect the Lawless case is also unique in that it is the single instance, out of the seven cases taken against Ireland, in which the complaint was dismissed whereas in the other cases it was decided that the Convention had been breached. In reviewing these cases it is worth remembering that from the very outset, when the draft Convention was merely at the promotion stage, two issues which were to become the subject of European Court of Human Rights decisions were clearly identified as possible issues of conflict. These were the powers of detention, which was in issue in the Lawless case, and the non-availability of state-funded legal aid, which was in issue in the Airey case. Of the five remaining cases, putting the *Ireland v United Kingdom* case to one side as being in a different category, two cases consisted of complaints regarding laws which had been in existence for many years prior to the establishment of the Irish Free State. The subject of the Johnston case[19] was the common law rules relating to the rights of illegitimate, or non-marital, children and the subject of the Norris case[20] was the criminalisation of certain sexual acts, particularly between adult males. Another case - that of Keegan, the latest decision of the Court against Ireland[21] - stemmed from a law which had been enacted very shortly after the Convention was signed.[22] As a small jurisdiction with limited resources and expertise, the executive and legislative organs of government could hardly have been expected to review every legal rule operating when the State either gained independence or when the State signed the European Convention. Having said that defensive word, it must be noted that by the time each of these particular topics was litigated before the Strasbourg organs - the status and rights to be afforded non-marital children,[23] the decriminalisation of certain sexual acts[24] and the rights to be afforded to non-marital fathers[25] - each had been widely discussed in the public domain in Ireland. Indeed, with regard to the continued criminalisation of certain sexual offences, the European Court had, in a very widely discussed decision, ruled against identical laws in Northern Ireland[26] on the ground that they invaded the right to privacy. A pre-emptive altering of the law, in each of these instances, would have avoided public condemnation by the European Court of Human Rights. In the Open Door and Dublin Well Woman case[27] it was a judicial act rather than a legislative or executive act which came under adverse scrutiny. This was the granting of an injunction to prohibit pregnant women from obtaining information concerning abortion facilities abroad and based on an interpretation of the Constitution. It was held to infringe the right to impart information. Given the complexity and suddenness with which the abortion issue arose it is a marvel, in a sense, that this infraction of the Convention was limited to such a narrow fault committed by an independent judiciary over which the other institutions of government had no control.[28] In the Pine Valley Development case[29] it is understandable that in dealing with the complex issue of the retrospective validation of planning decisions by legislation that the discriminatory provision of the Convention was overlooked. From a brief review of these cases it could be argued, as a general conclusion, that ample advanced warnings had been given to the State that, on the balance of probabilities, these various aspects of Irish law were suspect with regard to the Convention. These critical comments can only be made with hindsight because the executive and legislative arms of government did not take pre-emptive action to head off possible adverse court decisions. Had such a course of action been taken it would be impossible with certainty to claim that the Convention was the impetus for the change. By forcing a particular case to a conclusion before the European Court a clearer and easier assessment of the impact which the Convention has had on the shape of Irish law and administrative practice can be made. In the absence of further research it is impossible to calculate precisely the extent to which the Convention has been a modifying force on the proposals for legislative change and on proposed administrative action. In the early years of the Convention it is probable that its provisions had little influence in this regard though in more recent years it appears that the Convention, like the Constitution, has become a major influencing factor in the shape and content of Irish law.[30]

Of the seven decisions which the European Court has pronounced against Ireland, the Lawless judgment is the single case concerned with state security and aspects of the criminal legal system, another peculiarity of that case. The other cases litigated aspects of private law and private morality. At first impression, a striking feature of the relationship between Ireland and the Convention at European Court level, after the Lawless case, is the absence of any pronouncement on any aspect of the Irish criminal legal system, particularly when such issues are a regular feature of that court's jurisprudence. The first possible explanation for a lack of complaint against Ireland in this regard could rest with the ignorance by the criminal practitioner of the Convention and the extensive case law. A more accurate reason is the striking similarity between the relevant provisions of the Convention[31] and the principles of Irish criminal law and procedure when a comparison is made between both. This is hardly surprising since the relevant provisions of the Convention and Irish criminal law and procedure are both based on common law principles. Since the signature of the Convention the domestic courts have embedded many of these common law principles into a constitutional framework of rights. For instance, the Irish courts have enunciated principles on such matters as the right to be notified of the reasons for arrest or detention,[32] the presumption of innocence,[33] the right to an expeditious trial,[34] the right to legal aid,[35] and the right to bail either pending trial or pending appeal,[36] all issues which are expressly provided for in the Convention. These issues have been litigated before the European Court in cases coming from other signatory states. Accordingly, it has been unnecessary to invoke the jurisdiction of the European Court because the protections afforded by the Irish courts could not be further enhanced elsewhere.

Provided an Exception to the Principle of Secret Government

Since the foundation of the Irish Free State one of the singular features of public administration was the veiled and covert way in which the executive arm of government exercised its functions. This was despite the fact that the other two institutions of government, in the generally accepted tripartite division of governmental powers, the legislature and the judiciary, did, as a general rule, function under the glare of publicity. The clarion cry for generations had been that total and absolute secrecy was an essential ingredient for the proper exercise of executive powers.[37] Not only was that the view and practice of administrators, it was also the law of the land. The courts reinforced this rule that the executive arm of government could not be compelled to disclose the grounds on which decisions were made. Further attempts to lift the veil of executive secrecy, as in the Lawless case, proved futile. But that victory by the executive in the Irish courts, which ensured the survival of executive secrecy for a longer period in domestic law, had merely territorial effect and did not travel *sur la continent*. A cultural shock awaited the Government when the Lawless case moved into the Strasbourg system. Secrets that could be hidden behind the veil of executive privilege in Ireland, and supported by judicial pronouncement, could not remain a mystery before the Strasbourg organs, if the Government was to successfully defeat Lawless's claim. The Government was denied abroad a protection that could readily be availed of at home. Accordingly, denied this protective shield, the Government, for the very first time, was forced, in a public international forum, to produce and justify the grounds on which an executive decision had been made. The material produced successfully achieved the defeat of the claim. This does not detract from the fact that the Lawless case, in its European dimension, contributed to achieving a greater accountability and a greater transparency in the realm of the exercise of executive powers which was to prevail in an absolute form, in domestic law at least, until 1972. In that year the judiciary asserted its primacy in the exercise of judicial powers and seriously dented the common law principle of executive privilege.[38] Since that time, even the principle of cabinet confidentiality has been eroded.[39] The idea of government in secret has been further whittled away by legislation.[40]

The Lawless case reaped some benefits for administrative government. It ensured that an intimate knowledge of the provisions of the Convention was acquired. It also provided a definite understanding of the workings and procedures of the enforcement organs. Most importantly, the Government gained a general feel for and an easiness with the Strasbourg system which could only be achieved from a participatory experience. The encounter with the Lawless case was to stand the Government in good stead when, with courage and confidence, it initiated an inter-state application against the United Kingdom[41] in December 1971 which was successfully concluded in January 1978. Not only were breaches of the Convention exposed but human rights history was made in the process. Ireland was the first state to successfully indict another state before the European Court of Human Rights.

The Lawless Case and its Influences on Irish Law

Detention Powers Abandoned

Internment without trial has never been re-introduced since the 1957-1962 period, despite subsequent events that arguably might have justified its introduction. As the crisis in Northern Ireland deepened from the 1970s onwards there was a corresponding over-spill of violence into the Republic which necessitated, on public order grounds, the introduction of a wide range of measures to combat political violence. A state of emergency was declared,[42] statutory powers of seven-day detention were enacted as emergency laws,[43] special courts were introduced and extensively used,[44] and laws with extra-territorial effect were introduced to permit the trial in this State of certain offences committed in Britain and Northern Ireland.[45] There were changes in the law to the rules of evidence to provide easier methods for proving membership of unlawful organisations and increased penalty for membership of such organisations.[46] And a law to confiscate the property of unlawful organisations was passed.[47] But the traditional method utilised by the executive of dealing with political violence, indefinite detention without trial, was not resorted to as a weapon to suppress subversive activities. It is worthwhile to speculate why such powers were not invoked in recent years. Of course, as in all such situations, it was the political implications and repercussions that probably weighed most heavily in the decision whether or not to resort to internment without trial.

While an analysis of these political issues is outside the scope of a legal work such as this, some fairly obvious matters which are already well established in the public domain can be mentioned. Since the partition of Ireland, which had been forced upon the people of Ireland by Britain in 1922, a sizeable portion of the population of Northern Ireland and an overwhelming majority of the people on the whole island have favoured the political reunification of the island. Unfortunately, the Northern Ireland entity did not develop along, what can loosely be described as, traditional democratic lines. Instead, it reflected the demographic reality and developed on purely sectarian lines. One very distinct section of that community with a seemingly permanent and entrenched majority wished for continued political union with Britain. The other section of the community, with a large minority, were nationalist in outlook and were seemingly permanently excluded from political office and economic power in both parts of the island. The way the island was partitioned proved a disastrous settlement and the obvious manifestation of this failure was recurring political violence on the island. These events presented a dilemma for the Government of the Republic particularly when the violence reached a high level of intensity. Violence came from three diverse quarters within Northern Ireland: institutional violence, Loyalist violence and Republican violence. The Government of the Republic had adopted the role as the international voice of the nationalist community that could not be abandoned. To do so would be a desertion of the nationalist population and, more importantly, a surrender of the aspiration to national reunification. The courts of the Republic ruled that the unification of the island was a constitutional imperative.[48] On the other hand, the Government could not countenance political violence in Northern Ireland nor allow its territory to be used as a haven for violent activity against a neighbour. Thus in the 1970s a tightrope was constantly being walked between the various differing and conflicting obligations. While some steps were taken to control and suppress politically inspired violence, such extreme and ultimate step as the introduction of internment without trial or the use of the death penalty were never resorted to. The view may also have pertained within political circles in the Republic that the autonomy given to Northern Ireland following the partition of Ireland had not worked in an inclusive manner and that change could not be brought about through peaceful and democratic methods. On the other hand, violence, regrettable as it was, might lead inevitably to a realisation and acknowledgement, particularly by the British Government, that the governance of Northern Ireland as then constituted was a failure. Consequently, some other form of inclusive government was essential. A logical step at some future moment in time would be some form of new political settlement, in which the Republic would have a role. While that is precisely what has happened, it cannot be conclusively suggested that was envisaged. The lesson may also have been learned, from the period under review in this work, that the common and sole approach of the suppression of politically motivated violence did not result in any measures which made the governance of Northern Ireland more politically and economically inclusive for the nationalist population. If anything it may well have reinforced the intransigence of the Unionist and Loyalist political establishment.

Resort to such extreme measures not only exposed the Irish Government to the possibility of indictment before the European Court of Human Rights but may well have tied its hands in its ability to complain about the abuses of the British Government in Northern Ireland, as it successfully did. Over the years Ireland had endeavoured to carve out a moral and neutral voice for itself in international affairs. It has, for example, played an important role as an international peacekeeper. The introduction of detention powers would have damaged that reputation. Finally, a more immediate and less lofty reason existed why detention powers were not used. It may well have been feared that those against whom such detention powers would be used might argue, in an international forum, that the Irish Government had funded and thereby encouraged the armed conflict in Northern Ireland. Internationally that would have been a crushing indictment.[49]

Turning to the equally important legal reasons which would have made the introduction of detention powers difficult, issues which the author is more competent to deal with, these in the main, are directly traceable to the various issues raised in the Lawless case. This is understandable because, prior to that case and despite the widespread use of detention powers in the 1940s and 1950s,[50] there were only two cases in which these powers were judicially reviewed in Irish courts.[51] This was because of the policy of those against whom internment powers were used of not recognising the courts, yet another topic that surfaced during the course of the Lawless case. With the abandonment of this policy in modern times it was extremely likely that a huge volume of litigation would have ensued as a consequence of the introduction of detention powers and some of these potential legal issues which might have been litigated are explored here. The major obstacle facing the executive in any exercise of an administrative power that struck at the very heart of the fundamental human right of personal liberty was the existence of a more virulent and truculent judiciary. Their thinking on a wide range of human rights and governmental issues had, as already noted, radically altered since the late 1950s. Some of the judicial thinking exposed in the Lawless case, in the Irish courts, stood the chance of either being negatived and thereby abandoned, or, at least, seriously challenged as being of dubious authority.

First, the generally held belief that the Offences Against the State (Amendment) Act 1940 was beyond further constitutional challenge was extremely doubtful, a point which has been already been considered in detail.[52] That being so, the statute could have been challenged afresh on any number of grounds. The first major objection would have been to the nature of the detention powers sanctioned. Some understanding of the judicial mind on the subject might be found in what Walsh J had to say, on the related issue of bail. He remarked that:

> …it would be quite contrary to the concept of personal liberty enshrined in the Constitution that any person should be punished in respect of any matter upon which he has not been convicted...save in the most extraordinary circumstances carefully spelled out by the Oireachtas and then only to secure the preservation of public peace and order or the public safety and the preservation of the State in a time of national emergency or in some situation akin to that.[53]

The reference to the precondition of the existence of "extraordinary circumstances...in a time of national emergency or in some situation akin to that" which must be spelled out by the legislature, and not the executive, must have raised qualms within the executive branch of government that there would be constitutional and legal tricky times ahead if the powers of detention, as they then existed in Irish law, were resorted to.

The next major issue was the provision of some statutory mechanism that might ensure that the power to detain without trial was not abused. Such a statutory mechanism is the Detention Commission. The first difficulty is its nature. The view that it was merely an administrative body, as distinct from a judicial body, was open to serious doubt in light of the more modern case law. If it were held to be a judicial body then its powers would have to be limited.[54] Secondly, whether the notion that, because the ministerial opinion, on which a detention without trial was based, was couched in subjective language, which consequently placed it beyond judicial review, remained good law must have been in doubt and is considered separately later. Thirdly, even if the Detention Commission survived a constitutional challenge, the courts would have demanded the implementation of fair procedures. This was so because the presumption of statutory constitutionality carried with it an intention "that proceedings, procedures, discretions and adjudications which are permitted, provided for, or prescribed by an Act of the Oireacthas are to be conducted in accordance with the principles of constitutional justice".[55] The courts have also ruled that in any proceedings before any tribunal where a party is on risk of having his good name, or his person, or any of his personal rights jeopardised, "the State, in compliance with the Constitution, whether by its enactments or through the courts, must outlaw any procedures which will restrict or prevent the party concerned from vindicating these rights".[56] That could only be done by giving the person a copy of the evidence which reflected on him, leave to cross-examine his accusers, permission to give rebutting evidence and leave to address the tribunal.[57] This would result in a procedure that was clearly very different from that which was accorded to Lawless when he was before the Detention Commission. It would effectively have rendered that body inoperable, particularly, as happened with Lawless, where the State insisted on refusing to make the information on which it acted available to an applicant. Though the question may then arise as to whether the Detention Commission, or a similar review mechanism, was really necessary. And the answer was probably not.

The spectre of the Lawless case in its long traverse of the Strasbourg organs and its attendant publicity must have haunted the Government. The possibility of a reprise, with the probability of a greater numbers of applicants, must have been a major consideration against the introduction of detention powers. Lastly, apart from the possibility of a plethora of aggrieved applicants, there was always the likelihood that another of the signatory states of the Council of Europe would have initiated an inter-state application against Ireland, a practice which has become almost commonplace when states derogated in emergencies. The obvious way to avoid some of these difficulties would have been to introduce detention powers in an emergency statute, under the state of emergency that was then in existence, as had happened during the war years. That would have shut the door on legal repercussions on the domestic front. But the Strasbourg system could still have been invoked either by aggrieved persons or another signatory state.

Incorporation of International Law into Irish Law

An issue decided by the domestic courts in the Lawless case has continued to be highly influential ever since. That was the general principle that an international convention, treaty or agreement to which the State was a party, but which had not become part of the domestic law of the State as determined by the Oireachtas, could not confer rights on individuals which were enforceable in the domestic courts. This proposition has been rigidly adhered to since.[58] It would, of course, be a misunderstanding to suppose that principles of international law, contained either in customary rules or in conventions, treaties or agreements, may only find their way into domestic law *via* the legislative route. A generally recognised principle of international law governing the relations between states will be enforced[59] and the domestic courts have implemented this constitutional rule through the case law as the necessity arises.[60] In the Lawless case it was expressly decided that this route was solely applicable to rules governing the relations between states and that these rules could not confer any benefit on individuals.[61] The second way for a principle of international law to find its way into domestic law is where it was carried over when the Constitution was enacted and provided the rule was not inconsistent with any provision of the Constitution.[62] However, it must be admitted that the commonest way in which international conventions, treaties or agreements are given the force of law within the Irish State is by enactment into legislation.

European Convention vis-à-vis Irish Law

In the Lawless case, in the domestic courts, it was expressly decided that the European Convention of Human Rights had no enforceable status within domestic law. This conclusion has been consistently restated.[63] This principle has been extended to include decisions of the European Court of

Human Rights.[64] But it has been argued by a litigant, and vigorously contested by the State, in a recent case that, because of Ireland's membership of the European Union, the European Convention has become part of the domestic law of the State by virtue of the Maastrict Treaty which came into effect in 1992.[65] The High Court considered that it was not necessary to comment on this argument because it had not been established that any breach of the Convention had occurred.[66] It would be a most ironic twist of fate if the Irish courts, at some future time, were to rule that because of the changing landscape of Irish law and politics, the European Convention did have the force of law within the State and without any express legislative act. This was a proposition the courts refused to countenance in the Lawless case over forty-five years ago.[67]

All Administrative Action is Judicially Reviewable

While some of the principles enunciated in the Lawless case have survived to the present day, not all have stood the rigours of continuing judicial scrutiny. Another legacy of the Lawless case, in the sphere of judicial review of administrative action, has fallen foul of a change in judicial rethinking. The courts had earlier ruled that the exercise of discretionary powers by the executive could not be judicially reviewed where the enabling statute was couched in subjective language, a rule expressly followed and applied in the Lawless case.[68] But in the constant quest by the courts to ensure that all executive and administrative actions are subject to judicial review, this rule formulated in the earlier cases has been abandoned in modern times.[69]

Significance of the Lawless Case for the European Convention

Charter of Enforceable Rights

The initial signature and promulgation of the European Convention of Human Rights was widely and rightly acknowledged as a great achievement. The patently obvious, but nevertheless vitally significant, impact which the completion of the Lawless case had on the developing European human rights jurisprudence was the provision of the vital proof that the system established for the enforcement of engagements undertaken by the signatory states actually worked. The ability of the Strasbourg system to complete its first historic case went a great way towards restoring a flagging confidence in the Convention and helped to hide the critical fact that the Convention had been signed by the original signatory states more than a decade earlier. Until that first judgment was solemnly pronounced, the Convention had been seen merely as rhetorical, aspirational, inspirational, theoretical and symbolic in nature. Suddenly and irrevocably the Convention was imbued with a dynamic force which was to have deep and lasting implications for the governments and citizens of the states of Europe. Thus, once the Strasbourg system was finally in top gear the status of human rights was immediately propelled from the abstract plane of potential protection to the solid plane of real protection. The promotion and protection of a charter of human rights thus achieved a new status in the international sphere that was to have an enormous impact for signatory states both nationally and internationally. Not alone did the Convention itself achieve a new status but the Strasbourg organs correspondingly enhanced their standing and reputation. Until the Lawless judgment the signatory states could privately ignore with a certain impunity their obligations under the Convention while publicly paying lip-service to the place of human rights in European societies. While some states had incorporated the Convention into their domestic laws, there was, as already noted, a certain smugness within states that the Convention did not place individual states in peril before the Strasbourg system. The Lawless case, despite the victory going to a signatory state, must have sent a clear signal to the remaining signatory states that their assumed obligations, which had lain fallow for a decade, could now be enforced before a European forum. The right of individual petition resulted in the real possibility for the signatory states to find themselves indicted in the dock of an international forum for the breach of obligations towards individuals within their jurisdictions,[70] an uncomfortable place for any government. The signatory states had henceforth to worry about fulfilling their obligations under the watchful eye of the Strasbourg organs, the failure of which might result in an appearance before an international tribunal of human rights.

Undoubtedly, the real beneficiaries of the Lawless case were the millions of Europeans, each of whom was now placed on a level hitherto unrecognised in international law. The individual was now the recipient of rights which, when refused or denied in a national forum, could be internationally enforced. This single possibility irrevocably and drastically changed the face of human rights in Europe.

Reform of Convention Procedures

Abolition of the Sub-Commission System

The Lawless case took a little under four years to complete, from the lodgement of the application to the pronouncement of the final judgment. That period of time might be regarded as excessive. By comparison, it was hardly any longer than the length of time taken for a constitutional case to be completed before the Irish courts.[71] It must be remembered that the case was conducted in two languages, with part-time members of the Commission and Court living and working in the four corners of Europe and coming from different legal systems, and the otherwise heavy workload of the Commission. The fact that preliminary issues were raised further prolonged the proceedings. Having said that, it seems that those who followed the public debates before the Court admired the smooth way in which a totally unprecedented procedure had been conducted.[72] In those circumstances the time taken to complete the case was not excessive, though ideally it should have been much shorter. But from the very early days some procedural aspects of the Convention relating to the Commission were considered cumbersome and in need of change. An early criticism was made that the rigid division of competence between the Commission and the sub-Commission in regard to the investigation of the facts and the search for a friendly settlement was undesirable and a mistake. It tended to cause delay and to impede the smooth and effective handling of the case. It was suggested that it would be better simply to leave the two tasks within the competence of the Commission and give it discretion to work out its own procedure for discharging them.[73] It was also recorded that when only part of the Commission was working, in the form of a sub-Commission, there was a certain lack of balance. However informative the reports submitted, those members who only heard the case indirectly had an incomplete picture of it. Hence the opinions they were called upon to give before drawing up a report could not carry the same weight as those expressed by members of the sub-Commission at the conclusion of their proceedings.[74] These criticisms prompted the abolition of the sub-Commission system, and though this proposal was promulgated in 1963, it was only incorporated into the Convention on 21 September 1970.[75]

According a Role to the Individual before the Court

A major issue raised in the Lawless case, which consumed a large portion of the Court's time, was the status or role to be accorded to an individual applicant before the Court. Ranged on one side of the debate was the traditional attitude of governments that argued for total exclusion of the individual, and, on the other side, the understandably cautious attitude of the Commission, which favoured the granting of some role to the applicant, however limited. In the Lawless case, the Commission began a process to gain some standing for the applicant *via* the Commission's own role before the Court. Incidentally, much of the credit for the achievement of this innovation, adopted by the Court, must go to Waldock, President of the Commission, who as the Commission's principal delegate before the Court, defended these actions with great vigour at the insistence of the Commission.

To achieve the objective of affording a meaningful role for the applicant before the Court, the first avenue of attack was for the Commission to involve the applicant in some way in the written documentation that was prepared by the Commission for the Court hearing. As has been seen, the Commission invited Lawless's comments on the Commission report and on the Government's memorial to the Court. These views were subsequently incorporated into the body of the Commission's memorial to the Court. But this effort was rebuffed when the Court ruled that these comments were not to be considered part of the proceedings, though the Commission had all latitude, in the course of the hearing, to take those views into account in enlightening the Court, which the Commission did. But the Commission was not easily thwarted. In the next case after Lawless, on which there was a Court judgment on the merits, the *Belgian Linguistic* case,[76] the Commission repeated exactly what it had done in Lawless. It sent its report to the applicants, invited their views, and then included these in the body of the Commission's memorial and drew the attention of the Court "to the observations received, in so far as it considers them relevant to the task of establishing the truth". The Commission not only blandly ignored the Court's ruling in this regard in the Lawless case, but then rather cheekily expressly referred to other irrelevant portions of the Lawless judgment as authority for this very action. It quoted that the "Commission which, as defender of the public interest, is entitled of its own accord, even if it does not share them, to make known the applicant's views to the Court as a means of throwing light on the points at issue...".[77] The Commission blatantly ignored the central question which was *how* this information was to be brought to the Court's attention. The objection in the Lawless case was not to informing the Court of the applicant's views but including these in the Commission's written memorial to the Court. The Belgian Government did not make any objection to this course of action. The Court, while noting that the Commission's first memorial contained certain observations by the applicants, did not adversely pronounce on that procedure.[78] Already, in only the third case before the Court, a further shift towards the inclusion of the individual applicant was clearly established. The failure by the Court to repeat its express condemnation of this course of action was hardly an unintentional omission. On the contrary, it should be viewed as an expression of the deliberate policy of the Court to grant some role to the applicant. Regardless of the inference to be drawn, the Commission undoubtedly considered it had implicit approval for such action. Accordingly, thereafter this practice became the norm and commonplace.

The second avenue of attack against the proposition that the applicant should not be afforded any role before the Court was the initiation by the Commission of the practice of inviting the applicant to nominate a person to assist its delegates during the proceedings before the Court. This course of action was expressly approved by the Court in the Lawless case. With the passage of time, and the greater frequency of cases before the Court, it was probable that ways to expand the role of the applicant before the Court would be explored. That stage was reached in the *Vagrancy* cases[79] in 1970. For the first time, the Commission indicated that it was to be assisted by the applicants' lawyer, who would be asked to supply the Court with details on facts on which the Commission considered it was insufficiently informed. This was in light of some questions put by the Court that called for further explanation than was given in the Commission report.[80] Predictably, the Belgian Government "categorically" objected, though it admitted that a practice had been established since the Lawless case, which was not objected to, whereby the applicant or his counsel may, if they desired, come to the Court to be ready to assist the Commission delegates at any time.[81] Yet again, the Court rejected a government's argument in favour of those of the Commission. The Court noted that the Rules of Court[82] "does not place any limit on the freedom of the delegates in their choice of persons to assist them and it does not preclude them, *inter alia*, from having the assistance of the lawyer or former lawyer of an individual applicant...the Court has previously held in the Lawless judgment that nothing precluded the Commission from asking the applicant to nominate a person to be available to the Commission's delegates". The Court added a reminder that the role "of such a person so appointed consists of assisting the delegates of the

Commission whose main function is to assist the Court (Lawless)...the person assisting the delegates must restrict himself in his statement to presenting to the Court explanations on points indicated to him by the delegates, and this always subject to the control and responsibility of the delegates. It is the duty of the delegates to ensure the observance of this fundamental requirement by any person assisting them, in order to avoid any situation inconsistent with Article 44 of the Convention".[83] It is interesting to note that Waldock had become President of the Court and presided in the *Vagrancy* cases, and the principle of affording the applicant some status before the Court, which, as already noted, he pursued in the Lawless case, was expanded upon by the Court under his presidency.[84] The honour, as the first advocate unconnected with a government or the Commission, to address the Court fell to a member of the Belgian Bar, who made a very short address on the treatment of vagrants under Belgian law.[85] Once the legitimacy of permitting the applicant's lawyer to assist the Commission, by publicly addressing the Court was established, full use was made of that precedent, though not in every case,[86] not only to establish such a practice but to alter that role as the occasion arose. A further development occurred in 1975, in *Golder v United Kingdom*, when the applicant's lawyer before the Commission, addressed the Court both on the facts and on the interpretation to be given to Article 6 of the Convention.[87] In the same year, in *National Union of Belgian Police v Belgium*, the lawyer who had appeared for the applicants before the Commission addressed the Court.[88] In the following year, in *Swedish Engine Drivers Union* case,[89] there was a further innovation. Prof. Folk Schmidt of the University of Stockholm, an expert on Swedish labour law, who had not been previously connected with the case, addressed the Court,[90] as did the applicant's lawyer before the Commission.[91] In a connected case, *Schmidt and Dahlstrom v Sweden*,[92] there was another first for Schmidt when he had the distinction of being the first applicant in person to address the Court.[93] In the case of *Airey v Ireland* (1979),[94] Senator Mary Robinson, as she was then, made history by being the first Irish lawyer, unconnected with either a government or the Commission, to address the Court. She did so on the applicant's background and on aspects of Irish family law.[95]

In 1982 the inevitable step was taken to bring the Court's rules into conformity with the practice. The rules were amended so as to make specific provision for the presentation of the applicant before the Court.[96] Accordingly, the applicant gained standing before the Court, quite separately from, and not therefore subject to any limitation imposed by the

Commission. It is now commonplace for the applicant's lawyer to address the Court.

It is very clear that the groundwork for these developments was prepared by the Court's recognition, in the first exercise of its jurisdiction in the Lawless case, that if it was to perform its functions properly, the individual could not be excluded from its proceedings. If in the Lawless case the Court had decided that the applicant could not see the Commission's report, nor make comments on it, nor nominate a person to assist the Commission delegates, a impenetrable barrier would have been set up between the individuals of Europe and the Court. This would have had the effect of turning the proceedings into a private matter between the Commission and the government concerned. That would have been highly detrimental to the further development of the Convention as a charter for the protection of individual human rights. Confidence in the Strasbourg system, which at that stage was only emerging, would have been undermined to such an extent that it might never have recovered. By rejecting such a course in the Lawless case the Court, from the outset, laid the foundation for subsequent improvement in an applicant's position. It also demonstrated that it was committed to a concept and an application and an interpretation of the Convention in which the protection of the rights of the individual was to take priority over jurisdictional and procedural objections. Considerable progress has thus been made to redress the situation, first exposed in the Lawless case, whereby the applicant had no standing before the Court.

Applicant may Refer the Case to the Court

One of the obvious lacuna in the Convention from the beginning, and made noticeable in the Lawless case at the point when the Commission made its report, was the inability of an applicant to refer his or her case to the Court. This function was reserved to the Commission and the state(s) concerned. With the greater involvement of applicants before the Court, as explained in the previous paragraphs, it was inevitable that this particular inequality would eventually be tackled. It was in 1974, though it was not until 1990 before such a monumental change was effected.[97] The main effect of the change enables individuals to bring cases before the Court. However, this right is not automatic, but involves a preliminary screening procedure, though having regard to the more radical proposals to abolish the Commission and alter the Court,[98] the right of the individual before the Court is assured.

Application of the Convention

Power of Review and Margin of Appreciation

In the handful of cases where derogation from the provisions of the Convention have been pleaded, two inter-related concepts have permeated the basis of the reasoning in each of these cases. From the outset, the Commission, in *Greece v United Kingdom,* considered that, while it was competent to pronounce on the existence of a public danger, governments should be able to exercise a certain measure of discretion in such matters. These applicable principles were emphasised in the Lawless case, both by the Court and the Commission, the latter (though not the former) expressly using the expression "margin of appreciation" for the first time. The Commission, in the *Greek*[99] case, held that the burden lay on governments to show that the conditions justifying derogating measures had been met, having due regard to the margin of appreciation, which, according to the "constant jurisprudence of the Commission", a government had in judging the situation. The Court noted, in *Ireland v United Kingdom,*[100] that it fell in the first place to each signatory state with its responsibilities for "the life of [its] nation" to determine that life is threatened by a "public emergency" and, if so, how far it was necessary to go in attempting to overcome the emergency. The national authorities, by reason of their direct and continuous contact with the pressing needs of the moment, are in principle in a better position than the international judge to decide both on the presence of such emergency and on the nature and scope of derogation necessary to avert it. Accordingly, in this matter a wide margin of appreciation is left to those authorities. Nevertheless, the states did not enjoy an unlimited power in this respect. The Strasbourg organs were responsible for ensuring the observance of the engagements of states and were empowered to rule on whether states have gone beyond the "extent strictly required by the exigencies" of the crisis. The Court concluded, "the domestic margin of appreciation is thus accompanied by a European supervision".

Notification of Derogation

Because derogation from the Convention is such a fundamental step, notification is considered an essential link in the machinery provided for ensuring the observance of the engagement undertaken by the signatory states, because without information the other signatory states will not know their position. In the Lawless case, the Court ruled that the Strasbourg organs had the competence to examine whether a notice of derogation, and supporting information communicated by a state, was in conformity with Article 15 (3). Applying that principle in that case, the Court held that the communication of the legislative texts, together with an explanation of their purpose, within twelve days of the introduction of the derogation measure was sufficient compliance. The Commission, in the *Greek* case,[101] having expressly referred to Lawless, ruled that Article 15 (3) had been breached. The legislative texts, and full information of the administrative measures taken, were not communicated and the reasons for the derogation measures were not delivered for more than four months after they were first taken. The Court, in *Ireland v United Kingdom*,[102] noted that, in the light of the Lawless case, the British notices of derogation fulfilled the requirements of the Article 15 (3). In *Cyprus v Turkey* (1976) no communication of any sort was made. The Commission, having expressly noted that in the Lawless case the Commission had reserved its view as to whether failure to comply with the requirements of Article 15 (3) may "attract some sanction of nullity or some other sanction", expressly avoided deciding this particular issue. However, it decided that "Article 15 requires some formal and public act of derogation, such as a declaration of martial law or state of emergency. Where no such act has been proclaimed by the [state] concerned, although it was not in the circumstances prevented from doing so, Article 15 cannot apply."[103] Surely the invasion of one Council of Europe state by another is a sufficient public notice of derogation?

Interpretation of the Convention

Definition of Public Emergency

One of the major contributions which the Lawless case made to the interpretation of the Convention was the opportunity it afforded the Strasbourg organs of defining the expression "public emergency" contained in Article 15. This has been used as a authoritative precedent both in subsequent cases and, as will be seen later, in a wider international context. The expression was defined as "une situation de crise ou de danger exceptionnel et imminent qui affecte l'ensemble de la population et constitue une menace pour la vie organisee de la communaute composant l'Etat". The translation of the authentic French text into English, as we shall see presently, was not without incident. It read: "an exceptional situation of crisis or emergency which affects the whole population and constitutes a threat to the organised life of the community of which the State is composed." The Commission, in the *Greek*[104] case, "noticed that the notion of 'imminent' danger, which is represented in the French but not directly in the English text of the judgment, must be given weight because it is the French text which was authentic." In that case the Commission held that a public emergency must have four characteristics: (1) it must be actual or imminent; (2) its effects must involve the whole nation; (3) the continuance of the organised life of the community must be threatened; and (4) the crisis or danger must be exceptional, in that the normal measures or restrictions, permitted by the Convention for the maintenance of public safety, health and order, are plainly inadequate. In *Ireland v United Kingdom*[105] the existence of a public emergency was not in dispute though the Commission was satisfied that there existed at all material times a public emergency threatening the life of the nation because "the degree of violence...was on a scale far beyond what could be called minor civil disorder".

Impact on International Human Rights Jurisprudence

Lawless Case Part of an International Pool of Human Rights

As noted in this chapter's introduction, the international community commenced in the latter part of the last century to strength the international protection of human rights. The European Convention has made an enormous contribution, universally recognised, in the process towards this objective. Not only was the Convention one of the first charters of human rights to be promulgated, which acted as a model which could be imitated in other similar charters elsewhere, it more importantly contained an innovative enforcement mechanism. When this device came subsequently to fruition, for the first time in the Lawless case, it marked the beginning of a gradual building of what has become an impressive body of case law which stands as a persuasive and authoritative code of human rights law. This in turn plays an influential role in the development of an universal human rights jurisprudence.[106] In this global process the influencing factors are many and varied and nothing is done in isolation. From the swelling pool of human rights, fed by many tributaries, there are regular trickles and an occasional flood that ensures a constant rippling presence.

International Norms in States of Emergency

One of the major issues addressing the minds of international human rights jurists in recent years has been the drafting of international law norms to govern national states of emergency. The result of these endeavours has been the Paris Minimum Standards of Human Rights Norms in a State of Emergency,[107] which took eight years to draft and revise, and finally was adopted in 1984 by the International Law Association,[108] which has consultative status with the United Nations. These standards are intended to help ensure that, even in situation where a *bona fide* declaration of a state of emergency has been made, the state concerned will refrain from suspending human rights. Since the Lawless case was concerned with this very issue, it is only to be expected that the principles established therein would be obviously influential. The norms provide that "the existence of a public emergency which threatens the life of the nation, and which is officially proclaimed, will justify the declaration of a state of emergency".[109] They then go on to provide that "the expression 'public emergency' means an exceptional situation of crisis or public danger, actual or imminent, which affects the whole population [or the whole population of the area to which the declaration applies] and constitutes a threat to the organised life of the community of which the state is composed".[110] With the exception of the words in the brackets, this definition is lifted verbatim from the French definition laid down in the Lawless case.[111] It is interesting to note that the more specific definition pronounced by the European Court is preferred to the general words and expressions declared in the European Convention - "in time of war or other public emergency threatening the life of the nation" or in the International Covenant on Civil and Political Rights - "in time of public emergency which threatens the life of the nation".

There are, in addition, other issues, such as the notification of derogation and the rule of proportionality, covered in the Paris Minimum Standards and which were dealt with in the Lawless case, though the influence is not seen in the same detail as in the definition of a state of emergency.

Notes

[1] O'Donovan v AG [1961] IR 114 and Article 26 and the Electoral (Amendment) Act 1961 [1961] IR 169 (both concerned with the electoral issue of uniformity of representation); Educational Co.of Ireland v Fitzpatrick [1961] IR 345 (right to dissociate); Cowan v AG [1961] IR 411 (administration of criminal justice otherwise than by judge or court); Melling v O Mathghamhna [1962] IR 1 (definition of minor offence); Deaton v AG [1963] IR 170 (separation of powers - selection of punishment a judicial rather than executive matter); The State (Shanahan) v AG [1964] IR 239 (separation of powers - sending forward for trial notwithstanding judicial refusal to do so); The State (Quinn) v Ryan [1965] IR 70 (access to courts in extradition); The People (AG) v O'Brien [1965] IR 142; (admissibility of unconstitutionally obtained evidence); McDonald v Bord na gCon [1965] IR 217

(administration of justice otherwise than by judges or courts); Ryan v AG [1965] IR 294) (personal rights) and Conroy v AG [1965] 411 (definition of minor offence).

[2] The bulk of these cases were concerned with family rights: Art. 26 and the School Attendance Bill 1942 [1943] IR 334; In re Frost, infants [1947] IR 3; In re Tilson, infants [1951] IR 1; In re Doyle, an infant [1956] IR 217; Burke v Burke [1951] IR 216, and In re Blake, deceased [1955] IR 89. The State (Burke) v Lennon [1940] IR 136 and Buckley v AG [1950] IR 67 were mainly concerned with the separation of powers though Burke's case (see pp.18-19) touched on personal liberty and Buckley's case dealt with property rights. The remaining case, NUR v Sullivan [1947] IR 77 touched on freedom of association.

[3] J.M. Kelly. *Fundamental Rights in the Irish Law and Constitution*. 2nd edn (1967) foreword. p.vii.

[4] *Development in the Irish Legal System Since 1945* in *Ireland 1945-70*. Ed. J.J.Lee (1979). pp.83-95.

[5] For example, Martin Luther King was assassinated in 1968.

[6] In *Fundamental Rights in the Irish Law and Constitution* (1967), Kelly cited the Lawless case as The State (O Laighleis) v O'Sullivan and Minister for Justice, whereas in his later book, *The Irish Constitution* it is cited as In re O Laighleis.

[7] MacBride, Connolly and McGonigal appeared in the O'Donovan and the Electoral (A) Bill cases, Connolly and Sorahan appeared in Cowan's case, Connolly appeared in Melling's case, MacBride and McGonigal appeared in the Deaton and Shanahan cases, Connolly appeared in Conroy's case, MacBride and Connolly appeared in Ryan's case, Connolly and McGonigal appeared in Quinn's case. McGonigal was briefed by the State in these cases. The AG would have known of all these cases. (References are given at footnote 1, supra).

[8] Only O'Donovan and Melling had been decided before final judgment in the Lawless case. The Education Co.and Shanahan cases were partly heard at that point.

[9] In 1971, ten years after the Lawless case was decided, there was slighly fewer than 200 practising barristers in Ireland. Since five leading senior counsel (MacBride, Connolly, O Cuiv (the AG would, at that time, have continued his private practice), Walsh and McGonigal) and two leading juniors (Sorahan and Hederman) were involved it is hardly any wonder that the case was a topic of conversation and so influential.

[10] Cearbhall O Dalaigh, who had been a Supreme Court judge from 1953, replaced Conor Maguire as Chief Justice in October 1961. Brian Walsh was appointed to the Supreme Court from the High Court at the same time. It was this combination together with Kingsmill Moore and Haugh JJ and later with Budd J (who had been in the High Court from 1951) which was to prove so deadly. Another addition to the High Court in 1963, that of John Kenny, was also decisive.

[11] J.M.Kelly. *The Irish Constitution*. 1st edn (1980). Preface, p.xxx.

[12] In eight instances where statutes were judicially reviewed on constitutional grounds prior to 1960, the courts upheld four statutes: Pigs Marketing Board v Donnelly (Dublin) Ltd [1939] IR 413; Art.26 and the Offences Against the State (A) Bill, 1940 [1940] IR 470 (see p.20); In re MacCurtain [1941] IR 83 and In re Philip Clarke [1950] IR 235, and struck down four statutes: The State (Burke) v Lennon [1940] IR 136 (see p. 18); Art.26 and the School Attendance Bill 1942 [1943] IR 334; NUR v Sullivan [1947] IR 77 and Buckley v AG [1950] IR 67. Hardly the actions of a timid judiciary! Kelly might have been more accurate had he levelled his comments at the courts' more subservient attitude towards executive action: e.g. In re McGrath and Harte [1941] IR 68; In re MacCurtain [1941] IR 83 and The State (Walsh) v Lennon [1942] IR 112.

[13] See *Human Rights and Constitutional Law. Essays in Honour of Brian Walsh.* Ed. O'Reilly (1992). In particular *The Early Judgments of Mr Justice Walsh* by G.W.Hogan.

[14] Within DEA, though DJ was not that sanguine, see p.5.

[15] "When legislation was being proposed in the Netherlands for the purpose of ratification (1953) it was claimed, with a degree of indignation, that there was no need for such a Convention (as it was unnecessary and might in some cases even prove an inconvenience) but that there was equally nothing objectionable about it, as Dutch legislation was already completely within the spirit of the Convention. So no well-founded petitions were to be expected." K.de Vey Mestdagh *Reform of the European Convention of Human Rights in a Changing Europe* in *The Dynamics of the Protection of Human Rights in Europe: Essays in Honour of Henry G.Schermers* (1996) ed. Lawson & de Blois. (pp.337-360 at p.340).

[16] Speaking in the Icelandic Parliament, the Althing, in 1951, the Minister for Justice, Bjarni Benediktsson said: "As regards the rights enumerated here one can say briefly that in all aspects of any significance they are already expressly granted the citizens in Icelandic statute law and to some extent in the Icelandic Constitution itself, or that they are rights of such basic nature that they are deemed to be included in Icelandic general legal principle, even if they are not expressly stated." Quoted at p.191 in *International Human Rights Norms in the Nordic and Baltic Countries.* Ed. Scheinin, M. (1996).

[17] This attitude to the European Convention is not unique. Over the years, Ireland has "enthusiastically" signed international treaties and conventions which later was matched by a general amnesia about their ramifications for domestic law. For example, Ireland signed the Refugee Convention and Protocol, reduced these into statute law, and then when large numbers of refugees turn up wishing to avail of the rights under international law, which have been incorporated into law, the law was not implemented and instead some "*ad hoc*" arrangements were put in place.

[18] In the period 1960-1987 covered by V.Berger's *Case Law of the European Court of Human Rights,* Vol.1 and making a comparison between countries which accepted from the outset both the right of individual petition and the compulsory jurisdiction of the court, Iceland with 200,000 population had no case, Ireland with 3.5m. had 3 cases, Denmark with 5m. had 3 cases and Belgium with 10m. had 16 cases.

[19] ECHR Series A. Vol. 112. 18.12.1986. The complaint had been lodged on 16 February 1982 and was referred by the Commission to the Court on 21 May 1985.

[20] ECHR. Series A. Vol. 142. 26.10.1988.

[21] ECHR. Series A. Vol. 290. 26.5.1994.

[22] Adoption Act 1952.

[23] The Council of Europe Convention on the Status of Children Born out of Wedlock (1975), the Law Reform Commission's *Report on Illegitimacy* (1982). The Supreme Court had given its decision in O'B. v S. [1984] IR 316. The AG had been informed, on 6 November 1981, when the case was in its initial stages, that these common law rules would be coming under constitutional scrutiny. The reformed law is now the Status of Children Act 1987.

[24] These sexual acts have been decriminalised and the Criminal Law (Sexual Offences) Act 1993 contains the relevant law on the matter.

[25] As far back as the mid-1960s the Supreme Court refused to accord the non-marital father any rights to the adoption of his child: The State (Nicolaou) v An Bord Uchtala [1966] IR 69 In the Law Reform Commission's *Report on Illegitimacy* (1982) a proposed that the non-

marital father should acquire automatic guardianship rights was not incorporated into the Status of Children Act 1987.

[26] Dudgeon v United Kingdom. Series A. Vol. 45. 22 October 1981.

[27] ECHR. Series A. Vol. 246. 29 October 1992.

[28] The Constitution has since been amended by the 8th Amendment of the Constitution Act 1995 which inserted into Art.40.3.3° a provision that "this sub-section shall not limit freedom to obtain or make available, in the State, subject to such conditions as may be laid down by law, information relating to services lawfully available in another state". The Supreme Court, in Art.26 and the Regulation of Information (Services Outside the State for Termination of Pregnancies) Bill 1995 [1995] 2 ILRM 81, upheld this legislative proposal.

[29] ECHR. Series A. Vol. 222. 29 November 1991.

[30] For example, when introducing the Criminal Justice (Drug Trafficking) Bill in Dail Eireann the Minister for Justice said that "as well as having regard to requirements which arise under our Constitution we must have regard to our obligation under the European Convention on Human Rights". 462 DD 1364.

[31] See Appendix 1 for Articles 5 and 6 of the Convention.

[32] The People (DPP) v Walsh [1980] IR 294.

[33] O'Leary v Attorney General [1995] 2 ILRM 259.

[34] The State (O'Connell) v Fawsitt [1986] IR 362.

[35] The State (Healy) v Donoghue [1976] IR 325.

[36] The People (AG) O'Callaghan [[1966] IR 501. Following a constitutional amendment, a court may refuse bail to a person charged with a serious offence where it is reasonably considered necessary to prevent the commission of a serious offence by that person: Bail Act 1997.

[37] See *A Privilege of the State*. M.Russell. (1967) Irish Jurist, pp.88-99.

[38] Murphy v Dublin Corporation [1972] IR 215.

[39] An amendment to the Constitution in 1997, provides that while the confidentiality of discussions at meetings of the Government must be respected, it permits the disclosure of same where the High Court determines that disclosure should be made in the course of the administration of justice, or, by virtue of an overriding public interest, pursuant to an application by a tribunal appointed under the authority of the Houses of the Oireachtas to inquire into a matter of public importance. This change has partially negatived the Supreme Court decision in AG v Tribunal of Inquiry into the Beef Industry [1993] ILRM 81.

[40] The Freedom of Information Act 1997 though various records are exempted, such as law enforcement and public safety, and security, defence and international relations.

[41] The UK had also acquired similar experience - the first inter-state application under the Convention had been taken against the UK by Greece.

[42] On 1 September 1997 resolutions were passed by the Houses of the Oireachtas.

[43] Emergency Powers Act 1976.

[44] Part V of the Offences Against the State Act 1939 was brought into operation in May 1972 and has continued in operation since.

[45] Criminal Law (Jurisdiction) Act 1976.

[46] Offences Against the State (Amendment) Act 1972.

[47] Offences Against the State (Amendment) Act 1985, which was unsuccessfully challenged as to its constitutionality in Clancy v Ireland [1989] IR 670.

[48] McGimpsey v Ireland [1990] IR 441.

[49] The events surrounding the famous Arms Trial, where a number of persons, including former Government ministers, were acquitted of conspiracy to import firearms bought from public funds were never conclusively resolved. The background to these events are set out in the judgment of O Dalaigh CJ in In Haughey [1971] IR 317 at pp.243-244.

[50] This was because those detained traditionally did not utilise the courts as a method of redress, a policy which changed sometime in the 1970s.

[51] The State (Burke) v Lennon (see pp.18-19) and Article 26 and the Offences Against the State (A) Bill, 1940: (see pp. 20-21.).

[52] See pp.22-23.

[53] The People (AG) v O'Callaghan [1966] IR 501 at pp. 516-517.

[54] Article 37 of the Constitution.

[55] per Walsh J, speaking for the Supreme Court, in East Donegal Co-operative Livestock Mart Ltd v AG [1970] IR 317 at p.341.

[56] Per O Dalaigh CJ, in In re Haughey [1971] IR 217, at p.264.

[57] Ibid. p.263-264.

[58] In the Application of Woods [1970] IR 154 it was the UN Declaration of Human Rights; in Norris v AG [1984] IR 36 it was the European Convention; in Fakih v Minister for Justice [1993] 2 IR 406 it was the Convention and Protocol on the Status of Refugees - while these have been incorporated into the Refugee Act 1996, this statute has yet to be brought into operation by ministerial order; and Hutchinson v Minister for Justice [1993] ILRM 602 - it was the European Convention on Transfer of Sentenced Persons - which has been incorporated into the Transfer of Sentenced Persons Act 1995 and is in operation.

[59] Article 29.3 of the Constitution.

[60] The Supreme Court ruled, in Government of Canada v Employment Appeals Tribunal [1992] ILRM 325, that the doctrine of sovereign immunity was one of the generally recognised principles of international law which, by virtue of Article 29.3 of the Constitution had been incorporated into Irish law.

[61] Supreme Court, p.124. Followed by the High Court in The State (Sumers Jennings) v Furlong [1965] IR 70 where it was held that even if the rule of speciality in extradition matters was a generally recognised principle of international law the application of Article 29.3 prevented the conferring of any benefit on an individual.

[62] Article 50 of the Constitution. In ACT Shipping v Minister for the Marine [1995] 2 ILRM 30, the High Court held that the rule of customary international law whereby foreign commercial vessels in serious distress had a *prima facie* right of refuge in the waters of an adjacent coastal State had long since merged into domestic law.

[63] Carrigaline Community Television Broadcasting Co. Ltd v Minister for Transport [1997] 1 ILRM 241.

[64] In Norris v AG [1984] IR 36, the Supreme Court refused to accept Dudgeon v United Kingdom (1981), which decided that there had been a breach of the right to respect for private life guaranteed by Article 8 of the Convention, as a persuasive precedent.

[65] Title 1, Article F of which provides that "the Union shall respect fundamental rights, as guaranteed by the European Convention for the Protection of Human Rights...and as they result from the constitutional traditions common to the member states, as general principles of community law".

[66] Kavanagh v Government of Ireland [1996] 1 ILRM 133 at p.152. On appeal in the Supreme Court, [1997] 1 ILRM 321, this issue was not addressed.

[67] In the Belfast Agreement , the Agreement Reached in the Multi-Party Negotiations, signed on Good Friday 10 April 1998, while the UK Government undertook to complete the incorporation of the European Convention into Northern Ireland law (p.19), the Irish Government merely agreed to take steps to further strengthen the protection of human rights in its jurisdiction and these proposals will draw on the European Convention and other international legal instruments in the field of human rights and the question of the incorporation of the European Convention will be further examined in this context (p.20).

[68] In re O Laighleis [1960] IR 93 at pp.130-131.

[69] "While the opinion of the former Supreme Court, expressed in 1940 and 1957, reflected what was then current judicial orthodoxy, judicial thinking has since undergone a change." per O'Higgins CJ, in the Supreme Court, in The State (Lynch) v Cooney [1982] IR 337 at p.360.

[70] Article 1 of the Convention.

[71] For example, in Norris v AG [1984] IR 36, the plenary summons initiating the action was issued in November 1977 and the Supreme Court gave its decision in April 1983, a period of five-and-a-half years.

[72] See Valentine, D.G., in 10 International Comparative Law Quarterly (1961) pp.899-903.

[73] By the President of the Commission, Waldock, in an address on Council of Europe Day 1958, published in *The European Convention*: 34 BYIL (1958) pp.356-363.

[74] Madame Janssen-Pevtschin, in the Lawless case; Series B, para.95, p.100, noted that "a number of [her] colleagues" held the same view.

[75] Protocol No.3, which Ireland ratified on 12 November 1963.

[76] 1967. Series B, Vol I and Vol II, in Vol.I at pp.385-386.

[77] Ibid.

[78] Series A. Vol.5. 9.2.1967. para.5, p.8.

[79] De Wilde, Ooms and Versyp v Belgium, the first case to be referred to the Court by a government.

[80] Ibid. Series B. p. 352. per M.Sorensen, principal delegate.

[81] Ibid. p.353. Judge Favre noted in his judgment (Series A. Vol. 12. 18 June 1971p.10) that "the Court may have the assistance, according to Rule 29 (1)...of any person of its choice. It may therefore have the assistance of the applicant's lawyer, which is usually the case..." .

[82] Adopted on 18 September 1959. Rule 29 (1): "The Commission shall delegate one or more of its members to take part in the consideration of a case before the Court. The delegates may...have the assistance of any person of their choice."

[83] Ibid. Series A. pp.7-8. Judge Favre held (p.10) that "since the Commission's task is to defend the public interest it cannot be represented, even partially, by the applicant's lawyer who acts on the applicant's behalf. He may not speak at the Court hearing on behalf of the Commission or in order to submit an opinion different for the Commission. He could be heard by the Court...on what facts it desires explanation."

[84] The influence is obvious in that the judgment in English on this procedural point is the authentic one, whereas in all the judgments, from the Lawless case (1961) until Klass v Germany (1978) the authentic text is the French one.

[85] Series B. pp.367-369.

[86] For example, not in the next case of Ringeisen v Austria 16 July 1971. Vol.13 or in Kjeldsen, Busk Madsen and Pedersen v Denmark 7 December 1976. Vol.23.

[87] Series B. (1973-1975) (Vol.16) pp.233-242.

[88] (1973-75) (Vol.17) Series B. pp.176-184.

[89] (1974-75) (Vol.18) Series B.

[90] Ibid. pp.126-136.

[91] Ibid. K.Noorstrom. pp.136-139.

[92] (1974-75) (Vol.19). Series B.

[93] Ibid. pp.109-122.

[94] (1979) (Vol.32) Series A. Judgment. 9 October 1979.

[95] (1978-81) (Vol.30) Series B. pp.86-102.

[96] Adopted on 24 November 1982. Rule 30.1: "The applicant shall be represented by an advocate authorised to practise in any of the contracting states and residing in the territory of one of them, or any other person approved by the President. The President may, however, give leave to the applicant to present his own case, subject...to his being assisted by an advocate or other person as aforesaid".

[97] Protocol 9 became effective on 1 October 1994 when the tenth required ratification was made. Ireland ratified on 24 June 1994.

[98] Protocol 11 contains sweeping changes to the control machinery in that the Commission and the Court are to be replaced by a new permanent Court. It requires ratification by all contracting states.

[99] YBECHR 12, p.72.

[100] (1978) (Vol.25) Series A. p.79.

[101] op.cit. pp.41-43.

[102] op.cit. p.84.

[103] YBECHR 1976. pp.161-162.

[104] YBECHR (1969) Vol.13 pp.71-72.

[105] YBECHR (1976) Vol.19 p.512.

[106] For example, see *The Complementarity of the Covenant and the European Convention on Human Rights: Recent Developments.* M.G.Schmidt in *Influence of the European Convention and International Convention on Civil and Political Rights and UK Law.* eds Harris and Joseph (1995). pp.629-659.

[107] See in general, *Rule of Law in a State of Emergency: The Paris Minimum Standards of Human Rights Norms in a State of Emergency.* S.R.Chowdhury. (1989).

[108] See *The Paris Minimum Standards of Human Rights Norms in a State of Emergency.* R.B.Lillich. (1985) 79 American Journal of International Law. p.1072.

[109] Ibid. Section A. 1 (a).

[110] Ibid. Section A. 1 (b).

[111] The Lawless case is extensively discussed in Chowdhury, op.cit. e.g. pp.9-11, 13-14, 24, 29-32, 68, 96-97, 103-109, 112, 120, 176.

Appendix 1

Selected Articles of the European Convention of Human Rights

Article 5

(1) Everyone has the right to liberty and security of person. No one shall be deprived of his liberty save in the following cases and in accordance with a procedure prescribed by law:

(a) the lawful detention of a person after conviction by a competent court;

(b) the lawful arrest or detention for non-compliance with the lawful order of a court or in order to secure the fulfilment of any obligation prescribed by law;

(c) the lawful arrest or detention of a person effected for the purpose of bringing him before the competent legal authority on reasonable suspicion of having committed an offence or when it is reasonably considered necessary to prevent his committing an offence of fleeing after having done so.

(2) [*immaterial*]

(3) Everyone arrested or detained in accordance with the provisions of paragraph (1) (c) of this article shall be brought promptly before a judge or other officer authorised by law to exercise judicial power and shall be entitled to trial within a reasonable time or to release pending trial. Release may be conditioned by guarantees to appear for trial.

Article 6

(1) In the determination of his civil rights and obligations or of any criminal charge against him, everyone is entitled to a fair and public hearing within a reasonable time by an independent and impartial tribunal established by law…

(2) Everyone charged with a criminal offence shall be presumed innocent until proved guilty according to law.

(3) Everyone charged with a criminal offence has the following minimum rights:

(a) to be informed promptly, in a language which he understands and in detail, of the nature and cause of the accusation against him;

(b) to have adequate time and facilities for the preparation of his defence;

(c) to defend himself in person or through legal assistance of his own choosing or, if he has not sufficient means to pay for legal assistance, to be given it free when the interests of justice so require;
(d) to examine or have examined witnesses against him and to obtain the attendance and examination of witnesses on his behalf under the same conditions as witnesses against him.

Article 7

(1) No one shall be held guilty of any criminal offence on account of any act or omission which did not constitute a criminal offence under national or international law at the time when it was committed. Nor shall a heavier penalty be imposed than the one that was applicable at the time the criminal offence was committed.
(2) This article shall not prejudice the trial and punishment of any person for any act or omission which, at the time when it was committed, was criminal according to the general principles of law recognised by civilised nations.

Article 15

(1) In time of war or other public emergency threatening the life of the nation any High Contracting Party may take measures derogating from its obligations under this Convention to the extent strictly required by the exigencies of the situation, provided that such measures are not inconsistent with its other obligations under international law.
(2) [*immaterial*]
(3) Any High Contracting Party availing itself of this right of derogation shall keep the Secretary General of the Council of Europe fully informed of the measures which it has taken and the reasons therefor. It shall also inform the Secretary General of the Council of Europe when such measures have ceased to operate and the provisions of the Convention are again being fully executed.

Article 17

Nothing in this Convention may be interpreted as implying for any State, group or person any right to engage in any activity or perform any act aimed at the destruction of any of the rights and freedoms set forth herein or at their limitation to a greater extent that is provided for in the Convention.

Appendix 2

Biographical Notes

Judges of the European Court of Human Rights (1959-1961)

Arik, Kemal. Born Istanbul, Turkey in 1913. Studied law at Universities of Ankara, Geneva and Freiburg. Doctor of laws. Appointed to judicial office, 1937. Dean of the Faculty of Political Science and later Professor of Private International Law at University of Ankara.

Arnalds, Einar. Born in Reykjavik, Iceland in 1911. Studied law at University of Iceland and in England, Germany and Denmark. Barrister. President of Civil and Maritime Court.

Balladore Pallieri, Count Giorgio. Born in Acqui, Italy in 1905. Doctor of laws from the University of Turin, 1936. Professor of international law at the Catholic University of Sacre-Coeur in Milan, 1935. Author on constitutional law and international law.

Cassin, Rene. Born Bayone, France in 1887. Studied law at Aix-en-Provence and Paris Universities. Professor of international law at Lille (1920-9) and in Paris (1944-60). Represented France at the League of Nations. Increasingly concerned with safeguarding human rights in the Council of Europe. Vice-President Conseil d'Etat. Delegate to the United Nations. Played a leading part in the establishment of UNESCO. Awarded the Nobel Peace Prize in 1968.

McGonigal, Richard. Born in Ireland in 1902. Master of science from the National University of Ireland. Barrister 1925 and Senior Counsel 1940. Bencher of the King's Inns 1944.

Maridakas, Georges. Born in Siphnos, Greece in 1890. Studied at the University of Athens. Doctor of laws (1911) and advocate (1913). Professor of private international law, University of Athens (1925). Legal author. Member of the Permanent Court of Arbitration at The Hague.

Rodenbourg, Eugene. Born in Luxembourg in 1895. Studied at the University of Munich, Bonn, Louvain and Paris. Doctor of laws (1920). Member of Conseil d'Etat (1947) and judge of the Supreme Court of Luxembourg (1959).

Members of the European Commission of Human Rights (1957-1959)

Beaufort, L.J.C. Born Haarlem, Holland in 1890. Parliamentarian. Professor of Ethics at the Franciscan Seminary. Later Professor of Law at the University of Nimwegan. Delegate to the UN General Assembly.

Berg, Paal. Born in Hammerfest, Norway in 1873. Studied law at Oslo, Berlin and London. Judge of Supreme Court 1913. President of Industrial Court 1916. Minister of Social Affairs 1919-20 and Minister for Justice 1924-26. President of Supreme Court, 1929-40 and 1945-46.

Crosbie, James. Born in Cork, Ireland in 1902. Studied law at University College Cork and King's Inns. Barrister, 1925. Newspaper proprietor. Member of Seanad Eireann 1944-51 and 1954-1957. Member of the Consultative Assembly of the Council of Europe 1954-1955, and Vice-President 1956-57.

Dominedo, Francesco. Born in Rome, Italy in 1903. Studied at University of Rome. Doctor of laws. Professor of Commercial Law in Sienna and later professor of laws at Rome. Deputy in National Parliament. Under Secretary of State for Foreign Affairs. Member of Consultative Assembly of the Council of Europe.

Erim, Nihad. Born in Kandia, Turkey in 1912. Studied law at Istanbul and Paris. Professor of International law at Ankara. Member of Parliament and Minister for Public Works. Delegate to League of Nations.

Ermacora, Felix. Born Klagenfurt, Austria in 1923. Studied at Innsbruck and Paris. Doctor of laws. Professor at Innsbruck University and later Vienna. Legal author. Member of Parliament.

Eustathiades, Constantinos Th. Born in Athens, Greece in 1912. Studied at University of Athens and Paris. Professor of law at University of Athens, 1937-49 and Salonica 1949. Legal Advisor to UNESCO, 1948-49.

Faber, Paul. Born in Luxembourg in 1888. Studied law at Universities of Berlin and Paris. Doctor of laws. Advocate, 1917. Magistrate. Judge of District Court at Luxembourg. President of the High Supreme Court (1945-53).

Janssen-Pevtschin, Genevieve. Born in Belgium in 1915. Studied at Free University of Brussels. Advocate. Magistrate. Judge of the Court of First Instance.

Petren, Bror Arvid Sture. Born in Stockholm, Sweden in 1908. Studied at Universities of Lund, Upsal and Friborg. Judge of Court of Appeal, Stockholm (1943-48). Director of Legal Affairs at Ministry of Foreign Affairs (1949-63). Legal author. President of Court of Appeal, Stockholm (1962-67). Member of the Permanent Court of Arbitration. Judge of the International Court of Justice at The Hague. Later President (1962-67) of the European Commission of Human Rights.

Skarpedinnion, Fridjon. Born in Iceland in 1909. Studied law at the University of Iceland. Mayor of Hafnarjordur 1938-45. District judge 1945. Member of Parliament.

Sorensen, Max. Born in Copenhagen, Denmark in 1913. Studied in Copenhagen and Geneva. Attaché in Ministry for Foreign Affairs (1938-48). Professor at University of Aahus. Legal author. Member of the Permanent Court of Arbitration. Later President of the European Commission of Human Rights.

Susterhenn, Adolf. Born Cologne, Germany in 1905. Studied in Fribourg and Cologne. Doctor of laws. Advocate. President of Higher Administrative Court and of the Constitutional Court of Rhineland-Palatinate. Member of Parliament.

Waldock, Sir Claud Humphrey Meredith. Born in 1904. Studied law at Oxford. Barrister, 1928. Chichele Professor of international law at Brasenose College (1947-72). Fellow of All Souls College. Legal author. Queen's Counsel, 1951. Later judge of the European Court of Human Rights (1966-71) and President (1971-74). Judge of the International Court of Justice (1973-79) and President (1979-81).

Bibliography

Books

Beddard, R. (1993), *Human Rights and Europe*, Grotius Press, Cambridge.
Berger, V. *Case Law of the European Court of Human Rights*. vol. I. 1960-1987 (1989), vol. II. 1988- 1990 (1992), vol. III. 1991- 1993 (1995), Roundhall Press, Dublin.
Bonner, D. (1985), *Emergency Powers in Peacetime*, Sweet & Maxwell, London.
Bowyer Bell, J. (1972), *The Secret Army - A History of the IRA 1916-1970*, Sphere Books, London.
Campbell, C. (1994), *Emergency Law in Ireland 1918-1925*, Clarendon Press, Oxford.
Chowdhury, S.R. (1989), *Rule of Law in a State of Emergency: The Paris Minimum Standards of Human Rights in a State of Emergency*, Pinter, London.
Coogan, T.P. (1972), *The IRA*, Harper Collins, London.
Coogan, T.P. (1993), *Long Fellow, Long Shadow*, Hutchinson, London.
Delmas-Marty, M. (1992), *The European Convention of Human Rights for the Protection of Human Rights: International Protection versus National Restriction*, Martinus Nijhoff, The Hague.
Drzemczewski, A. (1993), *European Human Rights Convention in Domestic Law: A Comparative Study*, Clarendon Press, Oxford.
Eide, A. & Schou, A. (1968), *International Protection of Human Rights*, Interscience, New York.
Fawcett, J.E.S. (1987), *The Application of the European Convention of Human Rights*, Clarendon Press, Oxford.
Foley, J.A. & Lalor, S. (1995), *Annotated Constitution of Ireland*, Gill and Macmillan, Dublin.
Garvin, T. (1996), *1922-The Birth of Irish Democracy*, Gill and Macmillan, Dublin.
Golding, G.M. (1982), *George Gavan Duffy*, Irish Academic Press, Dublin.
Gormley, W. P. (1966), *The Procedural Status of the Individual before International and Supranational Tribunals*, Martinus Nijhoff, The Hague.

Heffernan, L. & Kingston, J. eds. (1994), *Human Rights: A European Perspective*, Roundhall Press, Dublin.
Hogan, G. & Walker, C. (1989), *Political Violence and the Law in Ireland*, Manchester University Press.
Jacobs, F.G. & White, R.C.A. (1996), *The European Convention on Human Rights*. 2nd edn, Clarendon Press, Oxford.
Jordan, A.J. (1993), *Sean MacBride*, Blackwater Press, Dublin.
Kelly, J.M. (1967), *Fundamental Rights in the Irish Law and Constitution*. 2nd edn. Allen Figgis, Dublin.
Kelly, J.M. (1994), *The Irish Constitution*. 3rd edn. eds. Hogan & Whyte, Butterworths, London.
Lawson, R. & de Blois, M. eds. (1996), *The Dynamics of the Protection of Human Rights in Europe: Essays in Honour of Henry G.Schermers*. (vol. III). Clarendon, Oxford.
Lee, J.J. (1989), *Ireland 1912-1985. Politics and Society*, Cambridge University Press.
Longford, Earl of & O'Neill, T.P. (1970), *Eamon de Valera*, Gill and Macmillan, Dublin.
Macardle, D. (1968), *The Irish Republic*, Gollancz, London.
Merrills, J.G. (1993), *The Development of International Law by the European Court of Human Rights*, Manchester University Press.
O'Leary, C. (1979), *Irish Elections 1918-1977*, Gill and Macmillan, Dublin.
Oraa, J. (1992), *Human Rights in States of Emergency in International Law*, Clarendon Press, Oxford.
O'Reilly, J. ed. (1992), *Human Rights and Constitutional Law: Essays in Honour of Brian Walsh*. Roundhall Press, Dublin.
Rafter, K. (1996), *The Clann: The Story of Clann na Poblachta*, Mercier Press, Cork.
Robertson, A.H. & Merrills, J.G. (1989), *Human Rights in the World*. 3rd edn. Manchester University Press.
Robertson, A.H. & Merrills, J.G. (1993), *Human Rights in Europe*. 3rd edn. Manchester University Press.
Sieghart, P. (1983), *The International Law of Human Rights*, Clarendon Press, Oxford.
van Dijk, P. & van Hoof, G.J.H. (1990), *Theory and Practice of the European Convention on Human Rights*. 2nd edn. Kluwer, Deventer.
Ward, A.J. (1994), *The Irish Constitutional Tradition*, Irish Academic Press, Dublin.
Whyte, J.H. (1980), *Church & State in Modern Ireland 1923-1979*. 2nd edn. Gill and Macmillan, Dublin.

Government Reports (Irish)

Report on Illegitimacy: Law Reform Commission (1982)
Report of the Committee on the Constitution (1967)
Report of the Constitution Review Group (1996)

Chapters in Books and Articles in Journals

Brownlie, I. (1962), 'The Individual before Tribunals exercising International Jurisdiction', *International Comparative Law Quarterly*, vol. 11, pp.701-720.

Brownlie, I. (1983), 'The Calling of the International Lawyer - Sir Humphrey Waldock and his Work', *British Yearbook of International Law*, vol. 54 pp.7-44.

de Vey Mestdagh, K. (1996), 'Reform of the European Convention of Human Rights in a Changing Europe', in Lawson and de Blois (eds), *The Dynamics of the Protection of Human Rights in Europe: Essays in Honour of Henry G. Schermers*, vol. III, pp.337-360, Clarendon Press Oxford.

Doolan, B. (1997), 'Ireland-Human Rights Defender of British Trade Unions', *Irish Law Times*, vol.14, pp.197-198.

Farrell, B. (1970-71), 'The Drafting of the Irish Free State Constitution', *Irish Jurist*, vol. 5, pp. 115-140 and 343-356, and vol. 6, pp.111-135 and 345-359.

Golsong, H. (1962), 'The European Convention before Domestic Courts', *British Yearbook of International Law*, vol. 38, pp. 445-456.

Golsong, H. (1963), 'International Protection of Human Rights', *Recueil des Cours*, vol. 110, pp.1-151.

Golsong, H. (1992), 'On the Reform of the Supervisory System of the European Convention of Human Rights', *Human Rights Journal*, vol. 13, pp.265-269.

Harris, D.J. (1961), 'European Court of Human Rights (the Lawless Case)', *International Comparative Law Quarterly*, vol. 10, pp.616-619.

Higgins, R. (1976-7), 'Derogations under Human Rights Treaties', *British Yearbook of International Law*, vol. 48, pp.281-320.

Higgins, R. (1984), 'European Convention for the Protection of Human Rights', in T.Meron (ed.), *Rights in Human Rights in International Law*, Clarendon Press, Oxford.

Hogan, G.W. (1992), 'The Early Judgments of Mr. Justice Brian Walsh', in J.O'Reilly (ed.), *Human Rights and Constitutional Law: Essays in Honour of Brian Walsh*, pp.37-48, Roundhall Press, Dublin.
Keogh, D. (1987), 'The Constitutional Revolution: An Analysis of the Making of the Constitution', *Administration*, vol. 35 (4), pp.4-84.
Lester, A. (1984), 'Fundamental Rights: The UK Isolated', *Public Law*, pp.46-72.
Lomas, O. (1980), 'The Executive and the Anti-Terrorist Legislation of 1939', *Public Law*, pp.16-33.
McMahon, B.M.E. (1979), 'Developments in the Irish Legal System Since 1945'in J.J. Lee (ed.), *Ireland 1945-70*, pp.83-95, Gill and Macmillan, Dublin.
McNulty, A.B. (1968), 'Practical Application of the European Convention', in A. Eide and A. Schou (eds), *An International Protection of Human Rights:Proceedings of the Seventh Nobel Symposium, Oslo, 1967*, pp.217-226, Interscience, New York.
O'Higgins, P. (1962), 'The Lawless Case', *Cambridge Law Journal*, pp.234-251.
Ost, F. (1992), 'The Original Canons of Interpretation of the European Court of Human Rights', in M. Delmas-Marty (ed.), *The European Convention for the Protection of Human Rights: International Protection versus National Restrictions*, pp.283-318, Martinus Nijhoff, The Hague.
Robertson, A.H. (1960), 'The First Case of the European Court of Human Rights: Lawless v Government of Ireland', *British Yearbook of International Law*, vol. 36, pp.343-359.
Robertson, A.H. (1961), 'Lawless v Government of Ireland (Second Phase)', *British Yearbook of International Law,* vol. 37, pp.536-547.
Robertson, A.H. (1967), 'The European Convention on Human Rights', in E. Luard (ed.), *The International Protection of Human Rights,* pp.99-131, Thames & Hudson, London.
Russell, M. (1967), 'A Privilege of the State', *Irish Jurist*, pp.88-99.
Schmidt, M.G. (1995), 'The Complimentarity of the Covenant and the European Convention on Human Rights: Recent Developments', in Harris and Joseph (eds), *Influence of the European Convention and International Convention on Civil and Political Rights and UK Law*, pp.629-659.
Soulier, G. (1992), 'Terrorism', in M. Delmas-Marty (ed.), *The European Convention for the Protection of Human Rights: International Protection versus National Restrictions*, pp.15-30, Martinus Nijhoff, The Hague.
Stefansson, S.M. and Aoalsteinsson, R. (1996), 'Iceland', in M. Scheinin (ed.), *International Human Rights Norms in the Nordic and Baltic Countries*, pp. 169-200, Martinus Nijhoff, The Hague.

Valentine, D.G. (1961), 'The European Court of Human Rights - The Lawless Case', *International Comparative Law Quarterly*, vol. 10, pp.899-903.
Waldock, C.H.M. (1958), 'The European Convention', *British Yearbook of International Law*, vol. 34, pp.356-363.

For Product Safety Concerns and Information please contact our EU representative GPSR@taylorandfrancis.com
Taylor & Francis Verlag GmbH, Kaufingerstraße 24, 80331 München, Germany

www.ingramcontent.com/pod-product-compliance
Ingram Content Group UK Ltd.
Pitfield, Milton Keynes, MK11 3LW, UK
UKHW022204190926
475702UK00003B/199

* 9 7 8 1 1 3 8 6 3 5 3 6 4 *